BIG DATA ON CAMPUS

BIG DATA ON CAMPUS

Data Analytics and Decision Making in Higher Education

EDITED BY KAREN L. WEBBER AND HENRY Y. ZHENG

JOHNS HOPKINS UNIVERSITY PRESS | *Baltimore*

Johns Hopkins University Press
2715 North Charles Street
Baltimore, Maryland 21218-4363
www.press.jhu.edu

Library of Congress Cataloging-in-Publication Data

Names: Webber, Karen L., editor. | Zheng, Henry Y., editor
Title: Big data on campus : data analytics and decision making
    in higher education / edited by Karen L. Webber and Henry Y. Zheng.
Description: Baltimore : Johns Hopkins University Press, 2020. |
    Includes bibliographical references and index.
Identifiers: LCCN 2019059971 | ISBN 9781421439037 (paperback) |
    ISBN 9781421439044 (ebook)
Subjects: LCSH: Universities and colleges—Administration—Data processing.
Classification: LCC LB2341.B4785 2020 | DDC 378.1/01—dc23
LC record available at https://lccn.loc.gov/2019059971

A catalog record for this book is available from the British Library.

Special discounts are available for bulk purchases of this book. For more informa-tion, please contact Special Sales at specialsales@press.jhu.edu.

Johns Hopkins University Press uses environmentally friendly book materials, including recycled text paper that is composed of at least 30 percent post-consumer waste, whenever possible.

CONTENTS

Amid declining enrollments, daunting resource constraints, and flagging public support, higher education leaders can still transform colleges and universities for the benefit of students and society. A renewed commitment to the institution-wide use of data analytics in strategic decision making has extraordinary potential to accelerate efforts to advance institutional goals, improve quality and efficiency, strengthen student outcomes, and enhance teaching, learning, and advising.

Data analytics adoption and use in higher education for decision making is currently stagnant and uneven—despite the rapid development of new information technologies, wider access to analytical tools, and the acceleration of the "data revolution" in other industries. In a recent survey of provosts and chief academic officers among US colleges, *Inside Higher Ed* (Jaschik and Lederman 2019) found that less than 20% of provosts across public and private institutions believe that their universities use data very effectively to inform institution decision making. Tom Davenport et al. (2001) lamented nearly two decades ago that "in the rush to use computers for all transactions, most organizations have neglected the most important step in the data transformation process: the human realm of analyzing and interpreting data and then acting on the insights" (18). The use of analytics to assist in the translation of data into actionable insights remains a major barrier at many colleges and universities.

To increase the sense of urgency for action, the leaders of three higher education associations—the Association for Institutional Research (AIR), EDUCAUSE, and National Association of College and University Business Officers (NACUBO)—developed a joint statement in 2019 prompting higher education leaders to reenergize efforts to unleash the power of data and analytics and support decision making for the benefit of students and institutions (changewithanalytics.com). Each of the three agencies strongly believes that using data to better understand students and institutional operations paves the way to developing innovative approaches for improved student recruiting, better student outcomes, greater institutional efficiency and cost-containment, and much more. The joint statement includes six principles of action to accelerate the meaningful use of analytics and take advantage of the insights derived from data to make the decisions and take the actions that set up higher education for a successful future. Our associations have made our own commitment to advancing and supporting the efforts of institutional leaders through the sharing of targeted resources, success stories, and implementation guides.

Webber and Zheng's book on data analytics in higher education reinforces the urgency and adds a valuable resource for higher education leaders. The book describes the conceptual underpinnings of the roles of data analytics within higher education as well as recent innovations in analytic models, new types of data and their curation, and digital media. Several chapters focus on the critical importance of processes and structures such as a mission-focused data strategy and robust governance policies. Importantly, a strong emphasis is placed on the human factors in successfully using data analytics for decisions such as an institution-wide commitment to a culture of data use and data literacy. The book will be valuable to researchers and practitioners alike. It is written by experienced higher education professionals who are recognized champions of data-informed decision making and provides case studies, examples of the application of data analytics, and helpful checklists for readers to scan their own institutional environments for opportunities.

AIR's core mission is to empower higher education professionals to use data and analytics to make decisions and take actions that benefit students and institutions and improve higher education. As executive director and CEO of AIR, I believe that Webber and Zheng's book reflects a core purpose of AIR and the values of our members and stakeholders. Each chapter brings practical and thoughtful insights from some of the best thinkers and leaders of data analytics in higher education. The book is a timely and useful resource for higher education leaders and stakeholders, and I am confident it will add to our ability to harness the power of data and analytics for the success of higher education institutions and students.

Christine M. Keller, PhD

Executive Director and CEO

Association for Institutional Research

References

Davenport, T. H., J. G. Harris, D. W. DeLong, and A. L. Jacobson. 2001. "Data to Knowledge to Results: Building an Analytics Capability." *California Management Review* 43 (2): 117–138.

Jaschik, S., and D. Lederman. 2019. "The 2019 Inside Higher Education Survey of College and University Chief Academic Officers—A Study by Gallup and Inside Higher Education." *Inside Higher Education*. January 23, 2019. https://www .insidehighered.com/news/survey/2019-inside-higher-ed-survey-chief-academic -officers.

Our sincerest appreciation is extended to Johns Hopkins University Press, particularly Editorial Director Greg Britton, who responded with encouragement to our initial inquiry about this possible volume. We also acknowledge JHUP's assistant editors Catherine Goldstead and Kyle Gipson, who patiently answered many questions throughout manuscript preparation, and the production team at the Press.

To our colleagues who contributed to this volume, we extend sincere gratitude. Without you, this book would not have been possible; your expertise in specific facets of data and analytics in higher education helped us develop full and meaningful information on this important and rapidly changing topic. Readers of this book will have a much better understanding of how higher education researchers and administrators are thinking about data analytics, and we hope that the implications discussed in each chapter urge readers to ponder the state of data analytics today and how it might contribute to its continued impact in higher education.

We thank IR colleagues who answered our email questions and offered insights that strengthened the discussion. Special thanks to Timothy Chow for his review and comments on portions of several chapters.

We also thank our work colleagues at the University of Georgia's Institute of Higher Education and the Ohio State's Office of Strategy Management, who kindly offered their support and assistance. We especially thank UGA's Institute of Higher Education doctoral student Amy Yandell for her assistance with manuscript preparation, IHE administrative manager Suzanne Graham for help with review of drafts, and the Lehigh University Office of Institutional Research and Strategic Analytics for its support and use of its experience in our writings.

We also thank our families for their support. They allowed us the freedom and quiet space to endeavor the development and finalization of drafts and edits to each chapter. We are better academic professionals because of your quiet patience and ever-present support.

PART I. Technology, Digitization, Big Data, and Analytics Maturity as the Enabling Conditions for Data-Informed Decision Making

Data Analytics and the Imperatives for Data-Informed Decision Making in Higher Education

Karen L. Webber and Henry Y. Zheng

HIGHER EDUCATION decision makers are keen to use the vast and still-growing volume of data on students, faculty, staff, and institutions themselves. More data, it may be reasoned, will produce better decisions. On the surface that can be true, and yet the larger volume of data does not necessarily ensure better decision making. Along with more data comes the need to use contextualized knowledge of the higher education organization and analytics strategies that account for the unique situation or population under study, and everyone must be mindful of privacy, ethical, and overall responsible use of the data. While the allure of vast quantities of data offer the possibility of greater student success and more effectively managed institutions, higher education leaders must consider how data analytics can be harnessed successfully, how strategies for good data governance and organizational strategies can support informed decision making, and how and where issues of privacy and security must be addressed.

In the article entitled "Data to Knowledge to Results: Building an Analytics Capability," Davenport et al. (2001) foresaw the impact of the data tsunami on organizational decision making and lamented that "in the rush to use computers for all transactions, most organizations have neglected the most important step in the data transformation process: the human realm of analyzing and interpreting data and then acting on the insights." According to Davenport et al., companies have emphasized important technology and data infrastructures, but they have not attended to the organizational, cultural, and strategic changes necessary to leverage their investments. In other words, having the data but not using them to generate actionable insights to achieve better organizational outcomes was the problem. Eighteen years later, that message has been heard loud and clear among organizations across the world. Intel Corporation CEO Brian Krzanich (in Gharib 2018) called data the "new oil" that is essential to organizational agility and survival. He further surmised that data and their use in analytics will have a fundamental impact on most industries across the board.

Like the business community, the higher education sector is feeling similar pressures from the data analytics movement. Facing growing competition, rising education costs, and shifting demographic trends, the highly pressurized and competitive higher education environment today has shown the importance of a deep commitment to data-informed decision support (Gagliardi and Turk 2017; Swing and Ross 2016). Scholarly publications on the status and challenges of learning analytics are becoming more frequent (e.g., Arnold and Pistilli 2012; Drachsler and Greller 2016; Khalil and Ebner 2015; Viberg et al. 2018) and issues related to data analytics have been featured prominently in recent years in EDUCAUSE's list of top 10 information technology (IT) issues. For example, in the 2019 list (Grajek 2019), issue #3 concerns privacy, issue #6 addresses the data-enabled institution, and issue #8 speaks to data management and governance. In a recent interview, Michael Crow, president of Arizona State University (ASU) and a nationally known innovator in higher education, commented on how data analytics informs decision making at ASU:

> For us, to be a public university means engaging the demographic complexity of our society as a whole. It means understanding that demographic complexity. It means designing the institution to deal with that demographic complexity. And it means accepting highly differentiated types of intelligence: analytical intelligence, emotional intelligence. Students are not of one type but are of many, many types. Taking all of

that and overlaying it with hundreds of degree programs results in so many variables and so many dimensions of complexity that you actually can't operate the institution unless you make a fundamental switch and say to yourself that, at the end of the day, it is just about analytics. (Bichsel 2012, 16)

Despite some newfound emphasis on data analytics, most higher education officials are not yet adept at using analytics to support institutional decision making. In a recent analysis of more than 250 conference papers and journal publications on learning analytics, Viberg et al. (2018) reported that although the field of learning analytics is maturing, there is little evidence that shows improvement of student outcomes from learning analytics or that analytics has yet to be deployed widely. Similarly, in a recent survey of provosts and chief academic officers among US colleges, *Inside Higher Education* analysts (Jaschik and Lederman 2019) found that only 16% of private university provosts and 19% of public university provosts believe that their universities use data very effectively to inform campus decision making. This predicament is often described as being "data rich but information poor" (Reinitz 2015), and precisely how Davenport et al. (2001) described the industry almost 18 years ago. Clearly, for data-informed decision making to take root in higher education, we must have conceptual clarity on what defines data-informed decision making and how it can be practiced. This and the subsequent chapters in this book seek to explain and illustrate how data analytics can support a data-informed decision making culture in higher education. While the focus of discussions in this book relates to data analytics that affect student success and institutional administration, we heartily acknowledge that Big Data and techniques such as predictive analyses are being used in faculty member research. The creation of new knowledge is indeed a vital endeavor, and Big Data labs and advanced computing centers with high-capacity computing are enabling researchers to investigate important questions such as changing weather patterns and their current and predicted impact on living conditions, food sources, and energy consumption. Data analytics has the potential to help researchers move society forward in many ways.

Further, the discussions in this book focus on data analytics in US higher education, but we fully acknowledge that similar trends and activities are happening in higher education around the world. Although the examples provided herein are from US institutions, data analytics poses similar challenges and opportunities in higher education across the globe.

Data-Informed Decision Making vs. Data-Driven Decision Making

In higher education and other industries, the terms *data-informed* and *data-driven* are often used interchangeably in describing how data analytics supports organizational decision making. However, these two terms carry different meanings, and therefore it is important to discuss their differences and similarities so that there is a conceptual clarity as we move on to discuss data-informed decision making in the remainder of this book.

- *Data-Driven Decision Making (DDDM)* gained strength in the 1980s. It focuses on decision algorithms, heuristics, and decision rules that empower decision processes and minimize human factors (let data speak for itself).
- *Data-Informed Decision Making (DIDM),* more recently introduced, focuses on leveraging data to generate insights to provide the contexts and evidence base for formulating decisions (let us figure out what data tells us).

According to Heavin and Power (2017), DDDM refers to the collection and analysis of data to make decisions. Data "drive" the decision making, and conclusions are made using verifiable data or facts. It is the practice of basing decisions on the analysis of data rather than purely on intuition (Provost and Fawcett 2013). DDDM is a decision process guided by a set of algorithms supported by both historical and current data elements. These algorithms can be a set of mathematical formulas, an engineering model, or a machine learning module. The decisions—typically routine and operational in nature—are supported and even suggested by the algorithms so that human decision makers do not need to add input; most algorithms produce decisions that are automatically accepted by the computer systems. For example, when student academic records are read and processed by a degree audit program, the algorithm built in to that program will evaluate the students' eligibility for degree completion. The program can generate a set of courses that need to be taken by each student and may even suggest different pathways for degree completion. When a student has completed all degree requirements and is eligible for graduation, an automated procedure may alert the student to file application for graduation and for inclusion in the next commencement.

While a number of articles or other written documents use the terms DIDM and DDDM interchangeably, we argue that the "drive" in DDDM implies that data determine the direction of the decision-making process and decision makers typically accept the decision recommendations. Many of the decisions made in business organizations are DDDM even though we may not even realize it. For example, Walmart stores nationally restock their shelves when inventory tracking systems detect low inventory and an order will be automatically placed for the suppliers to restock. In higher education, when students miss a deadline to pay fees or exceed the credit hours limit for the semester, an email will be automatically generated to remind the students and the system will block the students' ability to enroll for the semester. While DDDM systems exist and can provide some advantages in ensuring some proactive prompts (when decision logic is fully implemented), we believe that data-informed decision making is more helpful and robust in most decision situations when human intelligence and flexibility are required. Therefore, the focus of this book is more about DIDM and less on DDDM.

DIDM recognizes that human judgment is a key element in complex, dynamic, and strategic decision making. Because of the complexities, DIDM involves many more variables than a set of algorithms may be able to effectively address. Politics, human sensitivity, organizational values, and timing considerations are just some examples of why computer programs cannot fully be incorporated to make "data-driven" decisions for many dynamic decision situations.

We define DIDM as *the process of organizing data resources, conducting data analysis, and developing data insights to provide the contexts and evidence base for formulating organizational decisions.* In DIDM, data are just the evidence base, while the decision context is very much as important as, if not more important than, the data alone. Higher education leaders, even when equipped with sufficient data and excellent analysis, will need to draw on their professional experience, intuition, political acumen, ethical standards, and strategic considerations in making their decisions. Data are the important part of the decision equation but not the only part that drives the decision (Knapp, Copland, and Winnerton 2007). According to Maycotte (2015), "Being data-informed is about striking a balance in which your expertise and understanding of information plays as great a role in your decisions as the information itself. In the analogy of flying an airplane—no matter how sophisticated the systems onboard are, a highly trained pilot is ultimately responsible for making decisions at critical junctures. The same is true in a business organization" (1). Given the recent tragic loss of two Boeing 737 Max airplanes, seemingly due to faulty control algorithms, Maycotte's analogy is appropriate yet troubling.

The Importance of Clearly Differentiating between DDDM and DIDM

DIDM has its roots in the organizational learning theories in organizational management literature (Goldring and Berends 2009; Winkler and Fyffe 2016). Organizational learning is the process by which members of an organization acquire and use information to change and implement action (Beckhard 1969). Organizations that have knowledge systems distributed across functional units and individuals as well as embedded in the culture, values, and routines of the organizations are undergoing the process of organizational learning. In this way, data can serve as a catalyst to propel organizational learning. Leaders can use data to put into place mechanisms to support individual and collective learning surrounding data (Pfeffer 1998). A few more comments may help examine the differences between these two forms of decision making:

- DIDM is a more relevant and useful concept in the context of higher education because the decision context is dynamic;
- DIDM acknowledges that data are not perfect, in the sense that not all data are available and not all available data are accurate;
- DIDM acknowledges that analyses and algorithms are not perfect; models and algorithms are based on the information available, and human interpretation is needed;
- Organizational decision making is more nuanced than most algorithms can predict; and
- Human interactions and environmental factors are not as routine and are more likely to change.

No doubt, data are invaluable and critical sources of insights for higher education organizations today. However, data analytics alone does not drive decisions, especially those strategic and operational decisions that have complex and dynamic contextual factors. For example, many universities employ predictive models to help them identify and recruit students and make admissions decisions. However, these predictive models do not replace the careful review and reading of the admission files and supporting documents by the admissions counselors. Many intangible factors need to be accounted for in such decisions. It would be callous and arbitrary if admissions offices relied entirely on quantifiable data and decision algorithms.

In order to fulfill the missions of higher education that include teaching and learning, research and discovery, and public and community services, higher education officials engage in human interactions with constituents or stakeholders. The idea of having super-algorithms to drive decisions and actions may have some appeal in the routinized and stable decision situations such as degree audit. However, we believe that DIDM is a better paradigm and concept to embrace, particularly in strategic and operational decision making processes that involve human judgment, political sensitivity, and ethical considerations. For DDDM to work well, data need to be clean, stable, and consistent, and regularly updated. Such an ideal situation is often not available in higher education.

Many institutions, even those equipped with the best data warehouses and business intelligence systems, face many challenges in data management. Due to inconsistent data standards and definitions, varying efforts in data quality control, and lack of strong data governance practices, it is not unusual that different numbers are produced for a seemingly identical question. A classic example is the calculation of faculty full-time equivalents (FTEs). The Offices of Institutional Research, Human Resources, Faculty Affairs, and academic departments may all be able to produce their own FTE numbers. Depending on what data definition is used, it is possible that all answers are technically correct but each is derived for a different context (Zheng 2015).

Additionally, in the age of the Internet of Things (IoT),* the speed, volume, and variety of data available for decision analysis are overwhelming and they limit decision makers' ability to process all available data quickly enough to use predetermined algorithms to drive decisions. Chai and Shih (2017) point out that there is a growing belief that sophisticated algorithms can explore huge databases and find relationships independent of any preconceived theory and hypotheses. The assumption is: The bigger the data, the more powerful and precise are the findings. However, this belief may be misguided and risky. There is high potential for more data sources and new data elements for which the current algorithms cannot account. Algorithms can include small biases in data that may be compounded. Because many machine learning applications do not offer a transparent way to see the algorithms or logic behind recommendations (O'Neil 2016), some business leaders call for "explainable algorithms." Despite all the hype about Big Data, data cannot be very useful unless they can be analyzed in a timely way to develop contextualized meaning (Lane and Finsel 2014).

In its 2012 report "Analytics in Higher Education: Benefits, Barriers, Progress, and Recommendations," EDUCAUSE formally defined analytics as "the use of data, statistical analysis, and explanatory and predictive models to gain insight and act on complex issues" (Bichsel 2012, 6).

*For a brief definition and discussion on IoT, see: https://www.forbes.com/sites/jacob
morgan/2014/05/13/simple-explanation-internet-things-that-anyone-can-understand/#5318
c8971d09.

Analytics programs can offer institutions a way to be responsive to the increasingly challenging demands of organizational performance and strategic development they now face. EDUCAUSE's definition of analytics is in alignment with the data-informed decision making concept. It recognizes the need for data to be statistically analyzed, explained, and used to support complex decision situations.

DIDM is also important to organizational decision making in higher education because many strategic, operational, and management decisions that leaders face are dynamic, complex, and more nuanced than most algorithms can predict well. The organization's unique and nuanced issues make it difficult to suggest a perfect decision. According to a McKinsey survey of US companies (Marr 2018), only 18% of business leaders believe they can gather and use data insights effectively. Concerns include the need for proper analysis, how data are communicated to decision makers, who, in turn, act from the insights. This finding is similar to what we discussed earlier in this chapter: higher education leaders' perception that a small percentage of provosts and chief academic officers believe that their universities use data very effectively to inform campus decision making (Jaschik and Lederman 2019).

Enabling Conditions for DIDM in Higher Education Institutions

DIDM in higher education does not happen overnight, nor, in most cases, smoothly. It requires a strong push from the top down and a reciprocal enthusiastic support and participation from the bottom up. Data analytics is part of a university's decision fabric that requires strategic planning from an institutional perspective and the allocation of resources that reflect its growing importance in support of the institution's mission and vision for the future. To be successful in instituting a data-informed decision culture, there are three main conditions that enable DIDM to be accepted and practiced in the higher education environment. They are the people, the technology, and the process and culture.

People: Leadership and the Analytics Community

University leaders have a very important role to play in data-informed decision making. Their commitment, support, and willingness to use data in supporting their decision making are critical factors in ensuring the successful development of a data-informed decision culture. In its Leadership Agenda series, leaders of Achieving the Dream (ATD), a non-profit organization advocating for college access and success, urges institutional leaders to set the tone for commitment to data. ATD believes that committed leadership is central to establishing a culture of continuous improvement that is grounded in inquiry and evidence. Presidents, department heads, and other institutional leaders should model behaviors that support a culture of evidence and inquiry throughout the institutions. ATD further believes that institutional leaders should regularly review and explore student outcome data with diverse stakeholders in ways that spur thoughtful problem solving for student success (Achieving the Dream 2012). Similarly, Long Beach City College District (LBCCD) president, Reagan Romali, and her colleagues have made significant progress in student success measures including degree completions (Toda 2020). More importantly, she and her team have created a culture of exceptional student success, noted as the most improved among all California community college districts in the number of certificates awarded and eighth most improved in the number of degrees awarded (Toda 2020).

Institutional leaders can provide support for data analytics development efforts by relating analytics programs with the university's strategy and vision. In hiring new leaders, institutional officials may find it helpful to ask new leaders about their interest, vision, and experience in using data to support organizational growth and performance assessment. Trustees should hold senior leaders accountable for delivering accurate, reliable, and comprehensive data for strategy conversations. University leaders can demonstrate their support for DIDM by investing in data talents and analytical capabilities.

In 2016, leaders of Lehigh University conducted an organization-wide risk assessment and identified data analytics as a critical gap in their organizational capabilities. They immediately took action to appoint the chief information officer and the chief institutional research officer to assemble a planning team made up of senior administrative leaders and data stewards to develop a strategic analytics plan. The plan addressed some of the most critical areas of building a DIDM analytics culture, including the data management infrastructure, data governance, data reporting and collaboration, and the sharing of analytical insights. Most important, Lehigh University's leadership put resources behind these initiatives and enabled the hiring of key personnel and the acquisition of new data management and reporting tools. Actions included moving the business intelligence staff to co-locate with the institutional research and analytics staff, setting up a centralized data repository, establishing a Tableau server for generating data reports and data visualization, and hiring a data architect and a data governance manager. With positive outcomes, leadership support provided the momentum and resources that Lehigh University needed to embrace data-informed decision making.

Another important base of support for developing a data-informed decision culture is the existence of a critical mass of campus data analytics users and developers who are actively collaborating and sharing their knowledge and skills. Díaz, Rowshankish, and Saleh (2018) believe that analytical talents and users have different roles to play and the same individual can play different roles depending on the circumstances. These roles include:

- Business leaders: lead analytics transformation across organization;
- Data engineers: collect, structure, and analyze data;
- Data architects: ensure data quality and consistency of present and future data flows;
- Workflow integrators: build interactive decision-support tools and implement solutions;
- Visualization analysts: visualize data and build reports and dashboards;
- Data scientists: develop statistical models and advanced algorithms to solve problems;

- Analytics translators: ensure analytics addresses critical business problems; and
- Delivery managers: deliver data and analytics-driven insights and interface with end users.

Clearly, as organizations face the challenge of Big Data, they need analytical talents to help clean the data, organize it, and store it, along with training people to analyze and build models using data. High-performing organizations tend to support data sharing and encourage collaboration among different types of users. A data community is a mutually supportive environment where data users with analytical needs and appropriate security clearance can connect to all available data resources across different organization vectors to detect patterns or connections that a single data silo will not help. Mathies (2018) proposes that institutions develop a data sharing mandate, and Arellano (2017) recommends that a data user community be designed as a combination of people across the enterprise, whereas common data and analytical tools are shared. This networked approach helps share information and analytic results across interested groups and those with more skills being seen as a source of trusted analytics for the whole network. This combination of central governance and distributed data access and contribution can help everyone get needed information without slowing down the business by depending on the central IT team (Arellano 2017).

Technology

Another critically important enabling condition for DIDM is the availability and access to up-to-date and user-oriented data management and reporting tools, including but not limited to the following core components:

- Ability to integrate data from many different sources, including but not limited to enterprise resource planning systems (i.e., PeopleSoft, Banner, etc.), third-party software systems, and cloud-based platforms, both internal and external sources;

- A strong data governance system that helps standardize and systematically document data definitions, data dictionaries, data specifications, and data lineages;
- Availability of effective data reporting, data analysis, and data visualization tools; and
- Ability to harness the power of structured, semi-structured, and unstructured data resources through data architecture designs such as a data lake.

An enterprise-wide data management and sharing infrastructure typically comes in the form of an enterprise data warehouse (EDW). Traditionally, an EDW is installed on-site at the institution in a database server and managed by the IT department. Technological advances in the last several years have allowed organizations to move EDW operations to the cloud. For Big Data storage, the concept of a *data lake* or *data reservoir* may be considered. A data lake is a data management methodology enabled by a massive data repository based on low-cost technologies that improves the capture, refinement, archival, and exploration of raw data within an enterprise. This repository may contain unstructured, semi-structured, and structured data where the largest part of these data may have unrecognized value for the organization (Khine and Wang 2017; Watson 2015). Data lakes are often built by tapping into the vast storage space made available by cloud-based computing platforms such as Amazon's or Microsoft's cloud solutions.

The availability of more data and from many more sources not only poses a challenge for storage and access, but also for the documentation and standardization of data elements. No matter whether it is in an EDW environment or a cloud-based data lake environment, a data governance structure with strong enforceability is a must. As a collection of practices and processes that help to ensure the formal management of data assets within an organization (Knight 2017), data governance is an organizational process that involves other activities such as data stewardship, data quality control, and data security. Together, these activities help an institution gain better control over its data assets, including methods, technologies, and behaviors around the proper management of data. For more detail, Glasgal and Nestor systematically introduce the concept of data governance and share how the system was implemented at Northeastern University in chapter 6 of this volume.

Another technological must for DIDM is the wide adaption of data reporting and visualization tools in sharing data insights with constituent groups, especially with the senior leadership. Gone are the days when data reports come in with dozens of statistical tables and many pages. With data visualization tools such as Tableau (tableau.com) and PowerBI (powerbi.microsoft.com), data are now shown in different graphical formats, fitting the types of data used in the reporting. For example, to report historical trends in college enrollment, instead of using a table with columns and rows, data visualization tools now make the trend displayed in a line or bar graph, with many different filters to drill down to different colleges and departments and by different types of students. When done well, following principles of good graphic design, a data visualization page can replace a large number of traditional tables. Described in chapter 4, clear and concise communication is essential. Visualized data reports can deliver the data insights quickly and provide an interactive element that can be more useful than static tables. With newer data-reporting tools, key data reports such as management dashboards, factbooks, student profiles, and productivity reports can now be made visually attractive and easy to understand. For DIDM, data insights delivered in an easy to understand and easy to access manner are key to acceptance and utilization. An example of Lehigh University's enrollment report is given in a visually pleasing and highly intuitive format in figure 1.1. The visualization module enables a user to interactively query the data by many layers of data filters: semester, level of students, class of students, race/ethnicity, cohorts, on-campus vs. off-campus, and FTE vs. headcounts. This report replaces many detailed data tables in traditional paper-based or PDF-generated reports.*

Another technological advancement in data analytics is the collection and analysis of social media and human interaction data. This new

*Lehigh University's interactive data visualization tool can be accessed at https://oirsa .lehigh.edu/enrollment.

Selected Demographics

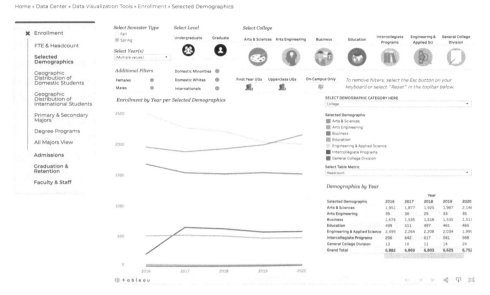

Figure 1.1. Lehigh University Enrollment Report (based on Tableau platform).
https://oirsa.lehigh.edu/fte-headcount

approach is best captured in the "connected campus" idea proposed by a number of companies such as Salesforce, Oracle, and Microsoft. Many higher education institutions are data rich and information poor. Institutions collect student data using enterprise resource planning (ERP) systems like Banner or PeopleSoft, but the data are mostly locked behind security layers and not utilized for analytical processing. Officials track high school students who visit institutional web sites, come for campus tours, and submit applications, but in most cases these data are not connected to predict and support their future success once they arrive on campus. Records are kept for students who participated in various campus activities, but the data are scattered and not utilized to personalize and enhance students' learning experience. Academic advisors meet with students regularly but are not equipped with the right data to individualize their interactions. They know that degrees are granted, but advisors have limited knowledge about students' career success and continued engagement with their alma maters.

While these data issues may not have been major barriers to student success in the past, institution officials' ability to improve retention, graduation, and lifelong engagement of students depends on improving their "connectedness." The connected campus idea is based on the customer relations management (CRM) platform (e.g., Salesforce.com), which acts as a communication tool for different campus departments to track their interactions with different stakeholder groups. A CRM stores data from all sources and organizes it in a way that facilitates personalized communications. For example, an academic advisor armed with a CRM will be able to interact with the student more effectively if he or she can access the student's academic records, student life, and career development opportunity data in one place. In chapter 9, O'Bryan explains how college officials can change their level of engagement with students by connecting the disparate data points to understand the full lifecycle of student engagement from the time of initial interest in the institution throughout the students' interaction with the institution before and after graduation.

Process and Culture

Leadership support, a community of analytics talents, and a strong technology infrastructure are the strong foundation for developing DIDM. To truly make DIDM a success, institution leaders must change their business processes and intentionally build an analytics culture. This cultural transformation starts with the articulation of the basic principle of treating data as an institutional asset and not a resource owned or monopolized by a department or unit. In a survey of higher education leaders, Bichsel (2012) found that the data silo is a particularly common problem in higher education. For an analytics program to be successful, organizational policies must be changed to encourage the sharing, standardization, and federation of data resources, balancing the needs for security with needs for access. For DIDM to take root, the following are key considerations:

- Senior leaders need to show commitment to using data to inform decisions by asking for and utilizing data analytics insights;

- DIDM requires the breaking down of the organizational silos to facilitate data sharing and collaboration—no individual unit or department "owns" the data, but rather it is part of the university's data resources and needs to be shared based on appropriate security and data governance rules;
- IT, institutional research (IR), and operational management should work in close collaboration to explore data and analyze data findings to discover actionable insights; organizational leaders must be willing to take the actionable insights to pilot test new organizational change or operational improvement ideas; and
- Given the large number of challenges facing higher education institutions, DIDM efforts will add greater value if such efforts can focus on institutional priorities (such as student success).

Data silos are often barriers to greater levels of transparency in performance assessment and institutional planning. Gagliardi and Turk (2017) point out that the democratization of data analytics might reveal some inconvenient truths about the performance of colleges and universities. However, a greater level of data transparency is needed as the higher education sector becomes more competitive and stakeholders demand greater accountability. Instead of letting organizational silos become barriers to needed changes, college and university leaders should empower change by providing critical operational and performance data to key stakeholders so that they can use the shared data resources to make informed decisions. For example, at a private college in the Northeast United States, a collegewide interactive dashboard project got stuck in the implementation phase when the deans and department chairs demanded that their data be kept from other deans and chairs. To meet the needs of the deans and chairs, the complexity of the data classification schema and access privilege rules increased almost exponentially, making the data programmers' job a nightmare. Even when the programmers were able to create data visualizations for the reports with multiple layers of administrative access rules, the resulting data reports lost all the connectivity and relative comparisons that a visualization tool is designed to deliver. To truly embrace DIDM, college leaders must break down the data silos and show some courage in enabling data transparency.

Enabling data analytics to be embedded in the institution's culture and be successful will also require plans for training and professional development. Training may be needed for the technical aspects of data storage and maintenance, for analysts who must be deeply knowledgeable of data definitions, techniques for manipulation of the data, and considerations of ethical and responsible uses of data. User groups may be one way to ensure that multiple users across a campus are consistent in their understanding of the data and how it applies within their specific contexts. Indeed, training and professional needs are an important part of the institution's long-term data analytics program, and more on this topic is discussed in chapter 12.

Another important aspect of cultural transformation in data analytics is the willingness to give data insights a chance to inform decision making. Leaders must have both the patience and the willingness to let data provide clues, to take some risk, and allow program experimentation. To have an innovation mindset is critically important because Big Data, artificial intelligence (AI), and machine learning (ML) will likely create disruptive changes. For example, one college's admissions office staff produced a well-designed and detailed glossy brochure to attract more applicants to help achieve its goal of expanding its enrollment for five consecutive years. Admissions officials sought to send the brochure to every applicant who visited their web site and requested additional information. Given the high cost of printing, the vice president for admissions decided to divide the prospects into two groups, with Group A prospects receiving the glossy paper brochure and prospects in Group B receiving a PDF version of the brochure through email with enhanced web-based contents. With the goal of finding out if an electronic brochure is equally effective in encouraging application, this experiment came with risk; if the electronic brochure was not well received, the college would have missed its enrollment target. College officials proceeded with the experiment and affirmed that it was a risk worth taking, because they believed that Generation Z students (the primary demographic group who are interested in this college) are more receptive to electronic materials. More important, they wanted to use data and results from this quasi-experiment to inform future admissions strategies.

Another key aspect of building a data-informed decision environment is the collaboration between the information technology (IT) and the analytics communities. IT is a critical partner that contributes to the strong and dynamic analytical environment of the campus. When asked, "What is your data strategy?" DalleMule and Davenport (2017) argued that a data strategy framework should distinguish between data defense and data offense—each with different objectives, activities, and architecture. A defensive data strategy focuses on ensuring data integrity, data security, data access, and data documentation. An offensive data strategy centers on generating insights from data to support business process, generate business value, and achieve organization objectives. In other words, defense is what IT is good at providing, and offense is what business users and analysts are good at developing. Defense and offense need to work well together to become effective in implementing organizational data strategies. All higher education institutions need both offensive and defensive data strategies to be successful in DIDM.

The Imperatives for DIDM in Higher Education

The Expectation Imperatives of DIDM

Many individuals hold high expectations for higher education. Stakeholders such as students and parents expect costs to be controlled, time to degree to be reasonably short, graduation rates to be high, and for employment to be secured soon after graduation. Business leaders expect universities to equip students with employable skills who can contribute to problem solutions. Government leaders expect universities to operate efficiently and contribute to regional and local economic development. With these expectations, universities are under scrutiny to prove their value. Many aspects of the university's operations will need to be supported by strong analytics programs. These include the six items described below:

Student Success and Outcomes

For all higher education institutions (HEIs), student success and outcomes should be the most important mission. The success of Georgia State University in improving student success using analytical insights (see chapter 8 of this book) is a great example of how DIDM can add value and truly make a great difference. Student success should be a core element of university strategy at the most senior level of the organization. Marketing and communications should highlight student success as a central piece of the institution's strategic mission. A sustainable plan should include data models and results showing return on investment at an institutional level. As the process scales, retention improvement will help improve revenue stream and improve instructional quality. Leadership should consistently communicate a vision of student success—this can, in turn, effectively align resources to support defined goals.

New Academic Program and Curriculum Innovation

Analytical tools such as learning analytics, customer relations management, machine learning, and artificial intelligence will create opportunities for new designs of academic programs and through mass customization. New developments such as stackable credentials, learning badges, and experiential transcripts are more connected with student learning needs and with demands of the job market. Davenport et al. (2001) have pointed out that, armed with Big Data analytics, more organizations will be able to better understand customers' needs and will, subsequently, create new products for those needs. Higher education can and should use Big Data analytics to support program innovations and changes that meet the changing needs of the students and employers.

Meeting the Needs of the Community and Industry

In discussing a university's relation with external communities Gavazzi and Gee (2018) use spousal relationships as a metaphor to argue that universities must cultivate relationships to have harmonious and prosperous interactions with their communities. To address the value propositions to their community and industry partners, university officials should work proactively to create and sustain programs that are mutually beneficial. In today's digital age and global competitions, a university cannot be an ivory tower isolated from its surroundings. University missions and programs are connected to communities and industry in large part as students acquire employable skills and knowledge that meet community and industry needs. DIDM will help by informing university leaders and faculty members about labor market trends, assessing students' learning experience and leadership capabilities, and measuring the effectiveness of different pedagogical approaches.

Operational Efficiency and Effectiveness

One of the biggest opportunities for the higher education sector in leveraging data analytics for decision making is the ability to improve operational efficiency and effectiveness. Big Data technologies, cloud-based solutions, machine learning, and artificial intelligence will make some of the older technologies and costly solutions obsolete. (See chapter 11 of this book for Wayt et al.'s discussion and examples of how analytics support financial and business operations in higher education.) For example, enterprise resource planning systems, including human resources, finance, research administration, and student information, will no longer need to be installed and operated on premise and budgeted as an expensive capital expenditure, saving a lot of resources and personnel cost. Instead, universities that migrate to new cloud-based solutions will be in a better position to allocate budget IT spending as operating expenses, which is easier to budget on an annual basis and minimizes cost surges for major upgrades. Data analytics can also help achieve operational efficiency and effectiveness by bringing data transparency and disciplines to performance assessment. As resources management and outcome measures become more accessible through dashboards and scorecards, the conversation on how to achieve better results and improve collaboration will lead to newer opportunities for shared services and reduction of redundancy.

Strategic Agility and Differentiation

More so than in the past, the next 10 to 20 years in higher education will test the ability of leaders to steer their institutions strategically. The challenges facing higher education and the rapid changes in the digital revolution and connectivity may bring disruptive innovations at a speed that is faster than anticipated. Senior leaders in higher education must identify the strategic challenges facing their institutions. Questions may include: What strengths or unique capabilities differentiate one institution from another?; what new programs are needed in order to stay competitive?; can one recruit the right number of students based on the desired student profiles given the significant demographic shifts to come?; and can one grow the institution's revenue base without relying heavily on tuition increases? University leaders and trustees must grapple with these and many other questions in their decision-making process. Marsh and Thariani provide critical insights into these questions in chapter 5.

Data Governance, Security, and Ethical Considerations

Another imperative for DIDM is the safeguarding, ethical, and responsible use of our data resources. It is important that data be used to generate analytical insights to inform decisions. It is equally important that this is done in a manner that protects the privacy and rights of our students and employees. Chapter 6 addresses important points related to data use and governance, and chapter 4 shares important insights on responsible and secure use of data. Prinsloo and Slade (2015) remind us that the traditional paternalistic HEI culture, along with the more recent enthusiasm for possible enhanced student success through analytics, has influenced attitudes and policies on data collection but has not adequately addressed issues of privacy. Strong data governance and a thorough plan for safe collection and storage of data are critical.

Cloud-based solutions and the proliferation of third-party applications will continue to create challenges for data management. Most of the policy and process questions need to be addressed through a data governance body to ensure legal and regulatory compliance and to reduce organization risk exposure. Similarly, as more data resources are being used to create predictive models and algorithms that impact students' lives and outcomes, greater attention and care need to be taken to ensure that the privacy rights of the study subjects are being safeguarded. In chapter 4, Webber and Morn also address some of the human factors and subjective judgments needed in the use of data. Many decisions require careful calibration of the political, financial, and social factors.

DIDM is a cultural change and not a one-time project. For DIDM to work well, university leaders and the user community need to embrace it as a platform and a culture, not a project that needs to be completed. DIDM is not just about the data tools or the newer technologies, it is more importantly about the data awareness and analytical insight acceptance and utilization mindset. Enabling this change will also require a strategy for personnel training for analytic techniques. EDUCAUSE (2012) recommends that higher education leaders ask the right strategic and operational decision questions and seek to use data evidence to answer these questions and find the right solutions: invest in data talents and data insight translators and foster a vibrant data user community on campus; do not let perfection be the enemy of data uses; make the best out of available data information resources; encourage closer collaboration between the IT and the analytics communities; and invest in analytical tools and technologies that will facilitate the integrated view of data insights across the campus.

Conclusion

Advances in technology, including storage for large volumes of data, are challenging the ways in which decisions are made in higher education. Nearly all, if not all, stakeholders desire more data, assuming that it will make better decisions. We believe that, unlike data-driven methods that rely heavily on predetermined algorithms, data-informed decision making will facilitate goal completion and help achieve greater effectiveness for higher education institutions. DIDM involves both top-down commitment and bottom-up support, strategic planning and resources that acknowledge the institution's mission and vision for the future, and lots of hard work. A strong foundation for DIDM rests on leaders who support and facilitate organizational programs and procedures that develop and build a community of analytics talents. University leaders have a critical role to play in data-informed decision making; their commitment, support, and willingness to use data to support decision making is among the most critical factors that will ensure the successful implementation of a data-informed decision culture.

Although the volume and variety of data continue to increase at a faster speed, institutional leaders as well as external stakeholders must consider the practical and ethical uses of data in higher education as they strive to stay ahead of the data tsunami. While vendor products abound, users or potential users should ask hard questions about the "what" can practically be learned from the data as well as the accuracy of the statistical models or algorithms being used. Users must guard against predictive analyses that include subtle biases or produce other unintended consequences (Ekowo and Palmer 2017; O'Neil 2016). An institution's comprehensive data governance plan is incredibly important. Officials may wish to review Mathies's (2019) proposed Data Bill of Rights, which requires a plan to protect individual data as well as practices that promote data definitions, rules of use, transparency, and shared governance.

Many aspects of the university's operation will benefit from a strong analytics program. Building partnerships with the local community and businesses and ensuring strong data governance and privacy policies are key drivers to the further advancement of data analytics in higher education that will facilitate student and institutional success. Analytic strategies of data will not be minimized, only further emphasized as we move forward.

References

Achieving the Dream. 2012. "Building Institutional Capacity for Data-Informed Decision Making." Public Agenda Series #3. Accessed December 31, 2018. https://www.achievingthedream.org/sites/default/files/resources/ATD_CuttingEdge_No3.pdf.

Arellano, P. 2017. "Making Decisions with Data—Developing a Community around Data in Your Business." IT Pro Portal. Accessed Feb. 21, 2019. https:www.itproportal.com/features/making-decisions-with-data-developing-a-community-around-data-in-your-business/.

Arnold, K., and M. Pistilli. 2012. "Course Signals at Purdue: Using Learning Analytics to Increase Student Success." *Proceedings of the Second International Learning Analytics and Knowledge Conference* (pp. 267–270). ACM Publications.

Beckhard, R. 1969. *Organization Development: Its Nature, Origin, and Prospects.* Reading, MA: Addison-Wesley.

Bichsel, J. 2012. "Analytics in Higher Education: Benefits, Barriers, Progress, and Recommendations." Louisville, CO: EDUCAUSE Center for Applied Research. http://www.educause.edu/ecar.

Brown, M. 2011. "Learning Analytics: The Coming Third Wave." (EDUCAUSE Learning Initiative Brief). Retrieved from EDUCAUSE library. https://library .educause.edu/resources/2011/4/learning-analytics-the-coming-third-wave.

Chin, J. K., M. Hagstroem, A. Libarikian, and K. Rifai. 2017. "Advanced Analytics: Nine Insights from the C-Suite." *McKinsey Analytics* (July): 1–8.

Chai, S., and W. Shih. 2017. "Why Big Data Isn't Enough." *MIT Sloan Management Review* (Winter): 57–61.

Chris Brady, C., M. Forde, and S. Chadwick. 2017. "Why Your Company Needs Data Translators." *MIT Sloan Management Review* (Winter): 14–16.

DalleMule, L., and T. Davenport. 2017. "What's Your Business Strategy?" *Harvard Business Review* (May–June). Accessed December 15, 2018. https://hbr.org/2017 /05/whats-your-data-strategy.

Davenport, T. H., J. G. Harris, D. W. De Long, and A. L. Jacobson. 2001. "Data to Knowledge to Results: Building Analytics Capability." *California Management Review* 43, no. 2: 117–138.

Díaz, A., K. Rowshankish, and T. Saleh. 2018. "Why Data Culture Matters." *McKinsey Quarterly* (September). Accessed April 2019. https://agribusiness .purdue.edu/quarterly-review/why-data-culture-matters.

Drake, B. M., and A. Walz. 2018. "Evolving Business Intelligence and Data Analytics in Higher Education." In *New Directions for Institutional Research*, 178, edited by C. Mathies. San Francisco: Wiley Periodicals, Inc.

Drachsler, H., and W. Greller. 2016. "Privacy and Analytics—It's a DELICATE Issue: A Checklist to Establish Trusted Learning Analytics." *Proceedings of the Sixth International Conference on Learning Analytics and Knowledge (LAK '16)*, 89–98. http://dx.doi.org/10.1145/2883851.2883893.

Dziuban, C., P. Moskal, T. Cavanagh, and A. Watts. 2012. "Analytics That Inform the University: Using Data You Already Have." *Journal of Asynchronous Learning Networks* 16, no. 3: 21–38.

Ekowo, M., and I. Palmer. 2017. "Predictive Analytics in Higher Education: Five Guiding Practices for Ethical Use." Educational Policy Paper. Washington, DC: New America.

Frick, W. 2014. "An Introduction to Data-Driven Decisions for Managers Who Don't Like Math." *Harvard Business Review.* May 19, 2014. https://hbr.org/2014/05/an -introduction-to-data-driven-decisions-for-managers-who-dont-like-math.

Gagliardi, J. S., and J. M. Turk. 2017. *The Data-Enabled Executive: Using Analytics for Student Success and Sustainability.* Washington, DC: American Council of Education.

Gavazzi, S. M., and E. G. Gee. 2018. *Land-Grant Universities of the Future.* Baltimore, MD: Johns Hopkins University Press.

General Accounting Office. 2016. "Data and Analytics Innovation—Emerging Opportunities and Challenges." September 2016. GAO-16-659SP.

Gharib, S. 2018. "Intel CEO Says Data Is the New Oil." *Fortune Magazine*. June 7, 2018. http://fortune.com/2018/06/07/intel-ceo-brian-krzanich-data/.

Goldring, E., and M. Berends. 2009. *Leading with Data Pathways to Improve Your School*. Thousand Oaks, CA: Corwin Publishing.

Grajek, S., and the EDUCAUSE IT Issues Panel. 2019. "Top 10 IT Issues, 2019: The Student Genome Project." Washington, DC: EDUCAUSE.

Heavin, C., and D. J. Power. 2017. "How Do Data-Driven, Data-Based and Data-Informed Decision Making Differ?" Blog post. Accessed February 11, 2019. http://dssresources.com/faq/index.php?action=artikel&id=392#.

Jaschik, S., and D. Lederman. 2019. "The 2019 Inside Higher Education Survey of College and University Chief Academic Officers—A Study by Gallup and Inside Higher Education." *Inside Higher Education*. January 23, 2019. https://www.insidehighered.com/news/survey/2019-inside-higher-ed-survey-chief-academic-officers.

Khalil, M., and M. Ebner. 2015. "Learning Analytics: Principles and Constraints." In *Proceedings of World Conference on Educational Multimedia, Hypermedia and Telecommunications 2015*, pp. 1326–1336. Chesapeake, VA: AACE.

Khine, P. P., and Z. S. Wang. 2017. "Data Lake: A New Ideology in Big Data Era." Paper presented at the Fourth International Conference on Wireless Communication and Sensor Network, Wuhan, China, December 2017. Accessed February 13, 2019. https://www.researchgate.net/publication/321825490_Data_Lake_A_New_Ideology_in_Big_Data_Era.

Knapp, M. S., M. A. Copland, and J. A. Winnerton. 2007. "Understanding the Promise and Dynamics of Data-Informed Leadership." In *Yearbook of the National Society for the Study of Education*: 74–104.

Knight, M. 2017. "What Is Data Governance?" Dataversity. Blog post. December 18, 2017. Accessed Feb. 13, 2019. https://www.dataversity.net/what-is-data-governance/.

Lane, J. E., and B. A. Finsel. 2014. "Fostering Smarter Colleges and Universities—Data, Big Data, and Analytics. In *Building a Smarter University: Big Data, Innovation, and Analytics*, 3–26, edited by J. E. Lane. Albany, NY: State University of New York Press.

Marr, B. 2018. "Forget Data Scientists and Hire a Data Translator Instead?" *Forbes Magazine Online*. March 12, 2018. https://www.forbes.com/sites/bernardmarr/2018/03/12/forget-data-scientists-and-hire-a-data-translator-instead/#48ade0b0848a.

Martin, D. 2016. "Data-Driven versus Data-Informed—What's Best for You?" Cleverism. August 12, 2016. https://www.cleverism.com/data-driven-versus-data-informed-whats-best/.

Mathies, C. 2018. "Ethical Use of Data." In *IR in the Digital Era: New Directions for Institutional Research* 178: 85–97, edited by C. Mathies and C. Ferland. Boston: Wiley.

Maycotte, H. O. 2015. "Be Data-Informed, Not Data-Driven, for Now." *Forbes Magazine Online*. January 13, 2015. https://www.forbes.com/sites/homaycotte/2015/01/13/data-informed-not-data-driven-for-now/#7ccdebc6f5b7.

McAfee, A., and E. Brynjolfsson. 2012. "Big Data: The Management Revolution." *Harvard Business Review* (October). https://hbr.org/2012/10/big-data-the-management-revolution.

O'Neil, C. 2016. *Weapons of Math Destruction: How Big Data Increases Inequality and Threatens Democracy.* New York: Broadway Books.

Peterson, R. J. 2012. "Policy Dimensions of Analytics in Higher Education." *EDUCAUSE Review* (July–August): 44–47.

Pfeffer, J. 1998. "The Human Equation: Building Profits by Putting People First." Cambridge, MA: Harvard Business School Press.

Picciano, A. G. 2012. "The Evolution of Big Data and Learning Analytics in American Higher Education." *Journal of Asynchronous Learning Networks* 16, no. 3: 9–20.

Prinsloo, P., and S. Slade. 2015. "Student Privacy Self-Management: Implications for Learning Analytics." In *Proceedings of the LAK 2015 International Conference on Learning Analytics and Knowledge,* 83–92. New York, NY: Association of Computer Machinery.

Provost, F., and T. Fawcett. 2013. "Data Science and Its Relationship to Big Data and Data-Driven Decision Making." *Big Data* 1, no. 1: 51–59. https://doi.org/10.1089/big.2013.1508.

Reinitz, B. T. 2015. "Building Institutional Analytics Maturity" (Summit report). Louisville, CO: EDUCAUSE Center for Analysis and Research.

Salesforce. 2019. "Software Company for Customer Relations Products and Tools." Salesforce. Accessed February 2, 2019. https://www.salesforce.com/crm/.

Smolan, R., and J. Erwitt. 2012. *The Human Face of Big Data.* Sausalito, CA: Against All Odds Productions.

Swing, R., and L. Ross. 2016. "A New Vision for Institutional Research." *Change* 48, no. 2: 6–13. https://doi.org/10.1080/00091383.2016.1163132.

Toda, S. (2020). Long Beach city college makes phenomenal progress in students earning degrees and certificates. Press Release from *Digital Journal,* February 4, 2020. Accessed February 12, 2020. http://www.digitaljournal.com/pr/4578138

Viberg, O., M. Hatakka, O. Balter, and A. Mavroudi. 2018. "The Current Landscape of Learning Analytics in Higher Education." *Computers in Human Behavior* 89: 98–110.

Waston, H. J. 2015. "Data Lakes, Data Labs, and Sandboxes." *Business Intelligence Journal* 20:4–7.

White, A. 2018. "Do You Really Want to Be Data-Driven?" *CIO Magazine.* November 21, 2018. https://www.cio.com.au/article/649883/do-really-want-data-driven/.

Winkler, M. K., and S. D. Fyffe. 2016. "Strategies for Cultivating an Organizational Learning Culture." Urban Institute White Paper. December 2016. https://www.urban.org/sites/default/files/publication/86191/strategies_for_cultivating_an_organizational_learning_culture_3.pdf.

Zheng, H. Y. 2015. "Business Intelligence as a Data-Based Decision Support System and Its Roles in Support of Institutional Research and Planning." In *Institutional Research and Planning in Higher Education—Global Contexts and Themes,* 159–173, edited by K. Webber and A. Calderon. New York: Routledge.

Zwitter, A. 2014. "Big Data Ethics." *Big Data & Society* 16: 1–6. https://doi.org/10.1177/2053951714559253.

Big Data and the Transformation of Decision Making in Higher Education

Braden J. Hosch

Gosh, you've really got some nice toys here.
—Roy Batty, *Blade Runner* (1982), set in 2019

IN THE summer of 1956, luminaries of mathematics and information sciences gathered at Dartmouth College for two months to hold in-depth discussions about what the group organizer John McCarthy termed *artificial intelligence*. McCarthy's proposal to the Rockefeller Foundation to support the summer meeting provocatively and presciently asserted: "If a machine can do a job, then an automatic calculator can be programmed to simulate the machine. The speeds and memory capacities of present computers may be insufficient to simulate many of the higher functions of the human brain, but the major obstacle is not lack of machine capacity, but our inability to write programs taking full advantage of what we have" (McCarthy et al. 1955).

Participants in this summer meeting included, among others, Arthur Samuel, who would later in the decade coin the term *machine learning* as he developed a computer program that could win a checkers game against a human being; Ray Solomonoff, who developed algorithmic information theory that machine learning is probabilistic and can be trained on existing data to solve new problems; Marvin Minsky, who would go on to co-found the AI Lab at MIT; and Claude Shannon at

Bell Labs, who developed information theory and would later in life quip that in computer-humans chess games, he was "rooting for the machines" (Shannon 1987). The meeting was significant not just because of the brilliance of its attendees but because of the problems addressed, which included discussion on automatic computers, how computers can be programmed to use a language, neuron nets, theory of the size of a calculation, self-improvement of data programs, abstractions, and randomness and creativity. These problems represented the central challenges of achieving artificial intelligence envisioned by Alan Turing (1950) several years earlier that a machine could mimic human behavior.

Solutions, however, remained elusive until improvements were made to computing power, data storage and management systems, and networking. The resulting developments are changing and will continue to change how organizations, including universities, operate and deliberate. This chapter provides historical context for how the transformation of computing from record keeping and administrative processing into what Agrawal, Gans, and Goldfarb (2018) call "prediction machines" affects how decisions are made and how Big Data represent a transformational means for colleges and universities to improve if not reimagine their operations. *Big Data,* in this respect, is a broad term that includes huge amounts of structured data (such as all the clicks of all students in all online learning materials at a university), but also unstructured data like social media feeds with text, images, and video files, as well as a set of non-hypothesis-driven analytical techniques applied to existing (smaller) data sets. This chapter asserts that resulting developments in machine learning, artificial intelligence, and the Internet of Things provocatively point toward a future for the higher education sector in which decisions made by students, faculty, and administrators are approached much differently from earlier periods.

The Evolution of Computing Power and University Decision Making

In the 1950s, colleges and universities were organizations of students, faculty, and staff, concentrated on a geographically defined campus, and who labored to produce voluminous textual material—articles, books, term papers, tests, and memos. World-class science occurred in laboratories, but results were recorded in quadrille notebooks and written up as lab reports, later typed up, submitted to and published in journals that would later be housed on the bookshelves of libraries. The walls of registrar's offices were obscured by beautiful wooden filing cabinets with reams of student files printed on paper (often handwritten) and stored in actual folders. Decisions about whom to admit or not, whom to hire or let go, what programs to start or retire were made largely on the basis of professional expertise and the judgment of experts who had spent entire careers at an institution. As Gladwell (2005) demonstrates, there is real value in the judgment of experts in their fields of expertise, but these judgments are also necessarily bounded by the knowledge of those making them.

Administrative computing became a reality at research universities following its deployment in academic computing in the late 1950s and 1960s, featuring large mainframe computers built by IBM and later Burroughs and Cray running with vacuum tubes adjacent to large cooling facilities. Initial processing power in the mid-1950s was measured in hundreds of instructions per second, increasing to millions of operations per second by the late 1960s (IBM 2003), several orders of magnitude slower than the personal mobile devices of the late 2010s, which record speeds of billions of operations per second (Simonite 2018). Data analysis became easier with the release of statistical software applications still in use today, such as the Statistical Package for the Social Sciences (SPSS) released in 1968 and the Statistical Analysis System (SAS) released in 1971. As faculty circulated through administrative roles, including the relatively new function of institutional research, these applications became widespread tools of choice among institutional researchers to prepare descriptive statistics informing institutional leadership about the past. This knowledge was invaluable to institutional decision making, and campus planning estimates made use of cohort attrition models for enrollment planning and segmented yield rates for admissions, but forecasting still relied heavily on professional expertise informed by population-level statistics.

Even though computing power was still relatively limited, the promise of artificial intelligence to transform education was under active exploration, as evidenced by Ellis Page's initiative (Page, Fisher, and Fisher 1968) to grade composition papers using the computing power of the day. Project Essay Grade, funded by the US Department of Education (Page and Paulus 1968), investigated the feasibility of automatically analyzing and evaluating student writing using a FORTRAN program for natural language processing after student papers were keyed into mainframes. Project Essay Grade demonstrated that computer programs were about as good as human raters at evaluating student writing, although the methods remained too costly for widespread adoption (Page, Fisher, and Fisher 1968). Page later revived the project in the 1990s, and with the exponential increase in computing power, the widespread use of computer terminals in testing, and the motivation of testing companies to cut costs, the basic infrastructure of Page's project became ubiquitous in the 2000s.

Data storage and processing also evolved markedly during the 1950s and 1960s, and the increased capacity to store data had implications for decision-making processes. Data and programs were created and stored on punch cards—technology from the nineteenth century to automate textile production. Use of magnetic tape to store data was introduced by IBM in 1951 and offered great advantages for increasing speed and volume but still carried the limitations of sequential storage. In the mid-1950s and with marked advancements in the 1960s, hard disks allowed for random access to the blocks in which data were stored, providing additional advances in storage capacity and retrieval speed. Importantly, the technology allowed development and commercialization of the floppy disk in the late 1960s and early 1970s, which allowed for the transport of data between microcomputers and mainframes. Direct access storage of data versus sequential storage on tape or a box of punch cards also allowed for development of data management systems, with the introduction of navigational databases in the 1960s and the relational database in the next decade by Edgar Codd (1970). These events were followed by the development of structured query language (SQL) later in the decade (Chamberlin and Boyce 1974), later to be commercialized by Oracle for release in 1979 and still in widespread use forty years later.

These intensive mainframe computing resources and data tools, however, were generally reserved for large research universities, not smaller colleges; it was not until the 1980s, with the proliferation of the microcomputer, or personal computer (PC), into faculty and administrative offices, that computing power became inexpensive enough to become widespread for management of colleges and universities. Gilbert and Green (1986) describe this era as the computing revolution, noting that almost half a million microcomputers were operating on campuses by the middle of the 1980s and over half of entering freshmen reported having occasionally or frequently written a computer program. Importantly, personal computers effectively pushed the ability both to generate and access data to every member of the university community, although the potential of this breakthrough was realized only over the succeeding decades. Gilbert and Green (1986) offered to campus leaders an overview of the challenges and opportunities of technology adoption as well as a taxonomy for making decisions about technology. However, their focus, and indeed the focus of administrative IT of the period, rested on how colleges and universities could and should manage information technology while remaining silent about how the computer revolution had the potential to improve management of colleges and universities.

The Advent of Enterprise Systems

Potential for more widespread application of computing power to manage the higher education enterprise advanced significantly in the 1980s and 1990s with the migration from locally developed administrative computing systems to broader adoption commercial enterprise resource planning (ERP) systems like Banner and PeopleSoft. University ERP systems brought together many of the basic business operations of universities into an integrated platform, so that registration and student records, billing, budgeting, and human resources management became entirely digitized processes, with data stored in common locations. These systems still notably omitted many mission-level functions of colleges and universities such as management of learning outcomes, teaching effectiveness, use of student services, and research activity and outcomes. In fact, the absence of these features within major higher education ERP systems has been the hobgoblin of efforts to measure and improve institutional effectiveness over the past two decades. Where ERP systems fell short for specific higher education functions, other vendors stepped into the breach with customer relations management (CRM) systems for admissions, learning management systems (LMS) for teaching and learning, assessment management systems for educational outcomes, and donor management systems for alumni affairs and advancement functions. (For more information on CRM systems, see chapter 9; for more information on LMS systems as part of learning analytics, see chapter 10.)

Nevertheless, the ERP systems were transformative for decision-making processes within the institution. Significant and insignificant transactional details about students and employees migrated from paper records or siloed spreadsheets to centralized repositories of digital records, every added and dropped course, every salary increase or extra service payment, every purchase and payment was assigned an effective date and stored as a row in a relational database for later retrieval. From these systems, IR offices, finance and budget offices, planning offices, and others extracted material for reporting, analysis, and forecasting. Decision making became reliant upon a culture of reporting that offered answers to questions in close to real time: How many applicants do we have now compared to the same time as last year? Is our spending for the month in each unit above or below what was budgeted? How many grant applications and for how much money do we have this year compared to the same time last year? Armed with this level of information, university leaders have been better able to adjust tactics and strategy to respond to current situations. Processes to access, analyze, and communicate this information to leadership are neither automatic nor systemically available, and they required human talent to extract data and transform it into information. Decision makers at institutions with the resources to invest in personnel devoted to analysis received better intelligence than those who did not.

The data warehouse also came of age in the 1990s as a response to the proliferation of data from transactional systems, which often yielded conflicting reports to senior officials because of issues of timing, differing and siloed analyst expertise, and imprecision in how questions were formulated. Bill Inmon (1992) offered the vision that a data warehouse could provide an organization with a "single version of the truth," and the star schema for warehousing introduced by Kimball and Merz (2000) became a standard still widely in use. From these systems, business intelligence (BI) units emerged on many campuses to provide data for decision support. BI units have generally been housed in university IT departments and typically provide a data and reporting infrastructure for client units across campus (Drake and Walz 2018). In some colleges and universities, this function is fulfilled by institutional research, in others institutional research is a client of the BI unit, and in some instances IR and BI units compete in providing information to other constituencies. In recent years, one approach has been to combine IR and BI units, and as Childers (2016) observes in an organizational and anthropological case study of such a merger at the University of Arizona, opportunities for synergy can be counterbalanced by cultural and disciplinary differences among personnel and even unit missions.

Setting the Stage for AI

Three subsequent advances led to the explosion of data in the last two decades that have set the stage for aggressive and increasingly prevalent use of machine learning and AI: near universal internet coverage, ubiquitous handheld devices, and the use of these devices for social media, internet access, and mobile applications. In the 1990s, transportation of data was accomplished through hard-wire connections on-campus, and at times via floppy disk and slower dial-up connections across campuses. In the following decade, extensive deployment of high-speed optic cable and high-speed internet access made sharing of larger data files convenient and cost effective, especially as creation of application programming interfaces (APIs) became standard practice among system developers. Satellite networks and mobile towers also contributed to increased connectivity to support the second key advance: the advent of the smartphone. Since the launch of the iPhone in 2007, which extended the email functionality of the BlackBerry to full internet and web-browsing access, an estimated 5.1 billion unique mobile users were active in 2018, with over 4 billion of them accessing the internet (Kemp 2018). The astonishing magnitude of this number of users becomes dwarfed when considering the amount of data each user generates as he or she browses web sites; accepts tracking cookies; allows data sharing among organizations; and provides data through "private" forms, transactions, and public posts. Effectively, every interaction even down to the click and keystroke is digitized and becomes data that AI needs to construct models and make predictions. It is this revolutionary social and transactional feature of the internet, enabled by Google, Facebook, and Twitter, that opened the world of Big Data to global corporate giants as an avenue to generate profits. And on a smaller scale, the university, through its administrative systems, LMS, and web site, collects data on students, faculty, staff, and visitors—data that are now available to identify patterns and to predict future outcomes. It is important to recognize that data collection is more prevalent than user-system interaction. Large stores of passive data are also being collected, if not yet substantively used, including digital video files from hundreds if not thousands of video security cameras, location and time tracking from the nodes of the wireless network, and repositories of license plates photographed with time stamps of vehicles that enter and exit parking facilities.

This amount of data exceeds the capacity and design of the traditionally structured data warehouse, and now, approaching 2020, college and university officials find themselves at the cusp of moving to more flexible data environments. Web 2.0 companies like Google, Facebook, and Amazon shifted away from data warehouses with the snowflake, or star, schema to data environments allowing distributed storage of disparate data types. These platforms, commercially available as products like Hadoop, SANA, and Amazon Web Services (AWS), offer a No-SQL environment in a nonrelational database, allowing for storage of unstructured data (e.g., Twitter feeds, video files, course assignments from the LMS) alongside structured data. The organization reflects an environment sometimes termed a "data lake," where data from all sources flow into a single location and then when needed are extracted, loaded, and transformed (ELT) to fit the analytical use case. This model for a university was outlined by computer scientists at Clemson University earlier in the decade (Ngo et al. 2012) and is in implementation at institutions like Arizona State University (Wishon and Rome 2016), Virginia Tech (Campbell, Smith, and Kumar 2018), and the California State University System (Aldrich 2018). Kellen (2019) observes that data modeling and design operate under new rules in the data lake environment: entity-based relationship modeling in star schema is replaced by streams of data in narrow tables with millions if not billions of records that represent a "replayable log." Enabled by superfast computing power, data architecture can represent maximum semantic complexity and be designed to capture everything, not simply data elements assumed a priori to hold operational importance. This amount of data becomes critical to machine learning, which requires tremendous amounts of "Big Data" to make predictions, and it is the advent of storage of this sort that will enable effective AI to begin to make predictions to guide university operations.

How the New Data Ecology Impacts Decision Making

These developments have prompted numerous institutional transformations that impact decision making. Data have become "democratized," in that they are widely available and comprehensible for campus constituencies to analyze and make their own decisions. Basic activities of departments and offices have transformed as they adapt to process, understand, and use these data. Individual students are assigned probability scores for "risk" to predict the likelihood that they will need support, and individual faculty are assigned productivity scores to assist with personnel decisions and unit development. Detailed data from sensors in buildings, from every online interaction or chat, even from metadata associated with stored files, can provide the raw material for AI to assist with monitoring operations and decision making. Digitization of virtually everything has led to an explosion of data beyond the capacity of systems to curate them.

Business Intelligence

At a number of higher education institutions in the United States, business intelligence units have pushed data to academic and administrative units so that they can directly access operational data about themselves. Some of this is simple: real-time budget information, real-time class rosters, and lists of advisees. Lists of individuals or expenditures represent some of the simplest information, but they can also be aggregated into reports than can assist with management, including grade distributions and analysis of courses where students struggle, student-faculty ratios and dashboards of faculty assignments to monitor educational quality and equitable work load, and spending per credit hour or FTE to monitor efficiency. Placed in the hands of unit leaders, such information assists with solid decision making, but it also challenges the "one version of the truth" vision from the centralized data warehouse. For example, Patti Barney, the vice president for Information Technology at Broward County Community College reported that implementation of a business intelligence system, a robust employee training initiative, and a cultural shift to value data-driven decision making significantly improved the effectiveness of decision making: "We no longer have management meetings where there are arguments over whose version of the data is correct, whose spreadsheet is correct, or whose report is correct . . . Now we see the metrics generated from the business intelligence applications and we can focus on the business issues we are facing, and what's preventing us from meeting key objectives, and what's the real impact on meeting the needs and success of the students" (Halligan 2009, 15).

Even if these data emerge from centralized sources in preprogrammed reports, however, the potential for the data to be recombined, filtered, analyzed over different time periods, and linked to other data sources leads to the eventuality that the unit will look at the data in a different way than others in the organization view the same data. Thus, localized decision making can assist with stronger management in the unit, but it can also add to confusion and opacity from a centralized perspective.

How Units Are Changing to Adopt AI

Additionally, the advances in data storage, computing power, and analytics have transformed university departments and business units from reliance upon paper file clerks to essential operations conducted by data professionals. Registrar functions and financial aid processing are the most salient examples, with the oaken file cabinets of the 1950s replaced with computer terminals for running batch processing for schedule preparation, prerequisite checks, and degree audits. Similarly, financial aid officials extract data from federal systems and run numerous programmed procedures to construct and optimize aid packaging, which is digitally communicated to the student and the bursar. Academic affairs officers use digital systems to review promotion and tenure; research administration offices maintain digital faculty profiles to identify optimal teams to pursue funding opportunities harvested from digital sources; and facilities and operations divisions monitor the physical plant in real time for energy usage, work order completion, and video footage. Because university personnel increasingly interact with the processes of the university as digital representations, these employees require increased data literacy, if not competency. The less obvious issues might include how Big Data will force the transformation of campus IT and data management infrastructure, how third-party software systems will disrupt the data management ecology on campus, how people who are more accustomed to working in silos must learn to collaborate more in the new digital environment, and what senior leaders need to know about what rapid changes in technology and digital content management process will mean to campus decision making.

Making Decisions about Individuals Based on a Score

The advent of machine learning and AI on top of Big Data and unit-level distribution of information is the introduction of the personalized "risk score" for educational progress or perhaps better phrased as predicted need for support. Much like credit scores, which were introduced in the late 1980s by Fair, Isaac, and Company (Kaufman 2018) to help financial institutions evaluate credit worthiness of borrowers, summarizing all of their credit history into a single number, the 2010s have seen the introduction of individualized scores for students, signaling their propensity to perform well and remain enrolled. Companies like the Education Advisory Board (EAB), which has its roots in the health care industry and population health care management through data analysis, and Civitas, which evolved more directly from higher education, offer services to colleges and universities to use their data to establish individual-level predictions of success, and various institutions have also approached this problem using their own resources (Arnold 2010). These approaches make use of demographic data, course performance data, and how students interact with the learning management systems. In some instances, non-academic data are brought to bear, such as Purdue's Forecast App, which uses wireless node data tracking students' cell phones to locate when students are physically present in academic buildings and how this relates to their success (Blumenstyk 2018).

Generally, models that create individualized scores use data mining techniques (including decision trees, clustering, and other methods discussed in chapter 3 of this book) to predict student success (discussed in chapter 8), or even their likelihood to enroll at all (discussed in chapter 7). Such models are extensible to the advancement function and to faculty recruitment and development. These sorts of predictions, of course, have been made in the admissions and hiring process very often, but with machine learning more data are brought to bear, ostensibly with a better chance of being correct more often than the use of more limited data combined with human judgment. They also bring with them potential for bias and replication of social inequality, and so they require some attention to what data are included and how the output of the algorithms treat various populations (discussed in chapter 4). The end result, however, is that personnel in university units (such as academic advisors, advancement officers, department chairs, and hiring committees) have specific and actionable information to work with individual students, donors, and faculty, so that the decisions they make can be tailored to individual needs. That said, university professionals will need to learn how to work with these new sources of data and how to treat probabilities and propensities assigned to individuals by machine learning algorithms, and universities will need to systemically learn how to make use of these without inadvertently causing harm.

Using AI to Improve Teaching and Learning

The digital enhancement of teaching and learning through extensive use of learning management systems like Blackboard and the complete digitization and delivery of courses online has also generated prolific amounts of data. When these data are harnessed and integrated with AI, they can offer insight into how students learn, what pedagogical methods will be effective and with whom, and how to adjust the teaching and learning process in real time (Popenici and Kerr 2017). For example, members of the Unizin consortium founded in 2014, which includes almost a million students across 11 member institutions, share data across a common learning platform called Canvas to become a massive learning laboratory. Partner institutions realize savings by sharing resources and also have access to anonymized data that allows for identification of general trends as well as class and assignment-level data for their own students. By 2018, the system had exhibited capacity to predict course-level success for some students within half a letter grade (Kafka 2019). The full-scale application of AI to identify markers for student success has the potential to individualize instruction for each learner in much the same way the medical field is being transformed by personalized medicine. Other examples include Georgia Tech's transformation of some of its graduate programs to incorporate massively online open courses (MOOCs), which include experimentation with computerized teaching assistants that appear to pass the Turing test, at least as far as student-teaching assistant interactions are concerned (Gose 2016). In another instance, the Mandarin Project at Rensselaer Polytechnic Institute teaches students Chinese in an interactive virtual world in which students can interact with simulated AI speaking in Mandarin and providing feedback about their performance (McKenzie 2018a). These uses of AI hold significant promise for improving the teaching and learning process but also raise ethical questions, and the use of algorithms always carries potential for bias and unintended consequences (O'Neil 2016). As AI is considered for student learning on campus, a number of important questions can be asked, including: Will student-level predictions of struggling in a course incentivize institutions to limit access for some students? Will they create self-fulfilling prophecies? Will AI teaching assistants neglect some groups of students who need extra help or help in different ways? Will virtual learning environments limit access to educational opportunities for students with disabilities? What happens when a large data breach occurs releasing terabytes of educational records and detailed information about how individuals struggled in class? Additional discussion on learning analytics is included in chapter 10 of this volume.

Using AI to Improve Campus Operations

Machine learning and AI are by no means limited to predicting individual success. Examples are already prevalent of how AI has allowed universities to replace or repurpose human decision making by substituting AI and using the Internet of Things (IoT). For instance, the University of Texas at Austin has successfully used AI to employ extensive sensor networks and climate data to operate its sprinkler system, and the University of Iowa has connected elaborate sensor networks in its buildings to detect potential maintenance and failure issues before they become problems (Gardner 2018). At Georgia State University, as discussed further in chapter 8 of this book, the university officials have successfully deployed automated admissions assistants (Gardner 2018). Community colleges in North Carolina rely on AI to connect, structure, and curate their digital content to improve real-time delivery of organizational learning across campuses (Schwartz 2019). In many of these instances, the technology and manner of use is novel enough to warrant news coverage and appear like the "nice toys" that Roy Batty references in *Blade Runner*, but caution is warranted in assuming widespread organizational transformation. It falls within institutional interests to publish and promote success stories and bury failures. Systematic investigation of the return on investment for AI in higher education has yet to be done, and even in the private sector, the technology consulting firm Gartner predicts that four out of five AI projects "will remain alchemy, run by wizards whose talents will not scale in the organization" (White 2019). Nevertheless, these deployments of AI and machine learning can be expected to increase exponentially, with some of the successful and scalable implementations resulting in significant monetization.

Data Proliferation and Data Governance

As functional areas of the university evolve and adopt their own systems that digitize more and more interactions, too much data are created to curate. Driven by the question, "Do you trust your data?" colleges and universities have rushed to advance their systems for data governance and data quality over the past decade, in part because the advent of inexpensive and widespread analytics on top of all data sources has exposed areas of invalid and incomplete data. These efforts are clearly needed, but as data continue to proliferate, there is a real possibility that some data used by university officials remain outside of a governance structure, or are allowed to remain in a state that accepts higher levels of error because the errors can be accounted for through AI prediction algorithms. As data proliferate and grow into Big Data and Bigger Data, the question "Do you trust your data?" will likely be supplanted with the question "Do you trust your algorithms?" leading to an entire additional set of higher-order control activities for monitoring the function of machine learning and AI. Data lake solutions adopted by institutions like Virginia Tech and the Cal State System attempt to address some of these issues, and while these solutions have clearly added value in the private sector, successful scale-based applications in higher education are still too early in development, as of the writing of this chapter, to demonstrate return on investment.

Given the resources and expertise required to design such systems, some institutions have turned to third-party vendors to provide predictive modeling, data integration, and even data lake environments. For instance, Rapid Insight was founded in 2002 to provide easy to use predictive analytics for financial aid modeling. Later in the 2000s, the

EAB grew out of a health care analytics operation to apply similar tools to student success, including an integration of service and usage data, with a host of competitors such as Civitas, Blue Canary, and ZogoTech. More recently, firms like HelioCampus and Snowflake offer colleges and universities data ecosystems ranging from traditional data warehousing solutions to full-blown data lakes integrating as many as 30 additional products with the ERP, with the data models ostensibly prebuilt. Especially where campuses lack maturity in data governance and management, such solutions appear attractive, although adoption of such products without substantial attention to organizational culture and process reform risks simply pushing poor-quality data from one system to another. Even where the garbage-in, garbage-out problem is overcome, institutional leaders should not be naïve enough to think that cutting a check to a technology company will substitute for the hard work of organizational transformation.

The Road Ahead for AI in Higher Education

The implications of widespread AI and machine learning in higher education certainly deserve some consideration. If AI can drive a car, then can AI run an institutional research office? Push-button compliance reporting for IPEDS (Integrated Postsecondary Education Data System) and other requirements has been a promise from many ERP systems, though rarely delivered because of institutional customizations. Such automation seems feasible with improved data governance and data quality, but successful application may still be far into the future. It also seems feasible that AI could be programmed to automate evaluation and optimize student success, course scheduling, faculty work load, and a range of other functions that extend beyond compliance reporting. Scores of vendors have supplied and continue to supply solutions of this sort to universities, but none of them run completely automatically, and when they work (and they do not always fully deliver on lofty promises) they often require additional, not fewer, personnel to supply data, evaluate output, and ensure that modifications are programmed into the applications. Further, because AI functions as a "prediction machine" that uses a set of historical data to predict the future, it is particularly ill equipped to handle new situations and smaller groups of students. Questions like "Is this new ranking of our university something to which we should pay attention or publicize?" "How will this proposed regulatory change affect our operations?" and "How will addition of this program position us in the marketplace?" are complex questions for human analysts to tackle, but they lie beyond the scope of today's AI to address.

However, assume for a moment that AI is able to substantially replace an institutional research office and a business intelligence unit—could it replace other administrative functions like a registrar's office or a financial aid office? Indeed, vendors already have solutions to optimize financial aid distribution for recruitment, student success, and so on. What advancements are needed to begin replacing personnel so that students interact with virtual financial aid counselors in adjusting financial aid packages? Can the decisions that a financial aid counselor make be replaced by AI with perhaps a summary review from an associate director or director level position? Can the financial aid director be replaced and dispute resolution simply be outsourced?

More provocatively, could AI replace executive functions—such as a provost or a president? In some respects, the AI presidency would carry a number of advantages. It should exhibit fewer ethical lapses (barring those of its programmers), fewer instances of sexual or personal misconduct, and fewer propensities to make decisions based on bias or personal preference. Conversely, AI could account for far more information about the organization than a college president could ever absorb and use this information to make decisions. All the sentiment from Twitter, Instagram, and so on could be monitored real-time to understand reaction and decisions made accordingly to optimize faculty work load, student enrollment, and staffing levels, and the list goes on ad nauseam. But again, when confronted with new situations, the AI of today struggles because when new situations arise it simply does not have historical data to provide reliable predictions about the future. There is also the very real challenge that an organization of human beings would resent or resist a set of computer algorithms leading their mission-driven educational activities (even more than human leadership of such activities is resisted). Nevertheless, it seems well within the realm of possibility that a governing board could set up an AI system to function as a check or regulating counterbalance to the president, or a president could have machine learning algorithms to monitor decisions of a provost or other vice president, offering independent predictions for what the institution could or should do. Such a working arrangement would again present challenges with an AI system, apparently second-guessing institutional leadership, but in some ways this dynamic exists today, just relying principally on human judgment rather than AI predictions.

Despite the directionality of some of these questions, the continuing adoption of AI on campus likely does not point toward a dystopian world where the machines are in control or their potential self-awareness is perceived as a threat to be eradicated, as suggested by the *Blade Runner* (1982) reference to technology in 2019 that frames this chapter. In part, evolution of educational systems and structures is by nature iterative and slow, and even the example of machine grading illustrates the slow and uneven adoption of the technology from Project Essay Grade in 1968 into educational environments, and when the computer-based systems make mistakes, they make the news and stir controversy (McKenzie 2018b). Such occurrences suggest that much like with acceptance of self-driving cars by society at large, adoption of AI in higher education may be more of a social science problem than a technological problem. The way that higher education professionals make decisions will undoubtedly change to incorporate these innovations and, in general, should continue to improve the quality and effectiveness of higher education, even as students are challenged to master an increasing body of skills, knowledge, values, and dispositions.

References
Agrawal, A., J. Gans, and A. Goldfarb. 2018. *Prediction Machines: The Simple Economics of Artificial Intelligence*. Boston: Harvard Business Review Press.
Aldrich, B. 2018. "Lead the Charge: CSU's Transformational Data Program." Paper presented at the EDUCAUSE Annual Conference, Denver, CO, 2018. Accessed Nov. 28, 2018. https://events.educause.edu/annual-conference/2018/agenda/lead -the-charge-transformational-data-leadership.

Arnold, K. 2010. "Signals: Applying Academic Analytics." *EDUCAUSE Review* 3. Accessed January 29, 2019. https://er.educause.edu/articles/2010/3/signals -applying-academic-analytics.

Blumenstyk, G. 2018. "Big Data Is Getting Bigger. So Are the Privacy and Ethical Questions." *Chronicle of Higher Education.* July 31, 2018. https://www.chronicle .com/article/Big-Data-Is-Getting-Bigger-So/244099.

Campbell, J., K. Smith, and T. Kumar. 2018. "Building an Analytics Infrastructure In-House." Paper presented at the Association of Public and Land-Grant Universities Annual Meeting, New Orleans, LA, 2018. Accessed November 24, 2018. http://www.aplu.org/members/commissions/information-measurement -analysis/cima-presentations-2018/In-House%20data%20infastructure.pdf.

Chamberlin, D., and R. Boyce. 1974. "SEQUEL: A Structured English Query Language." *Proceedings of the 1974 ACM SIGFIDET Workshop on Data Description, Access and Control,* 249–264. New York, NY: Association for Computing Machinery. Accessed December 29, 2018. http://www.joakimdalby.dk/HTM/sequel.pdf.

Childers, H. 2016. "Can Business Intelligence and IR Teams be Combined?" Paper presented at the Annual Forum of the Association for Institutional Research. New Orleans, LA.

Codd, E. 1970. "A Relational Model of Data for Large Shared Data Banks." *Comm. Association for Computing Machinery* 13, no. 6: 377–387.

Drake, B., and A. Walz. 2018. "Evolving Business Intelligence and Data Analytics in Higher Education." In *IR in the Digital Era. New Directions for Institutional Research* 178: 85–97, edited by C. Mathies and C. Ferland. Boston: Wiley.

Gardner, L. 2018. "How A.I. Is Infiltrating Every Corner of Campus." *Chronicle of Higher Education.* April 8, 2018. https://www.chronicle.com/article/How-AI-Is -Infiltrating-Every/243022.

Gilbert, S., and K. Green. 1986. "New Computing in Higher Education." *Information Technology Quarterly* 5, no. 2: 10–23.

Gladwell, M. 2005. *Blink: The Power of Thinking without Thinking.* New York: Little, Brown & Co.

Gose, B. 2016. "When the Teaching Assistant Is a Robot." *Chronicle of Higher Education.* October 23, 2016. https://www.chronicle.com/article/When-the -Teaching-Assistant-Is/238114.

Halligan, T. 2009. "Depending on Data: Business Intelligence Systems Drive Reform." *Community College Journal* 80, no. 3: 14–15.

IBM. 2003. "System/360 Model 91." Accessed January 24, 2019. https://www.ibm .com/ibm/history/exhibits/mainframe/mainframe_PP2091.html.

Inmon, W. H. 1992. *Building the Data Warehouse.* New York: John Wiley & Sons.

Kafka, A. C. 2019. "Colleges Are Banding Together Digitally to Help Students Succeed. Here's How." *Chronicle of Higher Education.* March 31, 2019. https://www.chronicle.com/article/Colleges-Are-Banding-Together/246002.

Kaufman, R. 2018. "The History of the FICO® Score." Blog post. Accessed April 7, 2019. https://blog.myfico.com/history-of-the-fico-score/.

Kellen, V. 2019. "21st Century Analytics: New Technology and New Rules." *EDUCAUSE Review* 54, no. 2: 31–39.

Kemp, S. 2018. "Global Digital Report." Blog post. Accessed January 29, 2018. https://wearesocial.com/us/blog/2018/01/global-digital-report-2018.

Kimball, R., and R. Merz. 2000. *The Data Warehouse ETL Toolkit: Practical Techniques for Extracting, Cleaning, Conforming, and Delivering Data*. New York: Wiley & Sons.

McCarthy. J., M. L. Minsky, N. Rochester, and C. E. Shannon. 1955. "A Proposal for the Dartmouth Summer Research Project on Artificial Intelligence." Accessed December 18, 2018. http://www-formal.stanford.edu/jmc/history/dartmouth/dartmouth.html.

McKenzie, L. 2018a. "Pushing the Boundaries of Learning with AI." *Inside Higher Ed*. September 26, 2018. https://www.insidehighered.com/digital-learning/article/2018/09/26/academics-push-expand-use-ai-higher-ed-teaching-and-learning.

———. 2018b. "Autograding System Goes Awry, Students Fume." *Inside Higher Ed*. November 30, 2018. https://www.insidehighered.com/news/2018/11/30/autograder-issues-upset-students-berkeley.

Ngo, L. B., A. W. Apon, P. Xuan, K. Ferguson, and C. Marshall. 2012. "An Infrastructure to Support Data Integration and Curation for Higher Educational Research." TigerPrints Publications 5. Accessed January 15, 2019. https://tigerprints.clemson.edu/computing_pubs/5.

O'Neil, C. 2016. *Weapons of Math Destruction: How Big Data Increases Inequalities and Threatens Democracy*. New York: Penguin Random House.

Page, E. B., G. A. Fisher, and M. A. Fisher. 1968. "Project Essay Grade: A FORTRAN Program for Statistical Analysis of Prose." *British Journal of Mathematical and Statistical Psychology* 21: 139.

Page, E. B., and D. H. Paulus. 1968. *The Analysis of Essays by Computer: Final Report*. Washington, DC: US Office of Education, Bureau of Research.

Paulus, D. H., J. F. McManus, and E. B. Page. 1969. "Some Applications of Natural Language Computing to Computer Assisted Instruction." *Contemporary Education* 40: 280–285.

Popenici, S., and S. Kerr. 2017. "Exploring the Impact of Artificial Intelligence on Teaching and Learning in Higher Education." *Research and Practice in Technology Enhanced Learning* 12, no. 22: 1–13.

Schwartz, N. 2019. "How Colleges Are Using AI to Save Time on Operations." Education Dive. February 27, 2019. https://www.educationdive.com/news/how-colleges-are-using-ai-to-save-time-on-operations/549277/.

Shannon, C. 1987. "Interview by Anthony Liversidge." *Omni Magazine* (August): 61–66.

Simonite, T. 2018. "Apple's Latest iPhones Are Packed with AI Smarts." *Wired*. September 12, 2018. https://www.wired.com/story/apples-latest-iphones-packed-with-ai-smarts/.

Turing, A. M. 1950. "Computing Machinery and Intelligence." *Mind* 59, no. 236: 1, 433–460.

White, A. 2019. "Our Top Data and Analytics Predicts for 2019." Blog post. January 3, 2019. https://blogs.gartner.com/andrew_white/2019/01/03/our-top-data-and-analytics-predicts-for-2019/.

Wishon, G., and J. Rome. 2016. "Institutional Analytics and the Data Tsunami." *EDUCAUSE Review*. December 12, 2016. https://er.educause.edu/articles/2016/12/institutional-analytics-and-the-data-tsunami.

[3]

Predictive Analytics and Its Uses in Higher Education

Henry Y. Zheng and Ying Zhou

As INSTITUTION leaders face pressure to increase student success yet under more and more challenging financial conditions, an environment of data-informed decisions becomes even more critical. Using data from the past to predict current and future conditions can help planning efforts to address these goals. When this is done properly, predictive analytics can help institution officials consider how current and prospective students perform academically, how institutions can meet their enrollment and revenue goals, and how they can retain leading faculty and support the institution's research and service missions. In analytics maturity hierarchy models, such as the one proposed by Davenport and Harris (2007), predictive analytics, alongside prescriptive analytics and optimization methods, is often viewed as part of the advanced analytics components as organizations become more sophisticated and effective in the use of analytics to inform their decisions. In university research programs, advanced computing resources and Big Data labs have become an integral part of many college campuses (e.g., see https://bigdata.uga.edu/), and these units enable researchers to assist in large-scale genomic, text mining, brain imaging, weather pattern analyses, and much more.

Although administrative units within most higher education institutions have more recently begun to consider predictive analytics as a way to move toward a greater level of maturity in analytics capabilities, the use of these techniques is not new. In 1997, when one of the authors of this chapter started his first job as an institutional researcher, one of his early projects was to help convert an enrollment projection model from a mainframe-based program to a personal computer–based system using a spreadsheet program. The model was based on the Markov Chain model, which is a matrix-based time series model of a stochastic process that estimates the dynamic changes of population over time. The model estimates the probability of events or object movements among different states or time periods. The basic assumption of the Markov Chain model is that patterns of past events or activities together with the current state information form the foundation for projecting what will happen next.

While the use of predictive models to address higher education decision situations is not new, the emergence of Big Data and more powerful methodological advances, such as machine learning and artificial intelligence algorithms, put predictive analytics in the spotlight as higher education leaders continue to find ways to leverage data analytics capabilities to inform their strategic and operational decisions. Browsing through recent annual conference agendas for organizations such as the Association for Institutional Research (AIR), National Association of College and University Business Officers (NACUBO) and EDUCAUSE (higher education IT network), it is hard not to see the omnipresence of *predictive analytics* as a key term in many conference sessions.

In this chapter, we define predictive analytics in the context of data-informed decision making in higher education. We will describe its connection to and differences from other core concepts such as machine learning and artificial intelligence; introduce some of the common approaches to predictive analytics and their uses in higher education; and illustrate the use of predictive analytics with select case studies.

What Is Predictive Analytics?

Predictive analysis is a general term that covers a range of analytical approaches and techniques to predict future events or behaviors. Some of these analytic models are used so commonly that people do not even think twice about them as being "predictive." For example, almost every adult has a credit score that is calculated based on a large number of variables such as income, consumption, payment records, and other personal data compiled by credit agencies using a set of algorithms. The credit score predicts a person's financial strength and is used in support decisions such as a bank's approval of a mortgage loan application.

A credit score, an enrollment projection, and an academic performance index used in college admissions all have some common characteristics (Ouahilal et al. 2016). They:

- aim to determine what is likely to happen in the future;
- rely on the use of data, especially historical data that provides trends or associations; and
- are analyzed using statistical techniques or computation algorithms.

The goal of predictive modeling is to provide predictions and forecasts about future business activities. According to Eduventures (2013), predictive analytics is "an area of statistical analysis that deals with extracting information using various technologies to uncover relationships and patterns within large volumes of data that can be used to predict behavior and events" (1).

Bari (2016) proposes a definition that is consistent with the Eduventures definition but goes further to indicate that it needs to include the rationale for predictive analytics. According to Bari (2016), data is one of an organization's most valuable assets and its value must be realized through its use to support decisions. Bari's formula for predictive analytics is:

Data mining + business knowledge = predictive analytics => value

In this sense, predictive analytics is the development of analytical insights through predictive modeling and by leveraging organizational data assets and business knowledge. Predictive models and algorithms do not by themselves constitute predictive analytics. The models and algorithms must be applied to organizational data and used to inform

Optimization · *What is the best result?*

Predictive modeling · *What will happen next?*

Forecasting · *What if trends continue?*

Statistical analysis · *Why is this happening?*

Alerts · *What action is needed?*

Query/Drill down · *Where is the problem?*

Ad hoc reports · *How many, how often?*

Standard Reports · *What happened?*

Competitive Advantage

Degree of Intelligence

Figure 3.1. Analytics Maturity Model. Adapted from Davenport and Harris 2007

decision making to be truly considered predictive analytics. This definition is consistent with views from other scholars on the use of data to inform decisions (Boyer et al. 2012; Davenport and Harris 2007; O'Flaherty and Heavin 2014).

In data analytics development, predictive analytics occupies an important space. In the data analytics maturity model developed by Davenport and Harris (2007) (figure 3.1), alerts, statistical analysis, forecasting, and predictive modeling can be generally considered the hierarchical building blocks of predictive analytics from a methodological standpoint. As colleges and universities continue to grow their analytics capabilities and pursue strategies to support data-informed decision making, it is imperative that they intentionally champion and support the progression of their analytical efforts toward the higher end of this maturity model.

Common Modeling Approaches to Predictive Analytics

There are many methodological approaches that fall under the predictive analytics umbrella. Table 3.1 summarizes some of the most common

Table 3.1. Common Approaches to Predictive Analytics Development

Predictive models	Descriptive models
• Regression analysis (inclusive of linear, Logit, and Probit regression)	• Cluster analysis
• Decision tree analysis	• Latent class analysis
• Neural network analysis	• Association analysis
• Random Forest	

Source: Adapted from Leventhal (2018) and Ouahilal et al. (2016).

approaches. Leventhal (2018) believes that modeling approaches to predictive analytics can be categorized into two groups: *predictive* and *descriptive* models. A predictive model is designed to anticipate certain outcomes or responses. For example, a predictive model for identifying promising donors in fundraising campaigns can predict the likelihood of giving and the size of the gift based on a large amount of data from previous years. Fundraisers will be directed by this model to prioritize which potential donors to spend more efforts on. Common modeling approaches under the predictive modeling category will include regression analysis, decision tree, neural network analysis, and random forest.

A descriptive model is designed to give a better understanding of individuals or their behaviors, without being directed to predict a particular outcome (Leventhal 2018). The applications of descriptive models tend to look into identifying clusters, groups, or segments, each containing people or events that are similar in terms of behaviors and patterns of changes. Common modeling approaches under the descriptive modeling category will include cluster analysis, latent class analysis, and association analysis. We will provide a high-level description of some of these common modeling approaches and how they are generally used in predictive analytics.

Regression Analysis

Regression analysis is perhaps the most commonly used statistical method for analyzing causal relationships between variables, specifically to predict how explanatory (independent) variables may influence and predict the changes in the target (dependent or outcome) variable. The basic concept of regression is to answer three questions: (1) is a set of explanatory variables effective in predicting changes in a target (dependent) variable; (2) which explanatory variables in particular are significant predictors of the target variable, in what way, and by how much; and (3) to what extent does the model in totality explain the causes to changing behaviors of the target variable. These regression estimates are used to explain the relationship between one dependent variable and one or more independent variables. The basic form of the regression equation with one dependent and one independent variable is expressed by the formula:

$$y = a + b^* x$$

where y = target or dependent variable, a = constant, b = regression coefficient, and x = explanatory or independent variable.

There are various regression techniques for modeling different types of data and relationships. Two methods used commonly in predictive analytics are multiple linear regression and logistic regression. Multiple linear regression models examine the influence of two or more explanatory variables on a desired outcome. The goal of the regression is to identify the effect and strength of independent variables on the dependent variable. For example, a multiple linear regression model can use hours of reading time, percentage of homework completed, and frequency of students participating in online group chats to predict a student's final course grade.

Logistic regression is the appropriate approach when the dependent variable is a dichotomous (binary) variable with values such as yes/no, pass/fail, win/lose, or stay/drop out. Unlike linear regression, where the relative strength and direction of changes are the focus, in the logistic model, the focus is on the probability, or odds-ratio. Logistic regression is one of the most popular ways to fit models for categorical data, especially for binary response data. Logistic regression provides probability estimates between the 0 and 1 interval. The coefficients of the model provide information on the relative importance of each input variable (Pampel 2000). For example, a logistic regression model can estimate the probability of student four-year graduation by accounting for variables such as student cumulative GPA, gender, academic major, financial aid status, and residential status.

According to Bari (2016), regression models in predictive analytics have the advantage of being straightforward in terms of establishing the relationship between the explanatory variables and target variable. The model builder can apply the model to make predictions for either the direction or magnitude of changes or the probability of changes. The main drawback is that regression models are generally more time consuming to develop than other techniques and require a deep understanding of statistical assumptions and technicalities. However, Bari's statement probably stands true for all predictive analyses, that is, all require a deep understanding of statistical assumptions and techniques.

Decision Tree Analysis and Random Forest

Decision tree analysis is used extensively in operations research and is often a tool of choice in predictive modeling. Decision tree analysis uses classification algorithms and data parameters to determine the possible risks and incentives of pursuing several different courses of action. Each course of action has a number of options and each option carries different payoffs. Potential outcomes can be visually presented as a flowchart through a treelike structure. A decision tree generally includes a root node, which is the starting point, along with leaf nodes and branches. The root and leaf nodes represent different decision scenarios or options.

In predictive modeling, decision tree is a good tool when data are available to estimate the parameters and decision alternatives, which include the following (Reid and Sanders 2010):

- Decision points—points in time when decisions are made, the nodes;
- Decision alternatives—branches of the tree off the decision nodes;
- Chance events—events that could affect a decision, branches or arrows leaving circular chance nodes; and

- Outcomes—each possible alternative listed and potential risks and payoffs.

Decision tree is perhaps the most appropriate predictive technique for new users because it is visual and straightforward (Bari 2016). In a more stable decision environment with relatively robust data support, a well-designed decision tree model can be very effective in supporting operational decisions such as exploring a variety of campus space and facility development plans (Reid and Sanders 2010). For example, in campus space planning, different projects have different price tags, serve different missions, have different construction durations, and are associated with different risks of cost-overrun or construction delay. A decision tree model can effectively represent these scenarios and options.

However, despite its visual appeals and straightforward logic, decision tree analysis can get very complicated when many values are uncertain and/or if many outcomes are interrelated and interdependent (Deng, Runger, and Tuv 2011). Liberman (2019) believes that decision tree models have several limitation. In particular, they require algorithms capable of determining an optimal choice at each node, which is often not possible given data issues. Decision tree analysis assumes that the modelers are able to use the algorithm to identify the best fit at each step, which is not easily achieved when uncertainty is present and data are not perfect. In such circumstances, decision tree models are less stable and misclassification errors tend to be larger than other modeling techniques.

In recent years, random forest analysis has been increasingly used as an extension of the decision tree approach. Random forest is an analytical approach that consists of multiple single trees each based on a random sample of the study data. In a random forest, many trees are generated automatically from the data—hence the term *forest* rather than *tree* (Bari 2016). Because multiple samples are taken to run the decision tree analysis to find the best fit, random forests are typically more accurate than single decision trees.

In a random forest analysis, observations are randomly sampled with replacement to create a so-called bootstrap sample the same size as the original data set. The observations are then repeatedly partitioned using binary decision rules. "These decision rules are characterized by a cut-point on a specific predictor in the data set. The predictor and predictor cut-point are chosen to split the observations into two groups" (He and Associates 2018, 2). Each tree in the forest is potentially suboptimal. However, by aggregating numerous suboptimal predictions over a collection of such trees, random forest may improve prediction accuracy by providing a ranking of important variables for prediction (He et al. 2018).

Clustering and Classification Models

Clustering and classification are descriptive modeling methods. When a model uses clustering and classification it sorts, filters, and identifies different groupings within the provided data. A cluster is a related set of data or objects. Clustering is the process of dividing a dataset into groups such that the members of each group are as similar as possible to one another, and different groups are as dissimilar as possible from one another. Clustering helps uncover inherent relationships among the observations in a dataset. For example, the frequently used Carnegie Classification of Institutions of Higher Education groups colleges and universities into many classes and subclasses using institution-based variables such as research intensity, highest degree offered, program size, and other variables. Each class is a cluster or segment of institutions with similar characteristics such as mission, program size, and degree offerings.

Classification models are similar to clustering models in that they both try to sort and assign groupings. Classification is a data mining technique that classifies observations in a data collection to various categories or classes. The goal of classification is to accurately predict the target class for each observation. Classification is different from clustering in how it treats the classification variable: classification analysis assumes that a variable or two can classify the observations and anticipate certain behaviors of the same class; whereas clustering lets the data analysis process evaluate and measure the clustering to find the groups, which is not predetermined.

Predictive Analytics and Machine Learning

Predictive analytics is tightly connected with an increasingly popular term, *machine learning*. Machine learning is the research and implementation of algorithms and statistical models that computer systems use to perform a specific task effectively without using specific human instructions, relying on patterns and inference to make suggestions, or predictions. Machine learning algorithms build a mathematical model based on sample data, also known as "training data," in order to make predictions or decisions without being explicitly programmed to perform the task (Bishop 2006).

Whereas machine learning makes predictions and updates the calculations in real time automatically when new data are added, predictive analytics is generally done manually based in the contextualized data environment. Predictive analytics includes the algorithms, analytical methods, and data processing considerations that are the foundation of machine learning. It may be suitable to consider predictive modeling techniques as the analytical engine that powers the computer learning machine, and machine learning, in turn, makes predictive modeling timelier, more useful, and more applicable.

Perhaps the most well-known application of machine learning is the recommendation systems used by companies such as Amazon or Netflix to detect consumer preferences and consumption patterns. In Amazon's system, personalized recommendations rely on a combination of clustering, classifications, and regression algorithms to develop its sophisticated and proprietary system. Madasamy (2019) explains that such a recommendation system is a machine learning process that is based on a number of factors or techniques:

1. *Popularity based*—recommending all the products that are popular, the more that a product is liked, the more often it shows up on top of the list.
2. *Classification based*—identifying groupings of users with types of products purchased to predict whether a product will be liked or not by the user.

3. *Collaborative filtering*—models that are based on the assumption that people like things similar to other things they like as well as those liked by other people with similar taste. A new user without prior history can be assessed using a similar profile of someone with similar attributes.

4. *Item-based collaborative filtering*—recommending items that are similar to the item the user has bought, similarity is based on co-occurrences of purchases.

Yates and Chamberlain (2017), believe that machine learning has huge potential in higher education. Their interest in machine learning started with a very simple question by a university donor to identify a group of students who needed an additional scholarship that would eventually lead to increased retention. Chamberlain and his team identified these students by constructing several machine learning models. After these students were awarded additional scholarships, retention rose from approximately 64% to about 90% (Yates and Chamberlain 2017). By using machine learning to find patterns in the data and testing hypotheses, this analysis helped identify the students with high retention risk due to financial reasons and assisted them with timely support.

The Uses of Predictive Analytics in Higher Education

Higher education institutions are turning to predictive analytics to improve their data-informed decision-making capabilities. There are many ways that predictive analytics can be helpful to institution officials, including the improvement of enrollment management, student engagement, advising effectiveness, student mental health and suicide prevention, academic major pathways and course selections, time to degree management, and alumni giving rate.

Predictive Analytics in Admissions and Recruitment Decisions

In chapter 7 of this volume, Gutman and Hinote provide a comprehensive review of analytics developments in admissions and enrollment management areas. They point out that the use of analytics to support enrollment management decisions is a necessity in today's competitive environment for colleges and universities. The combination of projected declines in demand for higher education, the increasing prevalence of discounting to attract new student enrollment, and the reality that many institutions face enrollment difficulties makes the use of data-informed decision making even more critical. Gutman and Hinote's chapter provides an in-depth introduction to both the theoretical and practical imperatives for the use of analytics in college admissions and recruitment practices. The following case study offers another example of how one university developed a model to predict admission yield rates.

CASE STUDY 1: LEHIGH UNIVERSITY'S ADMISSION YIELD RATE PREDICTION MODEL*

Prior to the development of a yield prediction model by the Office of Institutional Research and Strategic Analytics (OIRSA) at Lehigh University, the Office of Undergraduate Admissions at Lehigh would routinely calculate and examine a complex set of odds ratios to estimate which students had a high or low probability to accept an offer and matriculate at the university. With the proliferation of predictive analytics tools making their way into the world of institutional research, statistical algorithms and programming tools can now remove some of the guesswork that was previously involved, streamline the entire process, and provide reproducible results from year to year. Since February 2017, OIRSA has assisted the Office of Undergraduate Admissions in making yield predictions with the development of a continually evolving prediction model.

The original analysis, conducted for the fall 2017 first-year cohort, relied mostly on a logistic regression model with the goal of predicting which students out of all preliminary offers would matriculate to the university for the upcoming fall semester. A predicted probability was calculated from the final logistic regression model for each student. These probabilities were then ranked, and the results were shared with the Office of Undergraduate

*The authors would like to acknowledge and thank Mr. Zane Kratzer (data scientist) and Dr. Yenny Anderson (vice provost) of Lehigh University for the contribution of their case study in this chapter.

Admissions as each applicant's projected likelihood to yield. Recent iterations of the model have expanded to include tree-based algorithms, such as single decision trees and random forest models. The scope of the analysis has developed to consider not only the stage where preliminary offers become matriculated students but also to consider various approaches where one can predict the matriculated students directly from the entire application pool. In addition, a multistage approach was considered where offers were first predicted from the applicant pool and then matriculations were predicted from the resulting pool of offers. Future versions of the model will explore the ability to predict matrices directly from the larger preapplication inquiry pool.

The OIRSA has taken into consideration the strengths and limitations of logistical regression and decision tree models. Logistic regression is one of the most commonly used statistical approaches for classification problems. One of the main assumptions of logistic regression is the smooth linear decision boundary by which observations can be classified into a binary outcome. For a set of observations with a clear delineation between classes, logistic regression will provide accurate results. Decision trees, on the other hand, partition the observations into multiple nonlinear decision boundaries. Decision trees can create very complex decision boundaries with high levels of accuracy, but they are also prone to overfitting the training data. Depending on the complexity of the final decision tree, the results can be easier to interpret than logistic regression because they produce a visual representation of the decision boundaries used to partition the data.

In addition to testing all three statistical techniques, multiple approaches to validation were applied. For the logistic regression models, two different validation approaches were compared. In the first scenario, a validation set was held out from the original sample of training data. In the second scenario, tenfold cross-validation was performed on the full set of training data. In all iterations of the model, the tenfold cross-validation provided more accurate results on the test data. For this iteration, cross-validation was not used for the tree-based methods. Trees were built on the full set of training data and then applied to a test set of observations.

It should be noted that the random forest model was included for this particular purpose, to help with the imbalanced nature of the data. However, the results of the random forest predictions used at Lehigh up to this point have been unsatisfactory, so further exploration is required. In addition to the sampling techniques used to address the imbalance, future studies should consider cost-sensitive learning techniques.

Student Engagement, Career Success, and Outcomes

One of the main benefits of predictive analytics is adapting and personalizing the learning experience in a more efficient way. By leveraging predictive analytics, institutional officials can identify patterns of students' learning difficulties, roadblocks, and other critical issues. Specific programs and intervention strategies can then be employed to personalize academic coaching and support efforts to improve the learning experience. In chapter 10 of this book, Klein and colleagues discuss a number of programs and activities that are being used to engage students in their learning, and in chapter 8, Renick provides an institutional case study, outlining the history of how Georgia State University uses analytics and comprehensive student success strategies to improve student outcomes. Renick reports that using analytics to inform strategies, Georgia State has seen graduation rates improve by 23 percentage points even while doubling the number of low-income and non-White students it enrolls. At GSU, predictive analytics and data-informed systems are used in advising, financial aid, and student-support services that led to these gains.

Along with specific programs or activities, Klein et al.'s and Renick's chapters provide broader, institutional views on how leadership and strategies help guide analytical transformation. The following case study, on the other hand, tells a story about East Carolina University's attempt to develop predictive models to support student success.

CASE STUDY 2: EAST CAROLINA UNIVERSITY'S EXPERIENCE IN BUILDING PREDICTIVE MODELS OF STUDENT SUCCESS*

East Carolina University (ECU), a public four-year institution, serves a largely rural population in the coastal region of North Carolina. In recent

*The authors thank the staff at the East Carolina University Office of Institutional Planning, Assessment and Research, particularly Margot Neverett and Hanyan Wang for their contribution to this case study.

years, the provost of ECU has led a campus-wide Finish-in-Four initiative with participation of faculty and staff from academic affairs and student affairs. Student success–focused research, predictive analytics, and expanded data partnerships and collaboration are essential to this effort.

The Office of Institutional Planning, Assessment and Research (IPAR) at ECU launched its first predictive analytics project in 2015. From the very beginning, IPAR has attempted to use multiple data sources beyond the data stored in the Student Information System (SIS). Electronic platforms or electronic records maintained by academic and student support offices often store important indicators of students' academic and co-curricular engagement, such as the Starfish Early Alert System, the learning management system, writing center usage records, tutoring center usage records, participation records in student organizations, student surveys, and so on. Over the past four years, IPAR has explored large amounts of data from diverse sources to build models to predict student retention and graduation outcomes. In this process, it works closely with experts in academic and student support offices to understand the "local" data, incorporate their input in predictive modeling, and educate them about the power, limitations, and proper use of predictive analytics.

Building on the success of earlier work, ECU partnered with IBM in 2018 and 2019 to leverage its strengths in cognitive analytics. The joint project, called Cognitive Insights, distinguishes itself from similar studies by its extensive integration of structured and unstructured data sources, use of Watson technology for text analytics, and accompanying efforts to educate the campus about predictive analytics. One of the goals of the project is to identify, at the time of entry, students most likely to drop out or transfer at the end of the first year. The study included three cohorts of 12,786 first-time full-time students who entered in fall 2016, 2017, and 2018, and it integrated as much information as would have been collected about the students at the time of matriculation. Student data fall into the following categories:

1. Demographic Information (including gender, race/ethnicity, NC county or state of residence, home ZIP code, high school code, distance from home to ECU, NC economic region, and parents' education);

2. Academic Preparation (including weighted and unweighted high school GPA, SAT/ACT scores, and early college credits);
3. Application and Orientation (application date, acceptance date, orientation date, and application essay);
4. Financial Aid Information (Pell eligibility, filing FAFSA, grants, scholarships, loans, total need, and unmet need); and
5. First Semester in College (attempted credit hours and intended major).

Student data were supplemented by the American Community Survey (ACS; US Census Bureau), which provides the demographic characteristics, household income, household characteristics, housing, economic, and other data at the ZIP code level. Student's home ZIP code was used as the key to match with the ACS data. In addition, application essays submitted by 72% of these students were analyzed as unstructured data. The students responded to the same prompt, "How has your previous education prepared you for success in college?" IBM Watson generated a variety of variables, including total word count, word count without stop words, average number of letters in a word, key words, personality, sentiments, and emotions. Missing value imputation was used if a student did not submit an essay.

Methodology

A series of models were built to predict three outcomes: retained to the second year, transferred to another institution, and dropped out. A total number of 170 variables were tested, 46 from the structured data provided by ECU, 77 from the ACS, and 47 were generated using Watson's natural language understanding capabilities. Three modeling techniques were evaluated: multinomial logistic regression, classification tree, and neural network. Multinomial logistic regression was selected based on the goodness-of-fit measures: pseudo R squared, predictive accuracy, and K-fold cross-validation. The following variables, in order of importance, were found to be significant predictors of dropout and transfer risks: Weighted High School GPA, Unmet Need, Months between Application Date and Application Deadline, "Middle-Class" Score and "High Income" Score created from the ACS data, Distance between Home and ECU, Days between Application Date and Acceptance Decision Date, Credit Hours Attempted in Fall

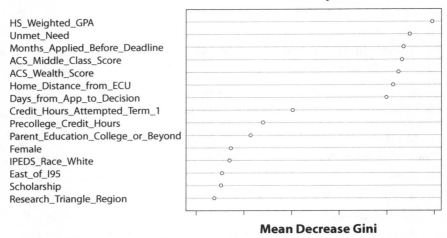

Variable Importance

HS_Weighted_GPA
Unmet_Need
Months_Applied_Before_Deadline
ACS_Middle_Class_Score
ACS_Wealth_Score
Home_Distance_from_ECU
Days_from_App_to_Decision
Credit_Hours_Attempted_Term_1
Precollege_Credit_Hours
Parent_Education_College_or_Beyond
Female
IPEDS_Race_White
East_of_I95
Scholarship
Research_Triangle_Region

Mean Decrease Gini

Figure 3.2. Variable Importance in Eastern Carolina University's Predictive Models

Semester, Precollege Credit Hours, and Parents' Education. Watson variables did not emerge among the top 10 predictors of one-year retention. IPAR will continue its work on unstructured data and further develop dictionaries to extract concepts and key words with higher predictive power. Figure 3.2 shows the importance of select variables in the model.

Communication and Use of the Results

Communicating results means engaging stakeholders across the campus and educating them about the power, limitation, and proper use of predictive analytics. An IBM data scientist was invited to present findings to multiple groups of people, including data providers, academic advisors, student affairs staff, the Finish-in-Four group, and the provost. The participants had lively discussions about how to use the results. One recommendation was to have designated staff (e.g., advisors) for at-risk student populations. Using different approaches to mitigating transfer and dropout risks has also gained support. IPAR staff also presented the results to deans and directors, and at a large student success conference held on campus. Then and now, university leaders have also quoted findings from the study in speeches and memos. These presentations, discussions, and messages elevated the study and helped promote a campus-wide interest in student success research and predictive analytics.

The negative impact of unmet need on student retention is not surprising to faculty and staff who work closely with students. Through the study, campus members gained insight on the magnitude of such impact: with every $1,000 increase in unmet need, the dropout risk increased by 8% and the transfer risk by 6%. That was a powerful message. The finding supported the ongoing discussions about a broad-based financial literacy program and an initiative to increase on-campus student employment opportunities. It also led to the creation of a new scholarship program to mitigate the impact of unmet need of some students.

Lessons Learned

ECU's predictive analytics project has been a challenge due to several factors. Multiple data sources used in the study are stored outside of the Student Information System. Data integration is labor intensive because variable definitions and data structures of different systems are often inconsistent. Because of the complexity of the study, it is challenging to communicate results to different constituents with varying levels of understanding about predictive analytics. From the methodology perspective, because data sparsity is unavoidable in such a large combined dataset, variable selection and missing data imputation are critical but tricky.

At ECU, data is seen as an institutional asset to support student success and the decision-making process. Understanding risk factors helps the campus evaluate and improve the effectiveness of student success programs and interventions. Individual risk scores allow for targeted student outreach and intervention. These benefits of predictive analytics make it an important tool to maximize student success.

Other Uses of Predictive Analytics in Higher Education
Optimization of Student Financial Aid

Colleges and universities provide millions of dollars every year to students in the form of institutionally funded financial aid. No matter whether it is merit-based or need-based, one of the key considerations in awarding the aid package is to ensure it looks attractive and is perceived to be affordable for the students when it comes to a final enrollment decision. In admissions and financial aid decision making, college officials have many competing considerations: they want to attain a higher yield rate; they hope to improve diversity; they want to continuously improve the academic profile; and most important, they want to increase net revenue. To meet these competing objectives, higher education officials can rely on predictive analytics to evaluate how each factor independently, and multiple factors interactively, will predict both enrollment decisions and student outcomes. The knowledge gained from these analyses can then be used to personalize financial aid offers at the individual student level. In other words, in the true optimization environment, each student's financial aid package is unique and tailored to the student's personal situation as well as the institution's admission policies and enrollment priorities.

Learning Analytics and Academic Advising

In chapter 10 of this book, Klein et al. discuss many important issues related to and examples of analytics being used in learning management systems, student advising, and other aspects related to student learning. In addition, Denley (2012, 2014) sought to improve the institution's academic advising process and to empower students to make informed choices that could lead to greater success. At Austin Peay State University, Denley and colleagues created an interface in the course audit and advising system (called Degree Compass) that successfully paired students with courses that best fit their talents and programs of study. The model combined many thousands of past students' grades with those students' transcripts to make individualized recommendations for each student. The algorithm interfaces with the institution's degree audit system to identify courses that would satisfy some of the unsatisfied degree requirement of a student. The system then selects the courses that are most applicable to the student's degree program and overlays a model that predicts the courses in which the student will achieve the best grades (seen by the advisor, not the student). Initial assessment of the Degree Compass system was positive, and replications of the original assessment in 2012 were similar. Data from Fall 2012 showed average grades were within 0.59 of the letter grade awarded, and 89% of those who were predicted to pass did so.

Curriculum Evaluation and Improvement

Predictive analytics can also be applied to one of the most important yet understudied areas in higher education: curriculum evaluation and improvement. In a national study conducted in 2012 US Department of Education officials identified predictive analytics as a key development in education innovation and curriculum improvement. Robust applications of educational data mining and predictive analytics techniques can effectively address some of the challenging questions in learning analytics (US Department of Education 2012), including:

- User knowledge modeling—What content does a student know (e.g., specific skills and concepts or procedural knowledge and higher-order thinking skills)?
- User behavior modeling—What do patterns of student behavior mean for their learning? Are students motivated?
- User experience modeling—Are users satisfied with their experience?
- User profiling—What groups do users cluster into?
- Domain modeling—What is the correct level at which to divide topics into modules and how should these modules be sequenced?
- Learning component analysis and instructional principle analysis—Which components are effective at promoting learning? What learning principles work well? How effective is the entire curriculum?
- Trend analysis—What changes over time and how?
- Adaptation and Personalization—What next actions can be suggested for the user? How should the user experience be changed for the next user? How can the user experience be altered, most often in real time?

Identify Key Donors and Investors

Fundraising for colleges and universities is very challenging work. In this highly competitive and relationship-driven arena, development officers require not only relationship-building skills but also patience, persistent efforts, and the ability to spot potential donors and the best opportunity to ask. With predictive analytics, development officers can arm themselves with more powerful and precise information to evaluate and identify higher-potential donors and therefore avoid unproductive efforts.

Armed with large volumes of data and a long history of donor behaviors, most analysts can leverage predictive analytics to analyze and provide detailed insight into the needs, preferences, and behaviors of donors. The model enables fundraising staff to anticipate how donors will respond to certain messages and estimate which contribution amounts donors—especially new donors—would be likely to give (Walcott 2014). Because predictive analytics learns from every donor interaction, it can also help build more loyal relationships over time and provide an "early warning system" of donors who may be dissatisfied and require extra attention (IBM Business Analytics 2014).

Help Improve Operational Effectiveness and Efficiency

Predictive analytics can also be used to reduce operating costs and improve organizational effectiveness. In chapter 11 of this book, Wayt and colleagues examine how analytics helps improve financial planning, optimize space and facilities planning, and support operational effectiveness and efficiency. It is no longer enough to review past and current financial data and perhaps cut expenses to stabilize the bottom line. Rather, higher education officials must strategically plan, be aware of economic models and constraints, and encourage long-range planning. In order for business and finance officers to best support their institutions in meeting their mission, remaining financially viable, and optimizing facilities use, leaders in college and university business and finance officers will need to leverage the advances in data analytics developments, particularly in the predictive analytics area.

Ethical and Responsible Use of Data and Predictive Analytics

As mentioned in chapter 4 of this volume, recent events such as the Facebook/Cambridge Analytica scandal (Granville 2018) are helping users become aware of the hidden dangers embedded in internet sites. Such events have prompted social media companies to be more transparent with the ways in which they collect and use data. Similarly, higher education officials are prompted to consider the ethics of how student and employee data are collected, stored, and secured as well as how the data are used and the effects of those data on individuals.

Indeed, as described above in this chapter, predictive analytics can be quite useful to help higher education students and institutions succeed. However, it is critical that predictive analytics be used ethically and responsibly. O'Neil (2016), Foer (2017), and other scholars ask us to be mindful of the ways in which predictive analytics can lead to unintended negative consequences. Without ethical practices, student data could be used to curtail academic success instead of improve it (Ekowo and Palmer 2016). Incorrect use of predictive analytics may intentional, or more likely, unintentional. For example, an analyst may not realize that data from the past are "building in" one or more points of bias, and subsequent analyses will only continue or perhaps increase that bias.

Ekowo and Palmer (2017) offer a framework for officials to examine how predictive analytics is formulated and whether it is used ethically. The authors believe that the ethical use of data is an iterative process; as college officials continue to use student and institutional data in innovative new ways, they will need to regularly reassess whether ethical standards address current data practices. The framework includes five practices that can guide the ethical use of predictive analytics (figure 3.3). The five practices are:

1. *Have a Vision and Plan.* Formulation of a vision and plan will facilitate the direction of the analytics effort. Without such planning, predictive analytics may do more harm than good, leave out key stakeholders, and/or fail to identify how success of this effort will be measured.

2. *Build a Supportive Infrastructure.* A supportive infrastructure ensures that processes are in place to assist the data effort and that predictive analytics is understood and welcomed by campus stakeholders.
3. *Work to Ensure Proper Use of Data.* Because predictive models and algorithms need data to build tools that will support student success, make sure that tools are built ethically, considering the quality of the data and their interpretation, as well as issues of privacy and security.
4. *Design Predictive Analytic Models and Algorithms that Avoid Bias.* Because predictive models and algorithms often inform interventions, it is crucial to reduce bias and improve accuracy.
5. *Meet Institutional Goals and Improve Student Outcomes by Intervening with Care.* How the institution acts as a result

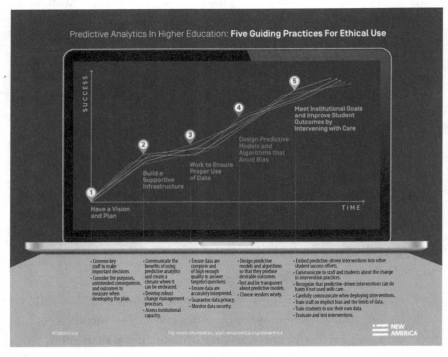

Figure 3.3. Five Guiding Practices for Ethical Use of Predictive Analytics
Ekowo and Palmer 2017, used with permission

of what it learns from predictive analytics is where the rubber meets the road. It is important that interventions are considered in the context of other supports offered at the institution and are communicated with carefully crafted messages. Staff deploying interventions should be trained on how to intervene appropriately, and assess the effectiveness of the interventions once deployed.

Along with considerations on the ethical use of data, higher education officials need to consider the responsible use of data and the practical use of results. For example, when many independent variables are used in a regression analysis, such as those used in ECU's study of student retention, it is likely that some of those variables will produce a statistically significant result. Human knowledge of the context is needed to ensure proper interpretation of the results for the specific institution. On Austin Peay's course selection system, Denley (2012) is wise to note its possible limitations. Nudging a student to select a particular course based on the predicted likelihood of greater success may increase the possible erosion of academic rigor by steering students toward easier courses. In addition, a system that is based on degree program requirements limits students' likelihood of taking nonrequired courses that may offer important insights into other aspects that are integral to a college education. Further, models that use past data to predict the future include the danger of perpetuating or reinforcing existing stereotypes and bias. In this example, Denley (2012) notes that demographic data were not used in the predictive models precisely to safeguard against such risk.

Concluding Remarks

As college and university officials build more effective data reporting and analytical capabilities, the development of more powerful predictive analytics capabilities is likely the next phase in the analytics maturity hierarchy. This transformation is critically needed if leaders believe in and support the building of a data-informed decision culture. Successes that occur when implementing predictive modeling in institutions such as those mentioned in this chapter lend credible support to the benefits of predictive analytics.

While we are excited about the potential for student and institution success that can come from predictive analytics, we are mindful of the challenges, particularly related to the ethics and responsible use of predictive analytics. As mentioned in several other chapters of this book, O'Neil (2016) has been outspoken in the potentials for discrimination that can occur, particularly through automated unsupervised analytics, and Ekowo and Palmer (2017) remind us that ethical use of data is complex, with many nuances to be considered. Their framework for the ethical use of predictive analytics can serve as prompts to important considerations and conversations on campus.

References

Bari, A. 2016. *Predictive Analytics for Dummies,* 2nd edition. Hoboken, NJ: John Wiley & Sons, 2016.

Bishop, C. M. 2006. *Pattern Recognition and Machine Learning.* New York: Springer, 2006.

Boyer, J., T. Harris, B. Green, B. Frank, and K. Van De Vanter. 2012. *5 Keys to Business Analytics Program Success.* Big Sandy, TX: MC Press.

Carmina, S., K. White, G. Orenstein, and C. Doherty. 2016. *The Path to Predictive Analytics and Machine Learning.* Boston, MA: O'Reilly Media, Inc.

Davenport, T. H., and J. G. Harris. 2007. *Competing on Analytics: The New Science of Winning.* Cambridge, MA: Harvard Business Press.

Deng, H., G. Runger, and E. Tuv. 2011. "Bias of Importance Measures for Multi-Valued Attributes and Solutions." Paper presented at the 21st International Conference on Artificial Neural Networks (ICANN), Espoo, Finland, June 15, 2011.

Denley, T. 2012. "Austin Peay State University: Degree Compass," edited by D. G. Oblinger. *Game Changers: Education and Information Technologies* (pp. 263–267). Louisville, CO: EDUCAUSE.

———. 2014. "How Predictive Analytics and Choice Architecture Can Improve Student Success." *Research & Practice in Assessment* 9 (2): 61–69.

Eduventures. 2013. "Predictive Analytics in Higher Education Data-Driven Decision-Making for the Student Life Cycle." Eduventures White Paper. January 2013. Accessed February 17, 2020. https://www.ecampusnews.com/resource-library/predictive-analytics-in-higher-education-data-driven-decision-making-for-the-student-life-cycle-2/.

Ekowo, M., and I. Palmer. 2016. "The Promise and Peril of Predictive Analytics in Higher Education: A Landscape Analysis." Educational Policy Paper. Washington, DC: New America.

———. 2017. "Predictive Analytics in Higher Education: Five Guiding Practices for Ethical Use." Educational Policy Paper. Washington, DC: New America.

Emigh, J. 2019. "Predictive Analytics Techniques: Seeing the Future." Blog post at Datamation. Accessed June 8, 2019. https://www.datamation.com/big-data/predictive-analytics-techniques.html.

Foer, F. 2017. "World Without Mind: The Existential Threat of Big Tech." New York, NY: Penguin Press.

Grace-Martin, K. 2019. "What Is Latent Class Analysis?" Blog post at the Analysis Factor. Accessed on June 11, 2019. https://www.theanalysisfactor.com/what-is-latent-class-analysis/.

Granville, K. 2018. "Facebook and Cambridge Analytica: What You Need to Know as Fallout Widens." *New York Times*, March 19, 2018. Accessed on April 26, 2019. https://www.nytimes.com/2018/03/19/technology/facebook-cambridge-analytica-explained.html?module=inline.

He, L., and Associates. 2018. "Random Forest as a Predictive Analytics Alternative to Regression in Institutional Research." *Practical Assessment, Research and Evaluation* 23 (1): 1–16.

IBM Business Analytics. 2014. "IBM Predictive Fundraising Analytics." IBM White Paper. Accessed on June 14, 2019. https://www.ibm.com/downloads/cas/Y8JK D0GO.

Kho, J. 2018. "Why Random Forest Is My Favorite Machine Learning Model: Discover the Real World Advantages and Drawbacks of the Random Forest." Blog post in Towards Data Science. Accessed on June 11, 2019. https://towardsdatascience.com/why-random-forest-is-my-favorite-machine-learning-model-b97651fa3706.

Leventhal, B. 2018. *Predictive Analytics for Marketers: Using Data Mining for Business Advantage.* London, UK: Kogan Page Publishers, 2018.

Liberman, N. 2019. "Decision Trees and Random Forests." Blog post in Towards Data Science. Accessed on June 11, 2019. https://towardsdatascience.com/decision-trees-and-random-forests-df0c3123f991.

Madasamy, M. 2019. "Introduction to Recommendation Systems and How to Design Recommendation Systems That Resemble Amazon." Blog post at Medium. Accessed on June 13, 2019. https://medium.com/@madasamy/introduction-to-recommendation-systems-and-how-to-design-recommendation-system-that-resembling-the-9ac167e30e95.

Norris, D., and L. Baer. 2014. "Leveraging Analytics to Optimize Student Success." Strategic Initiatives, Inc. White Paper, 2014. Accessed on June 8, 2019. https://wcet.wiche.edu/sites/default/files/docs/events/bootcamp/LeveragingAnalyticstoOp timizeStudentSuccess.pdf.

O'Flaherty, B., and C. Heavin. 2014. "Positioning Predictive Analytics—A Design Evaluation: Frontiers in Artificial Intelligence and Applications." December 2013. Accessed on June 9, 2019. https://www.researchgate.net/publication/270817465 _Positioning_Predictive_Analytics_-_A_Design_Evaluation.

O'Neil, C. 2016. *Weapons of Math Destruction: How Big Data Increases Inequality and Threatens Democracy.* New York, NY: Crown Publishers.

Ouahilal, M., M. El Mohajir, M. Chahhou, and B. E. El Mohajir. 2016. "A Comparative Study of Predictive Algorithms for Business Analytics and Decision Support Systems: Finance as a Case Study." Paper presented at the 2016 International Conference on Information Technology for Organizations Development, February.

Pampel, F. C. 2000. *The Logic of Logistic Regression*. Thousand Oaks, CA: SAGE Publications, Inc.

Reid, R. D., and N. R. Sanders. 2010. *Operations Management,* 4th edition. New York: Wiley and Sons.

US Department of Education. 2012. "Enhancing Teaching and Learning through Educational Data Mining and Learning Analytics: An Issue Brief." Washington, DC: National Center for Education Statistics.

Walcott, M. 2014. "Predictive Modeling and Alumni Fundraising in Higher Education." Doctoral Dissertation, Illinois State University. Dissertations #285.

Yates, H., and C. Chamberlain. 2017. "Machine Learning and Higher Education." *EDUCAUSE Review,* December 18, 2017. Accessed on June 11, 2019. https://er.educause.edu/articles/2017/12/machine-learning-and-higher-education.

PART II. The Ethical, Cultural, and Managerial Imperatives of Data-Informed Decision Making in Higher Education

[4]

Limitations in Data Analytics

Potential Misuse and Misunderstanding
in Data Reports and Visualizations

Karen L. Webber and Jillian N. Morn

R APID INCREASES in technology have led to an escalating demand
for and use of data and advanced analytics to inform decision making in higher education. Data analytics related to students and their
experiences in admissions, enrollment management, financial aid funds
disbursement, and activities related to academic learning and performance has evolved quite rapidly (Lester et al. 2017), and it continues
to evolve each day as the field of data science captures more attention
across the education, government, and business sectors. The growing
ubiquity and granularity of data offer new opportunities for research
and decision making. There are significant benefits but also risks associated with the increased availability of data as the higher education
sector shifts toward a greater reliance on Big Data analytics and open
access (Mathies 2018a). In particular, many decision makers in higher
education lack formal training and/or expertise with educational data
(Horta, Bouwma-Gearhart, and Park 2017), resulting in a data knowledge gap within senior institutional management (Ransbotham, Kiron,
and Prentice 2015). In addition, there are an increasing number of data
analyses or visualizations that, when presented without the proper context, result in inaccurate conclusions. Context is critical, as there are
many questions around the legitimacy, intentionality, and even the ideology of data use within higher education (Calderon 2015). Inaccurate

conclusions can lead to incorrect discussions that can affect student performance, possible program development, and/or policy changes.

There are a number of important considerations that should be addressed related to the growing use of data and analytics in higher education, and some of these topics are covered in other chapters of this book (e.g., data governance, appropriate use of predictive analytics, and institutional policies on data distribution). In this chapter, we examine another important topic—the potential for misuse or misunderstanding of data reports or visualizations. The ease with which data can now be collected and stored tempts institution officials to gather more data, often before decisions are made for how the data will be used. Senior leaders in higher education may lack formal training or expertise with educational data (Horta, Bouwma-Gearhart, and Park 2017) and may be less familiar with details of the data elements or advanced statistical treatments of data. The confluence of these issues certainly prompts the need and value for data experts, often those in institutional research (IR), who can provide context-based information presented in ways that can be meaningfully interpreted and used.

Even though large volumes of data can be stored easily and often, at low cost, data analysts should be mindful of some important limitations that can plague analytics and the effective presentation of data for decision making. Following an overview of the uses and misuses of data, we examine three limitations related to the use of data and analytics in higher education. First, we examine some principles of cognitive science that remind us of practices to ensure accurate presentation and interpretation of data and visuals. Second, we discuss how misunderstandings and misinterpretations occur through the use or misuse of data definitions, through mathematical calculations, through data visualizations, and by intentional manipulation or falsification of data. A third and final point discussed in this chapter focuses on the ethical use of data in higher education.

Overview of the Uses and Misuses
of Data within Higher Education

Individuals in higher education institutions (HEIs) use data in a variety of ways, from financial and resource management to learning more about the activities of community members. Parnell et al. (2018) report that student information systems (admissions, financial aid, and academic course data) are the most frequently used data systems in higher education. However, the fastest-growing segment of data use in higher education relates to student behaviors and their experiences, particularly on academic performance (i.e., student success and institutional engagement; Lester et al. 2017). The evolution of data use within HEIs is arguably no different from what is occurring in the rest of society: the movement into a digital era where technologies are collecting, processing, and presenting information at high speeds (Government Accountability Office 2016; Shepherd 2004).

In higher education, there are strong arguments for using data for evidence-based decision making (Calderon 2015; Webber 2018). However, data have been misused or misinterpreted on a number of occasions, even publicized in national news outlets. Most cases highlight a lack of data protocols or poor administrator judgment, leading to data misuse (recent examples include misreporting of business school scores at Temple University and misreporting of undergraduate student admissions scores at Claremont College). While these past data misuses cause concern, there are other impending data challenges that require our attention as well. Mathies (2018b) examines two recent disruptions in particular: the layering of coding within software systems (Somers 2017) and platform capitalism (Robertson 2018; Srnicek 2016), which will likely lead to future data misuses in higher education. These are discussed below.

Cognitive Science and the Use of Data and Visualizations

Along with considerations given to what data are collected and how they are used, attention must be given to principles of cognitive science and how an individual may benefit or be hindered in designing or interpreting reports and data displays. Whether poor data visuals are intentional or unintentional, both essentially lead to misinterpretation or misunderstandings. Well-designed visualizations are the goal for accurate interpretation. They can convey complex data or information and can minimize data misuse (Drake, Pytlarz, and Patel 2018). With the increasing use of data and analytics software in higher education, understanding how data are visualized and what they show is becoming increasingly important. This is particularly relevant with regard to third-party analytics tools, as their core elements are proprietary and often not shared with clients (Alamuddin, Brown, and Kurzweil 2016).

Data Visualizations

Data visualizations consist of the tools, technologies, techniques, and methodologies to display, explore, and communicate data and information in a graphical form (Drake, Pytlarz, and Patel 2018). Reviewing research on cognitive science and humans' understanding of visuals is helpful in developing better data visualizations in higher education.

Although visual-spatial displays are ubiquitous in human communication (Hegarty 2011), recent advances in computer graphics and human-computer interaction techniques, dynamic and interactive displays have become commonplace and have changed the way we think about and display data. Cognitive scientists argue that representations that are informationally equivalent (contain the same information) are not necessarily computationally equivalent (Larkin and Simon 1987). In the case of visual-spatial displays, Hegarty (2011) reports that there is substantial evidence that task performance can be dramatically different based on varying visual displays of the same information.

A visual system helps the viewer sense the features of an image or display such as color and shape. The system encodes these features to the viewer's brain constructing an internal (cognitive) representation of the image or display. Exactly which of these features are encoded depends on the viewer's attention, one's goals and expectations, and the salience of the display (Hegarty 2011). For example, one difficulty in display comprehension is viewer distraction by highly salient but task-irrelevant information; a viewer will fail to encode the critical information although it is present. In addition to basic perceptual, attentional, and encoding processes, which construct a representation of the external display, the user of a display typically applies knowledge to construct a representation of its referent (Hegarty 2011). This includes knowledge of the display conventions such as the meaning of the X- and Y-axes in a graph, which types of information are typically included or omitted, and which aspects can be taken literally (such as the relative length and configuration of roads on a road map) and which cannot (such as the color and width).

According to Tversky (2001), an individual's intuitions about the effectiveness of a display do not always conform to the display's actual effectiveness. Intuitively, animations of physical processes, such as the workings of machines, and biological mechanisms should be a good means of communicating how processes work. In animations of physical processes, the shapes, locations, and movements of parts of the representation should correspond directly to the shapes, locations, and movements of their referents. However, in a review of several papers comparing animated to static displays, Tversky et al. (2002) indicated that there were no advantages to animations over static displays, pointing out that animations are often ineffective because they are too fast or too complex for the brain to process well.

The Application of Cognitive Science in Data Visualization

Several scholars offer important information on how the human brain processes information, including Edward Tufte, Daniel Kahneman, and Stephen Kosslyn. Other scholars, including Alberto Cairo and Stephen Few add their insights on effective and misguided visual presentations of data. As a leading scholar in visual displays, Tufte (1990, 2001) believes that statistical graphics, just as statistical calculations, are only as good as they are created. A graphic (or calculation), no matter how clever or fancy, cannot rescue an ill-specified (preposterous) model or limited sample size data set (2001). Further, Tufte (2001) asserts that graphics, when done well, can reveal data and be more precise and informative than conventional statistical computations. He offers several important points related to data displays, among these points, graphics should:

- Induce the viewer to think about the substance rather than about methodology, graphic design, or graphic production;
- Make large data seem coherent;
- Encourage the eye to compare different pieces of data;
- Be closely integrated with the statistical and verbal descriptions of a data set; and
- Show the data.

Graphic excellence is important. According to Tufte (2001, 92) graphic excellence has the following characteristics:

- Substance, statistics, and design—presentation of data must be well-designed and interesting;
- Clarity, precision, and efficiency—complex ideas are communicated clearly, with little extraneous or unnecessary information;
- Parsimonious—the graphic gives the viewer the greatest number of ideas in the shortest time with the least in smallest spaces;
- Multivariate—most graphics will review more than one variable at a time; and
- Truthful—the graph tells the truth about the data.

Tufte (2001) is also concerned with how accurately visual elements represent the data at hand. *Graphical integrity* may seem straightforward, but because data are representable in a variety of ways, there is a tendency to scale data disproportionately in order to make them fit in the space allowed. This can lead to false representations of the data and incorrect conclusions. Because of variations in the ways data are presentable and, often, the limits in space Tufte (2001) offers six principles of graphical integrity:

- Representation of numbers should match the true proportions;
- Labeling should be clear and detailed;

- Design should not vary; show only data variation;
- To represent money, use well-known units;
- The number of dimensions represented should be the same as the number of dimensions in the data; and
- Context is essential; graphics must not quote data out of context.

Another scholar who has studied judgment and decision making, Daniel Kahneman (1983, 2011), argues that individuals too often use "gut instincts" to reach speedy conclusions when reading graphics. The fallacy of this "fast thinking" is that the survival process looks only at the information at hand and does not actively look for additional information. Fast thinking accounts for different understandings by how vividly data points appear in one's mind and not according to their objective importance. Kahneman (2011) believes there is a premium on presenting a coherent and logically structured narrative; we are very good at remembering it, as logic and association tie different components together.

Although people often make and remember associations, Tversky and Kahneman (1974, 1986) believe that individuals systematically violate the requirements of consistency and coherence when making decisions. This can lead to inaccurate decisions or misunderstood information. Tversky and Kahneman (1986) trace these violations to the psychological principles that govern the perception of decision making and the evaluation of options. Decision making in this way aligns with expected utility. They argue the value function is S-shaped and when faced with a choice "a rational decision-maker will prefer the prospect that offers the highest expected utility" (453).

Alberto Cairo (2013, 2016) also addresses principles of good data presentation. Cairo (2013) believes that mistakes can lead to misinterpretation/bad design; those mistakes include truncated axes, key variables omitted, oversimplification, using the wrong data visualization form for the data, and lacking key annotations. According to Cairo (2013), an infographic seeks to tell the story that its designer seeks to explain, but a data visualization lets people build their own insights based on the evidence provided. Cairo believes that interactive graphics highlight relevant facts first (e.g., the relationship between income and life expectancy across countries) and then allows the viewer to explore the data set underlying those facts (by presenting a set of numbers). As such, interactive graphics are simultaneously infographics *and* visualizations of data with at least two layers: a presentation one and an exploration one.

Organizing the works of other relevant scholars, Hegarty (2011) summarizes a number of principles for effective graphics. Through five principles that include relevant points from other major experts such as Tufte (2001), Kosslyn (1994), and Tversky (2001), Hegarty astutely points to a number of important considerations, reinforcing the need to think about the requirements and capabilities of the audience. Principles related to expressiveness of displays, for example, speak to the importance of presenting reports or visuals that display only the relevant data or information so that the viewer can focus on the intended numbers or image (Hegarty 2011). Like any good writing, the principles of pragmatics urge the analyst or visual designer to make the most important information easy to see and understand. Being mindful of scale as well as the use of consistent colors, symbols, and other conventions helps the reader/user to understand the meanings intended.

The above discussion points to how and why some presentations of data can fall prey to misuse or misinterpretation. While this can happen via basic numeric tables, the advances in data analytics and infographics have facilitated the increased likelihood of misuse or misinterpretation. While Mathies (2018a) organizes into four groups, Webber (2018) reasons that data in higher education have the potential to be misused or misunderstood in six ways. Misinterpretations or misuse can occur when the following are carried out incorrectly: (1) statistical treatment of data; (2) use of data definitions; (3) use of color, scale, and size or proportion; (4) type of chart or graph; (5) representation of context; and (6) multiple challenges that exist from the previous five categories. Sometimes the data user may lack knowledge of data definitions or may lack access to the data. Flawed data governance may allow data to be used not as intended or when accessible by outside entities (e.g., data breaches). These instances often violate the privacy of individuals as well as the institution itself. In many cases of data misuse within these three categories, it is often a definitional, mismanagement, or misapplication issue (Mathies 2018a). While some good examples exist (e.g., for Northeastern University, see https://provost.northeastern.edu/uds /data-access/overview, or for the University of Georgia, see https://oir .uga.edu/governance/), many HEIs do not have organizational structures or policies adequately addressing the organization-wide perspective on data governance and its distribution. The lack of policies, protocols, and structures can be remedied by instituting new procedures and guidelines that address data misuse. Mathies (2018b) suggests that institutions develop and implement a data sharing mandate that can help build broader groups of data users on a campus. Indeed, such a mandate might be helpful to reduce or eliminate data silos, but we agree with Mathies (2018b) that well-written policies and strong data governance will be required.

Charts or Graphics That Can Lead to Misinterpretation

As data visualizations become more frequent in higher education, so too is the possibility of visuals that lead to misinterpretation. Below are two examples of how data visuals mislead consumers within the context of other important information on higher education policy, process, and practice. When the proper context for data is used, there is legitimacy and greater accuracy of conclusions drawn (Calderon 2015). Due to limited space, this section includes just two structured examples of how data, when reported or visualized, have been misused. (Additional examples of poorly designed visuals for quantitative information by Stephen Few are available at http://perceptualedge.com/examples.php.)

Misinterpretation Based on Different Calculations Used. To interpret table 4.1 correctly, it is particularly important to know how a mean or average score was derived. The figures below show the Mean Debt of *all* students versus only *borrowers*. These are not significantly different groups, as the *borrowers* are a subset of the *all* group. In short, this is not a comparison between two distinct groups. Perhaps a better graphic would be to include data on the *nonborrowers* group, allowing for

Table 4.1. Cumulative Amount Borrowed for Graduate Education, US Institutions, 2012

Graduate Degree Recipients	2011–2012		
Graduate Degree	% Borrowing	Mean Debt $ (All)	Mean Debt $ (Borrowers)
Total	63.85	34,412.80	53,894.33
Degree Type			
Master's degree (all)	62.95	25,075.66	39,837.16
Professional degree (all)	84.76	109,385.40	129,053.20
Doctoral degree (all)	49.72	36,587.93	73,582.36
Gender			
Male	62.97	34,778.65	55,234.19
Female	64.45	34,167.62	53,017.00

Source: NPSAS 2012 data from Webber and Burns (2019).

comparisons between two distinct groups as well as to the whole group mean.

Misinterpretation Based on Y-axis Scale. Figures 4.1 through 4.4 show two bar and two line charts with different Y-axis scales that can lead to different interpretations of the same data. In the first chart, the Y-axis is much smaller (300 points) while in the second chart the Y-axis is much bigger (1,200 points). The Y-axis in figure 4.1 makes the change over time appear more dramatic because the amount of change accounted for (roughly 125 points) allows for a 42% change graphically (out of the 300 points). The Y-axis in figure 4.2 makes the change over time appear smaller due to the larger possible change available (1,200 points) and thus accounts for only about a 10% change graphically. The line charts in figures 4.3 and 4.4 emphasize the same point on perception based on scale. Beginning the Y-axis scale at zero is often advised, but it can lead consumers to infer a smaller change. The difference in comprehension could lead to dramatically different policy interventions.

Dashboards and infographics can be especially challenging to design clearly. Dashboard designers often seek to include different metrics or charts about multiple subgroups on one page. Dashboards and infographics that attempt to provide information on multiple points require the viewer to see and understand multiple items, often leaving the reader to do too much mental work, likely not taking in all the information.

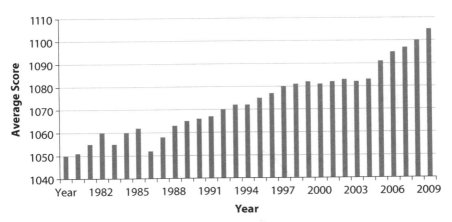

Figure 4.1. Fictitious Admissions Score Data, with Y-Axis Scale from 1040 to 1120

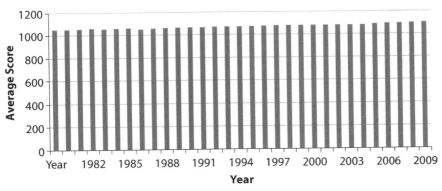

Figure 4.2. Fictitious Admissions Score Data with Y-Axis Scale from 0 to 1500

Readers who are interested in examples of infographics with design issues may wish to follow principles of good graphics design expressed by Taei (2019) at Visme.co. Additionally, readers may wish to review Chibana's (2018) or French's (2018a) version of mistakes commonly made with infographics. Chibana (2018) purports that interactive graphics require readers to do too much mental work. For example, she believes a common mistake is to separate the legend from the main data, forcing the reader to look back and forth between the central visualization and the meaning of each icon or color. (See more at http://blog.visme

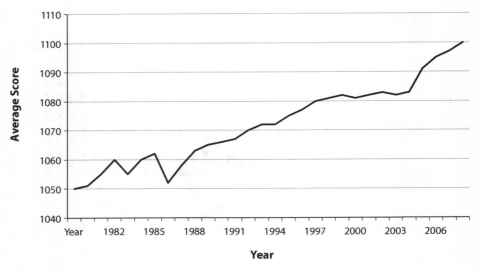

Figure 4.3. Fictitious Admissions Score Data with Y-Axis Scale from 1040 to 1120

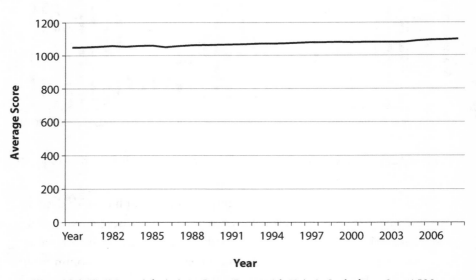

Figure 4.4. Fictitious Admissions Score Data with Y-Axis Scale from 0 to 1500

.co/bad-infographics/#2UFZW4vCLrJADu0p.99.) Mistakes include: showing too many visual points that limit the brain's ability to focus (visual data junk); using too many colors and/or too little white space; using inaccurate scales; and having no hierarchy of data or placement of information. To see French's (2018a) full list of mistakes and ways to fix them, see https://www.columnfivemedia.com/how-to-fix-the-15 -common-infographic-design-mistakes.

Ethical and Responsible Use of Data

Finally, in this chapter, we turn our attention to the need to be mindful of ethical and responsible use of data. As with the ethics of human subjects in research, higher education officials must wrestle to balance the benefit that can be achieved from more data with respect to and beneficence of the individual involved. Recent events such as the Facebook/Cambridge Analytica scandal (Granville 2018) are helping users become aware of the hidden dangers that are deeply embedded in internet sites and have prompted social media companies to be more transparent with the ways in which they collect data to enhance user experience. Authors such as Foer (2017) urge extreme caution, or at least user acknowledgment, that companies such as Google, Facebook, and Amazon are very strategic and effective at guiding individuals' access to information, further arguing that these companies' algorithms suggest items for purchase or information to read on that web site are modifying the way individuals think and behave. In the age of Big Data and predictive analytics, so too must higher education officials consider the ethics of how student and employee data are collected, stored, and secured, and how the data are used and the effects of those data on individuals.

The technological advancements that have enabled greater data collection and analysis of higher education activities and outcomes have opened the doors for new ethical dilemmas. To some degree, more data points can provide a more robust picture of a person or an activity, but it seems likely that there is a point of diminishing returns that higher education officials should seek to find. In addition to the need for greater institutional resources (including advanced technical instruments, policies to ensure proper use and storage of data, and staff members to complete analyses), officials should consider the value-added benefits as well as the possible infringements on privacy and the potential for algorithms that may heighten unintended bias. Some scholars agree with the value of anonymous data yet ponder how to do that well; Pardo and Siemens (2014) assert that "data can be either useful or perfectly anonymous, but never both" (2014, 447). Other scholars such as Khalil and Ebner (2016) point to the value of data de-identification as a way to ensure privacy and still provide students with information on their progress via learning analytics.

Collecting and using large volumes of data on students, indeed, is a double-edged sword. Accurate data on today's college students can contribute to informed decision making. It can help officials consider ways to ensure student success from application and entry through the degree or certificate experience, and into postinstitution career success. However, while good data can assist in making better decisions, the excitement about or enthusiasm for the ease of data collection and possibilities to increase student success may cloud one's thinking on issues of privacy and/or responsible use. The collection of data from learning management systems as well as "swipe card" data from building entry is now being used to examine the relationships between academic study (time in class or out-of-class study) and time spent on extracurricular activities (e.g., use of athletic facilities or student unions). Knowing when and how to report from data collection is important. Entrance into a building from swipe card data or logging in to a course management system (CMS) lacks detail on what is happening when the student is inside the building or the CMS and may prompt the use of many erroneous assumptions. User knowledge of how and when data are being used is important. In the K–12 sector, Reidenberg et al. (2013) reported, schools failed to inform parents about the use of data in the school's cloud services, including learning analytics programs. These authors argue that the lack of effective transparency undermines accountability to school communities and to the public.

Ethical and Privacy Considerations

Ethics and privacy in data use in higher education are incredibly important. There are a number of reasons why data are used for decision support, and it is necessary to consider the implications for their use for both individual students and staff as well as for institutional management. Palen and Dourish (2003) propose that privacy in digital environments be considered in three ways: via discourse, identity, and temporality. Ekowo and Palmer (2017) remind us that "using data ethically is complex, and no magic formula exists" (3). Ethical and responsible use of data can be established across campus with a good data governance program. Establishing policies and procedures can help campus colleagues know that adopting an ethical framework to engage with data is important as the continued interest in data-informed decisions pushes for the collection and storage of more personal data.

The emerging ethical considerations for higher education administrators and researchers center on data privacy, complacency with algorithms and vendor products (including e-learning vendor products), and the ways in which the results of data analysis are used. With greater data collection, higher education institutions and researchers may be empowered to address questions and issues, uncover patterns of behavior, and help students, staff, and organizations thrive. However, with more data collection efforts comes a higher risk of unintentional disclosures or leaks. Administrators need to consider the ways in which data are stored in the long and short term as well as how they will be managed, accessed, and protected.

Privacy of student information is important for education due to the possible adverse impact that inappropriate use or disclosures may have on student learning and social development as well as the possible impact on students' well-being by amplifying performance-related stress (Reidenberg and Schaub 2018). As with notions of stereotype threat (Steele and Aronson 1995), early awareness systems could prematurely label a student in a failing category that may prompt a student to be less motivated or be hesitant to seek tutoring due to fear of being labeled a failure. Learning analytics programs may gather large amounts of data on student performance in a variety of contexts, from student performance on specific exam questions to overall course assessments to large-scale measures at the institution or school system level. The variation in curriculum, instructor, pedagogy, classroom conditions, and/or mix of student demographics makes it very difficult to compare student performance. This variation may call into question the validity of analytic methods that have not accounted for the variance inherent in these and other moderators.

HEI officials should consider how the data they collect may be subject to compliance/alignment with regional, national, and supranational policies. Under the Family Educational Rights and Privacy Act (FERPA), students have a right to request access to view their academic record. The use of online course click-through data, GIS (geographical information system) data on card swipes, and the results of early awareness systems rest in a fuzzy area of interpretation, and it seems likely that institutional or federal guidelines on student protections will be revisited in the near future. While the European Union's Data Protection Directive (DPD; Directive 95/46/EC) regulates the processing of personal data and the movement of data in EU institutions, the General Data Protection Regulation (GDPR) affects US institutions enrolling and employing EU citizens, and should be added to HEI discussions on student privacy. In addition to codifying the right to erasure, EU GDPR requires institutions and companies to document consent or a stated business purpose for processing data on EU citizens.

While respect for privacy is important, Prinsloo and Slade (2015) urge us to consider the implications of students' "opting out" of data collection. These authors proffer that higher education officials must determine if and when students should have the choice to opt out of institutional surveillance. In light of an institution's role to ensure appropriate support and guidance to students, these authors ask important questions such as how opting out may impact the institution's fiduciary role.

Prinsloo and Slade (2015) found that some institutions are creating specific policies on ethical uses of analytics, and while they believe these policies are helpful in creating transparency and "boundary concerns"

(84), further issues remain that are related to issues of informed consent and how and when students can opt out of data collection. They recommend that HEI officials learn from the privacy issues of social media data and, despite a traditional paternalistic approach, engage more proactively with students to inform and more directly involve them in ways in which both individual and aggregated data can and should be used. Greater engagement with students, Prinsloo and Slade (2015) believe, will engender trust and cooperation.

In *Weapons of Math Destruction,* O'Neil (2016) provides chilling detail on the ways in which large volumes of data and intentions to identify student success can go wrong. Algorithms are conceived as fair, objective, and efficient forms of analysis (O'Neil 2016). Predictive analytics can be a beneficial aid that produces data-informed decision making in higher education. However, algorithms are constructed by people, and therefore they reflect the judgments and priorities of their creators (O'Neil 2016). Algorithms can encode human prejudice, misunderstanding, and bias into systems that determine access and outcomes and when they are not continuously updated and/or they rely on inaccurate proxy measures can lead to destructive outcomes (O'Neil 2016). Like Harel Ben Shahar (2017), O'Neil (2016) argues that destructive effects abound in ill-conceived algorithms, many of which discriminate or further stratify individuals, particularly students in education.

We agree with the scholars who recommend that, when constructing algorithms, variable selection should be based on direct measures (not proxies) whenever possible. Administrators selecting vendor products should be mindful of data sharing, privacy, and intellectual property, not providing vendor collection of data unless all forms of use are specified. End users of these products should know what is going to the measurements and be able to evaluate whether these are suitable measures. Further, products should be continuously updated based on new data.

Recommendations for Responsible Use of Data

Following O'Neil's (2016) proposal to implement a Data Bill of Rights, and similar to Calo's (2013) recommendation for a "consumer subject review board," Mathies (2018b) urges higher education officials to consider a data sharing mandate that would allow institutional data to be more accessible to campus colleagues but within a data governance plan. In such a data bill of rights institution officials would be required to develop a plan that respects and protects individuals' data, requires programming language that limits coding failures, and includes a data ethics board to review and ensure good data practices.

As higher education officials consider the value and potential consequences of vendor products (e.g., enrollment management, student learning assessment, and advising), we recommend that higher education officials evaluate the analyses that underlie predictive models, use caution in implementing early awareness systems, and strategize on how to react to the results of analysis. In addition to good data governance, institution officials should be firm in fully understanding how the vendor product completes calculations (when unknown referred to as the "black box") and how one vendor product (e.g., one used for admissions or enrollment management) relates to data being used in another vendor product (e.g., used for student advising). Ekowo and Palmer's (2017) guidelines for ethical uses of predictive analytics in higher education may be helpful for general structures and may be especially helpful for providing support to minimize inaccurate model use.

Conclusion

Evidence-based decision making requires access to, proper use of, and accurate interpretation of data. The volumes of data available today tempt us to use and share information frequently, and in a variety of ways. The complexities of HEIs and today's students can benefit from the use and analysis of many data points, but users must be mindful to use data in ethical ways, using statistically correct analyses and proper visuals. Large volumes of data and new technologies have allowed greater insight into student and senior leader decisions that reflect institutional behaviors, but proper data management and policies on the use and release of data are critical. Data governance policies require regular review and modification, as processes and protocols become dated. This is particularly true as pre-platform governance frameworks often lack the conceptual tools to envision data technology progress (Weatherby 2018). Both past and likely future data misuses highlight the need for foresight as well as oversight, from a technical as well as a contextual perspective. This is where planning and institutional research professionals can play an important role. Most senior institutional leaders rely on a small group of senior associates to provide context-based information to manage an institution; if IR or planning professionals are not in this select group it compounds data issues with possible misinterpretations and/or data nuances, quirks, and policy implications that might go unnoticed or ignored (Webber 2018).

As discussed above, cognitive psychologists and other scholars remind us of important principles related to how one "sees" data and how the brain interprets those data into information. Color, spacing, scale, and the calculation of numeric data are important to consider when designing graphs and charts. Today's new infographics, while intuitively appealing, may offer challenges to read and understand fully. Tufte's (2001) words still ring true: *above all else, show the data.* Tips to improve data visualizations include removing superfluous information that do not support the study, being mindful of placement (i.e., spacing) of images to facilitate comparisons, using callouts wisely, ensuring sufficient contrast between colors and patterns, including a zero baseline if possible, and designing for comprehension (French 2018b). Following these suggestions can reduce a great deal of misunderstanding. Tufte's principle on clarity, precision, and efficiency is particularly important; however, it can be challenging to communicate complex ideas clearly and with little extraneous or unnecessary information added. Additionally, parsimonious graphics that provide the greatest number of ideas in the shortest time and in the smallest spaces (Tufte 2001) aligns with Kahneman's (2011) fast-thinking process; encouraging individuals to look only at the information at hand and not to actively look for additional information.

Higher education officials have a duty, often a legal one, to protect student and staff data. They also have a duty to provide the higher education community with the most accurate data and information in a timely manner. Appropriate data governance procedures are essential, and senior personnel who are responsible for institutional research tasks should be integral in data governance policies on campus. Along with data policies that allow access to institutional data, good visual presentations are increasingly popular; when done well, they are a good way to share information to the internal as well as the external community. When data visualizations do not follow principles of good design, they can cause confusion or provide misinformation. The examples above illustrate how data and visualizations are misused or misinterpreted. Seeing these examples and understanding how they have been ineffective or misused can hopefully lead to better data visualizations in the future.

Implications

The use of data and the desire for continued larger volumes of data for informed decision making will only increase in the years ahead in higher education. While there are significant benefits that can serve to improve one or more aspects of higher education, there are also risks. When data are misused or misinterpreted, senior leaders may make the wrong decisions, ineffective or unproductive policies may be enacted, and students may not be as successful.

Once reports or visualizations are completed, data analysts or unit leaders should also strive to engage with users to ensure a full understanding of data definitions, the context in which the data reside, and any nuances that affect the data. Most often, a face-to-face meeting to discuss a new data table, visual, or infographic can be a highly effective way to ensure that the users understand the information presented, and it offers a great opportunity to answer questions that may arise, or to engage in discussions that may relate to new policies and programs.

While data analytics in higher education has great potential to help students and institutions succeed, it also presents the need to be strategic in ensuring ethical and secure use of data. Reidenberg and Schaub (2018) suggest that transparency, accountability, and security should be integral in learning analytics technology rather than afterthoughts, and that higher education officials and commercial learning vendors establish appropriate safeguards to govern appropriate access to and use of learning analytics data. They further suggest that legal safeguards for education privacy should reflect the reality of data-driven education by expanding privacy protections to clearly cover learning analytics. These are important points that can help move the use of data analytics in higher education to a stronger and more effective position in data-informed decision making.

References

Alamuddin, R., J. Brown, and M. Kurzweil. 2016. "Student Data in the Digital Era: An Overview of Current Practices." Resource document. Ithaka S + R. Accessed April 27, 2017. http://www.sr.ithaka.org/wp-content/uploads/2016/09/SR_Report _Student_ Data_Digital_Era-090616.pdf.

Breslow, L., G. J. Trafton, and R. M. Ratwani. 2009. "A Perceptual Process Approach to Selecting Color Scales for Complex Visualizations." *Journal of Experimental Psychology: Applied* 15: 25–34.

Cairo, A. 2013. *The Functional Art: An Introduction to Information Graphics and Visualizations.* Berkeley, CA: New Riders.

———. 2016. *The Truthful Art: Data, Charts, and Maps for Communication.* Berkeley, CA: New Riders.

Calderon, A. 2015. "In Light of Globalization, Massification, and Marketization: Some Considerations on the Uses of Data in Higher Education." In *Institutional Research and Planning in Higher Education: Global Contexts and Themes,* 288–306, edited by K. Webber and A. Calderon. New York: Routledge Press.

Calo, R. 2013. "Consumer Subject Review Boards: A Thought Experiment." *Stanford Law Review Online* 66: 97. Accessed November 19, 2018. https://www.stanford lawreview.org/online/privacy-and-big-data-consumer-subject-review-boards/.

Chibana, N. 2018. "11 Common Infographics Mistakes." Blog post. Visme. Accessed June 10, 2018. http://blog.visme.co/bad-infographics/.

Directive 95/46/EC of the European Parliament and Council, 1995. Retrieved on May 25, 2019 at: https://eur-lex.europa.eu/LexUriServ/LexUriServ.do?uri=%20 CELEX:31995L0046:EN:HTML.

Drake, B., I. Pytlarz, and M. Patel. 2018. "Let Me Paint You a Picture: Utilizing Visualizations to Make Data More Accessible." In *Building Capacity in Institutional Research and Decision Support in Higher Education,* 81–93, edited by K. Webber. Knowledge Studies in Higher Education, 4. Cham, Switzerland: Springer.

Ekowo, M., and I. Palmer. "The Promise and Peril of Predictive Analytics in Higher Education: A Landscape Analysis." New America. Accessed September 7, 2018. https://files.eric.ed.gov/fulltext/ED570869.pdf.

Few, S. 2012. *Show Me the Numbers: Designing Tables and Graphics to Enlighten* (2nd edition). Oakland, CA: Analytics Press.

Foer, F. 2017. *World Without Mind: The Existential Threat of Big Tech.* New York: Penguin Random House.

French, K. 2018a. "How to Fix the 15 Most Common Infographic Design Mistakes." Column Five. Accessed October 23, 2017. https://www.columnfivemedia.com /how-to-fix-the-15-common-infographic-design-mistakes.

———. 2018b. "25 Tips to Instantly Improve Your Data Visualization Design." Accessed August 25, 2018. https://www.columnfivemedia.com/25-tips-to-upgrade -your-data-visualization-design.

Gattis, M., and K. J. Holyoak. 1996. "Mapping Conceptual to Spatial Relations in Visual Reasoning." *Journal of Experimental Psychology: Learning, Memory & Cognition* 22: 231–239.

Government Accountability Office. 2016. *Data and Analytics: Emerging Opportunities and Challenges.* Government Accountability Office. Accessed February 2018. https://www.gao.gov/assets/690/680265.pdf.

Granville, K. 2018. "Facebook and Cambridge Analytica: What You Need to Know as Fallout Widens." *New York Times.* March 19, 2018. https://www.nytimes.com /2018/03/19/technology/facebook-cambridge-analytica-explained.html?module =inline.

Harel Ben Shahar, T. 2017. "Educational Justice and Big Data." *Theory and Research in Education* 15, no. 3: 306–320.

Hegarty, M. 2011. "The Cognitive Science of Visual-Spatial Displays: Implications for Design." *Topics in Cognitive Science* 3: 446–474.

Hegarty, M., M. Canham, and S. I. Fabrikant. 2010. "Thinking about the Weather: How Display Salience and Knowledge Affect Performance in a Graphic Inference Task." *Journal of Experimental Psychology: Learning, Memory and Cognition* 36: 37–53.

Horta, M., J. Bouwma-Gearhart, and H. Park. 2017. "Data Driven Decision Making in the Era of Accountability: Fostering Faculty Data Cultures for Learning. *Review of Higher Education* 40, no. 3: 391–426.

Jaschik, S. 2018." Lies, Damned Lies and Rankings." *Inside Higher Education.* July 10, 2018. https://www.insidehighered.com/news/2018/07/10/temple-ousts -business-dean-after-report-finds-online-mba-program-years-submitted.

Khalil, M., and Ebner, M. (2016). De-Identification in Learning Analytics. *Journal of Learning Analytics* 3 (1): 129–138. http://dx.doi.org/10.18608/jla.2016.31.8.

Kahneman, D. 1983. *Attention and Effort.* New York: Prentice Hall.

———. 2011. *Thinking, Fast and Slow.* New York: Farrar, Straus and Giroux.

Kellen, V. 2019. "21st-Century Analytics: New Technologies and New Rules." In *EDUCAUSE Review,* May 20, 2019. https://er.educause.edu/articles/2019/5/21st -century-analytics-new-technologies-and-new-rules.

Kosslyn, S. 1994. *Elements of Graphic Design.* New York: W. H. Freeman & Co.

Larkin, J. H., and H. A. Simon. 1987. "Why a Diagram Is (Sometimes) Worth a Thousand Words." *Cognitive Science* 11, no. 1: 65–100.

Lester, J., C. Klein, H. Rangwala, and A. Johri. 2017. "Learning Analytics in Higher Education." *ASHE Higher Education Report* 43, no. 5: 9–135.

Mathies, C. 2018a. "Uses and Misuses of Data." In *Building Capacity in Institutional Research and Decision Support in Higher Education,* 95–111, edited by K. Webber. Knowledge Studies in Higher Education, 4. Cham,, Switzerland: Springer.

———. 2018b. "Ethical Use of Data." In *IR in the Digital Era: New Directions for Institutional Research* 178, edited by C. Mathies and C. Ferland. Boston: Wiley.

Novick, L. R., and S. M. Hurley. 2001. "To Matrix, Network, or Hierarchy: That Is the Question." *Cognitive Psychology* 42: 158–216.

O'Neil, C. 2016. *Weapons of Math Destruction: How Big Data Increases Inequality and Threatens Democracy.* New York: Broadway Books.

Palen, L., and Dourish, P. (2003). Unpacking Privacy for a Networked World. *Proceedings of the SIGCHI Conference on Human Factors in Computing Systems.* New York, NY: Association for Computing Machinery, 129–136.

Palmer, S. E. 1978. "Fundamental Aspects of Cognitive Representations." In *Cognition and Categorization,* 259–303, edited by E. Rosch and B. B. Lloyd. Mahwah, NJ: Lawrence Erlbaum Associates.

Pardo, A., and G. Siemens. 2014. "Ethical and Privacy Principles for Learning Analytics." *British Journal of Educational Technology* 45, no. 3: 438–450. http://dx.doi.org/10.1111/bjet.12152.

Parnell, A., D. Jones, A. Wesaw, and C. Brooks. 2018. *Institution's Use of Data Analytics for Student Success.* National Association of Student Personnel Administrators, Inc.; The Association for Institutional Research; and EDUCAUSE. Accessed April 2018. https://www.naspa.org/rpi/reports/data-and-analytics-for -student-success.

Peebles, D., and P. C-H. Cheng. 2003. "Modeling the Effect of Task and Graphical Representation on Response Latency in a Graph-Reading Task. *Human Factors* 45: 28–46.

Prinsloo, P., and S. Slade. 2015. "Student Privacy Self-Management: Implications for Learning Analytics." In *Proceedings of the LAK 2015 International Conference on Learning Analytics and Knowledge,* 83–92. New York, NY: Association of Computer Machinery.

Ransbotham, S., D. Kiron, and P. K. Prentice. 2015. "Minding the Analytics Gap." *MIT Sloan Management Review* (Spring): 63–68.

Reidenberg, J. R., N. C. Russell, J. Kovnot, T. B. Norton, R. Cloutier, and D. Alvarado. 2013. *Privacy and Cloud Computing in Public Schools.* Center on Law and Information Policy, Fordham University School of Law. http://ir.lawnet .fordham.edu/clip/2/.

Reidenberg, J. R. and F. Schaub. 2018. "Achieving Big Data Privacy in Education." *Theory and Research in Education* 00: 1–7, doi:10.1177/1477878851885308.

Robertson, S. 2018. "Platform Capitalism and the New Value Economy in the Academy." *Culture, Politics, and Global Justice Research Cluster Working Paper.* Cambridge University. Accessed February 2018. https://cpgj.files.wordpress.com /2018/04/cpgj-working-paper-12.pdf.

Royal Society. 2010. *The Scientific Century: Securing Our Future Prosperity.* Policy document 02/10. London: Royal Society.

Schwartz, D. L. 1995. "Reasoning about the Referent of a Picture Versus Reasoning about the Picture as the Referent: An Effect of Visual Realism." *Memory & Cognition* 23: 709–722.

Shah, P., and P. Carpenter. 1995. "Conceptual Limitations in Comprehending Line Graphs." *Journal of Experimental Psychology: General* 124: 337–370.

Shepherd, J. 2004. "What Is the Digital Era?" In *Social and Economic Transformation in the Digital Era,* 1–18, edited by G. Doukidis, N. Mylonopoulos, and

N. Pouloudi. Accessed September 14, 2018. http://www.igi-global.com/chapter/digital-era/29024.

Somers, J. 2017. "The Coming Software Apocalypse." *The Atlantic.* September 26, 2017. https://www.theatlantic.com/technology/archive/2017/09/saving-the-world-from-code/540393/.

Srnicek, N. 2016. *Platform Capitalism.* Cambridge, UK: Polity.

Steele, C., and J. Aronson. 1995. "Stereotype Threat and the Intellectual Test Performance of African Americans." *Journal of Personality and Social Psychology* 69, no. 5: 797–811.

Strauss, V. 2012. "Elite University Lies to College Rankers for Years." *Washington Post.* August 23, 2012. https://www.washingtonpost.com/blogs/answer-sheet/post/does-it-matter-that-an-elite-university-lied-to-college-rankers-for-years/2012/08/22/e89b39d2-ec68-11e1-aca7-272630dfd152_blog.html?utm_term=.48cabc d2a554.

Taei, P. 2019. "A Beginner's Guide to Shareable Infographics." Visme. https://www.visme.co/wp-content/uploads/2017/03/How%20to%20Make%20an%20Infographic%20-%20A%20Visual%20Guide%20for%20Beginners%20By%20Visme.pdf.

Tufte, E. 1990. *Envisioning Information.* Cheshire, CT: Graphics Press.

———. 2001. *The Visual Display of Quantitative Data.* Cheshire, CT: Graphics Press.

Tversky, A. 2001. "Spatial Schemas in Depictions." *Spatial Schemas and Abstract Thought,* 79–112, edited by M. Gattis. Cambridge, MA: MIT Press.

Tversky, A., and D. Kahneman. 1974. "Judgement under Uncertainty: Heuristics and Biases." *Science* 185, no. 4157: 1124–1131.

Tversky, A., J. B. Morrison, and M. Betrancourt. (2002). "Animation: Can It Facilitate?" *International Journal of Human-Computer Studies* 57: 247–262. https://doi.org/10.1006/ijhc.2002.1017.

———. 1986. "Rational Choice and Framing of Decisions." *Journal of Business* 59, no. 4. Part 2: The Behavioral Foundations of Economic Theory (October): 5251–5278.

Weatherby, L. 2018. "Delete Your Account: On the Theory of Platform Capitalism." *Los Angeles Review of Books.* Accessed April 2018. https://lareviewofbooks.org/article/delete-your-account-on-the-theory-of-platform-capitalism/#!.

Webber, K. L. 2018. "The Future of IR and Decision Support: Ensuring a Seat at the Table." In *Building Capacity in Institutional Research and Decision Support in Higher Education,* 261–276, edited by K. Webber. Cham, Switzerland: Springer.

Webber, K. L., and R. A. Burns. 2019. "Graduate Student Debt 2000 to 2016: Trends and Implications." Submitted for consideration to peer-reviewed journal.

Yeh, M., and C. D. Wickens. 2001. "Attentional Filtering in the Design of Electronic Map Displays: A Comparison of Color Coding, Intensity Coding, and Decluttering Techniques." *Human Factors* 43: 543–562.

[5]

Guiding Your Organization's Data Strategy

The Roles of University Senior Leaders and Trustees
in Strategic Analytics

Gail B. Marsh and Rachit Thariani

IN 2017 Clayton Christensen, who is well known for his theory of "disruptive innovation," predicted that as many as half of American universities would close or go bankrupt within 10 to 15 years. The basis of his argument was that education via digital formats would undermine traditional institutions' business models to the point that many will not survive (Lederman 2017). Higher education is facing many challenges, including rising education costs, dwindling federal and state funding support, demographic shifts, and most important, rapid increase of education content delivery via digital technologies. A 2016 research study from Ernst & Young identified eight risk factors that are associated with failing colleges, and it classified a total of 805 colleges or universities as either "small and at risk" or "large and languishing" (Parthenon-Ernst and Young Education Practice 2016).

While Christensen's prediction may sound farfetched, higher education has many examples of rapid declines that should give university leaders and trustees a reason to ponder what the new digital order will mean to the future of their campuses. Fifteen years ago, few people would have predicted that the rapid rise and dominance of e-commerce companies such as Amazon would lead to the subsequent bankruptcies of retail giants like Blockbuster Video, Borders Bookstore, Sears, and Toys R Us, who were too slow to innovate. In higher education, we have already seen some of the early signs of disruptive innovations. For example, Georgia Tech's $7,000 Master of Computer Science program* attracted over 17,000 applications worldwide for fall 2017 and enrolled over 6,000 students as of spring 2018.

In the 2018 Survey of College and University Business Officers, respondents reported growing concerns about financial pressure facing colleges, private colleges in particular (Lederman 2018). Just under half (44%) of the chief financial officers at four-year undergraduate colleges said they were confident in their institution's financial stability over the next 10 years, down from 54% in 2016. More than two-thirds of the 2018 survey respondents (68%) acknowledged that their tuition discount rates are no longer sustainable (Lederman 2018).

Senior leaders and trustees may wish to review current challenges and formulate a strategy to ensure successful operation of their institutions. For example, senior leaders strive for program alignment that will best ensure student interest and economic need, how to recruit the right number of students based on desired student profiles, and how to grow the revenue base without relying heavily on tuition increases. To address these issues effectively, university leaders and trustees must leverage data resources and strategic analytics to fully understand the decision contexts and to objectively evaluate the trade-offs, cost-benefits, and long-term impacts of major organizational decisions. Davenport (2006b) argues that organizations need to compete based on their competency in analytics capabilities not only because they already have all the data resources and talents but because it matters to their organizational strategy and business performance.

What Is Strategic Analytics?

EDUCAUSE defines analytics as *the use of data, statistical analysis, and explanatory and predictive models to gain insights and act on complex issues* (Bichsel 2012, 6). When aligned with strategic planning in an organization, this definition points to several key components of data

---

*See http://www.omscs.gatech.edu/.

analytics activities, including: identifying a set of complex issues or questions to address using data evidence; finding or collecting the appropriate and relevant data, further analyzing the data with an eye toward prediction and insight; presenting data findings in ways that are both understandable and actionable; and making data analytics a constant part of the strategy development and implementation cycle, with each iteration elevating the organization's analytics maturity (Bichsel 2012).

Extending EDUCAUSE's definition, we believe that strategic analytics involves the use of data, statistical analysis, and explanatory and predictive models to gain insights and act on complex, long-term, and generally enterprise-wide issues that have strategic consequences. Strategic analytics is concerned with how an organization is positioned in the competitive environment, how resources and assets are mobilized to achieve organizational objectives, how the performance management system is leveraged to support strategic initiatives, and eventually, how an organization can stay agile and competitive for sustainable growth.

Strategic Analytics Extends the Capabilities of Institutional Research*

Strategic analytics is a relatively new concept in higher education. Only a limited number of universities have a dedicated group of data specialists and analytics experts who are specifically tasked with using data from multiple sources to explicitly support organizational strategy development and implementation. The growth of strategic analytics is a recognition that institutional research operations at many university campuses need a paradigm expansion. The Association for Institutional Research (2017) identified the following as the core functions and roles of institutional research offices:

- *Identify information needs.* This reflects the iterative process of identifying relevant stakeholders and their decision support

*The authors would like to thank Dr. Henry Y. Zheng for sharing his insights on strategic analytics as related to university institutional research and planning.

needs. It includes anticipating questions through review of data, information, and research and policy studies.

- *Collect, analyze, interpret, and report data and information.* This reflects the technical tasks employed to provide data, information, and analysis for decision support.
- *Plan and evaluate.* This may include operational, budgetary, and strategic planning in which institutional research collaborates with other units at the institution, state, or related organizations.
- *Serve as stewards of data and information.* This highlights institutional research's role in ensuring an institution-wide data quality, data use policy, and compliance.

Among these core functions for institutional research, "plan and evaluate" overlaps with the scope of strategic analytics. Strategic analytics includes the collaboration with key stakeholders in operational, budgetary, and strategic planning. It also includes program review and organizational performance assessment. However, strategic analytics includes other areas that institutional research traditionally does not address—competitive intelligence, market research, and integrative analyses that combine data from different domains of the institution.

Strategic Analytics Is about Data-Informed Strategy Management

A key consideration in strategy management is how external competitive forces shape an organization's strategic choices. Recognizing that "peer institutions" may also be competitors is a step forward in strategic analytics development. Strategic analytics includes the need for analytics professionals to be aware of plans and programs at competing institutions and how those plans and programs might affect one's home institution. For example, if college A offers a new online master's degree program in nursing, it may affect college B's fully in-person master's degree program in nursing. In this example, strategic analytics capabilities can be used to anticipate how the new competing program within the same city will attract potential students, thus affecting college B's own enrollment and projected financial positions.

Levenson (2015) argues that central to the mission of strategic analytics is the identification of the sources of your organization's competitive advantage. How does one's organization compare to direct competitors? Which organizational assets and processes of a university are more central for competitive advantage? These questions are important because strategy is concerned with differentiation and trade-offs. Differentiation is about the unique activities and assets that are distinct and challenging for competitors to replicate. Strategic decision is also concerned with trade-offs. When an investment is made in one area, there will be less to invest in others. These trade-offs need to be made based on careful data analysis and focus on what competitive advantages one can create.

In order to achieve the organization's strategic and operational goals, leaders need to focus on developing the capabilities that enable a university to provide programs and services in a way that is superior to or at least equally strong as its competitors. Competitive advantage comes from the organizational capabilities that enable strategic goals to be reached (Levenson 2015). Competitive analytics allows institution officials to leverage data analytics when coordinating planning efforts, when aligning strategies with actions, and when managing performance using advanced analytics capabilities. With the goal of supporting data-informed strategic decision making, strategic analytics includes some key characteristics as described by Davenport (2006b): widespread use of modeling and optimization algorithms in their strategic decision analysis; a culture of using data analytics to inform strategy conversations; analyzing situations from an enterprise perspective rather than from a subunit angle; and monitoring and anticipating how changes in the environment will affect organizational responses.

The Positive Feedback Loop of Strategy and Data Analytics

In effective organizations, data analytics capabilities support strategy development, and effective strategy execution incentivizes greater use of data analytics capabilities. Mazzei and Noble (2017) found that, rather than corporate strategy dictating which data should be collected and analyzed, studies suggest that in some instances the data collected and analyzed are having a dramatic influence on corporate strategy. Mazzei and Noble believe that data analytics and digitalization offer three tiers of value to an organization.

- *Tier 1: Data as a tool.* Data analytics at the operational level (such as supply chain and human resources management) supports greater levels of operational efficiency that offer tangible benefits to individual customers. In higher education, an example of Tier 1 capability is the use of data analytics to inform and personalize first-year experiences for the freshman class.
- *Tier 2: Data as an industry.* Data resources, analytics tools, and talents enable the creation of organizations specializing in Big Data analytics, leading to a new industry segment. In higher education, examples of Tier 2 capability are companies like HelioCampus or Academic Analytics, which specialize in using higher education data to support campus operations and decision making.
- *Tier 3: Data as a strategy.* Visionary leaders develop their organizations to build strong data analytics infrastructure and acquire talents to support business model and product innovations. In higher education, an example of Tier 3 organization is Georgia State University's heavy reliance on data analytics to significantly improve student success (see chapter 8 of this book).

Tier 3 organizations are where strategic analytics is at its best. Tier 3 organizations use data capability as a driver to support competitive strategy. These are learning organizations that are growth oriented and intentionally work to become more agile based on the knowledge and experience generated by their data analytics capabilities. They put data to full use in major decision making situations and use data to monitor outcomes of strategic and operational decisions. Quality decisions are supported by strong data and in turn generate greater need for more data. Mazzei and Noble (2017) describe this process as a "positive feedback cycle."

Several studies have identified data analytics as a key factor in supporting the success of organizations like Facebook, Amazon, and Google

(Alphabet) (Faggella 2019; Hewage et al. 2018). These firms are highly successful because they convert data insights into escalating competitive advantage. These are the Tier 3 organizations as identified by Mazzei and Noble. Aspirations to reach Tier 3 require an organizational focus on continuous learning through increased data flows as the means to create and enhance competitive advantages. Data analytics assets in this case are turned into valuable and nonsubstitutable strategic assets, thereby generating competitive advantage (Vidgen, Shaw, and Grant 2017). In higher education, a primary question in developing strategic analytics involves how to develop and implement cohesive and systematic data and analytics strategies that will be utilized by campus stakeholders who traditionally are more accustomed to decentralized decision making.

The Importance of Strategic Analytics to Senior Leaders and University Trustees

As institutional strategy development continues to evolve, the process relies on experience of key stakeholders such as members of the board of trustees, president, provost, deans, and senior administrators of the university. As custodians of the institutional strategy development and execution processes, trustees and senior leaders must gather as many facts as possible about the strategic landscape and organizational position, and then evaluate it against their experiences and opinions to develop a robust path forward. To infuse facts into the strategy-making process requires focus on and willingness to invest in data and analytics.

In addressing the Big Data revolution in the industry, the Association for Governing Boards (Pelletier 2015) urged governing board members to understand data analytics, "because in an era in which competition for students is fierce and the economics of running an institution are challenging, data mining and analysis create new tools that can help institutions better serve students and sharpen their competitive edges by making better strategic decisions" (Pelletier 2015, 3). The effective use of data analytics at the board level depends on whether officials for the college or university have developed a culture of inquiry that is open to leveraging the full benefits of what data reveal. The desired environment is one that enables continuous improvement and does not use the numbers to find fault or assign blame. From the institution's managerial perspective, board members require assistance to develop that understanding.

For trustees and senior officers of the university, focusing on the high-level findings and actionable insights from strategic analytics is crucial for data-informed strategic decision making. To use data analytics most effectively for strategy management decisions, we believe there are several actions or events that should prompt concern for board members and senior administrators. These include:

- *Obtaining early alerts on major trends and changes in higher education.* The higher education landscape, like many other industries, is constantly evolving and is impacted by many forces outside the industry. By using objective and subjective data analytics, trustees and leaders position themselves to obtain insights on key drivers, new technologies, new pedagogical methods, affordability issues, student and consumer selection processes and how they are changing the higher education landscape. Absent these insights, the strategy development process is inadequate.
- *Assessment of institutional capabilities and core competencies.* Higher education institutions are inherently complex in nature, with a wide variety of stakeholders working together to achieve results. Oftentimes, there is not a consistent and common understanding of institutional capabilities and core competencies across these stakeholder groups. As a result, executive discussions and decision making slow down and become complicated. Trustees and senior leaders must therefore insist on using data and analytics to build a common understanding of capabilities and competencies. For example, a SWOT (strength, weakness, opportunity, and threat) analysis may use subjective survey data but should also include more objective benchmark data that compare an institution to its peers as well as how these comparison data points are trending.

- *Objective evaluation of competitive forces and strategic trade-offs.* Data and analytics can help trustees and senior leaders obtain an unbiased, objective assessment of the operating competitive landscape of higher education. This can be accomplished through benchmarking performance on a set of attributes relative to leading industry players, thus leveraging multiple data sources easily accessible to most higher education institutions. This information can also help the institutional leaders make strategic choices and trade-off decisions, which is the essence of strategy. For example, data analytics and benchmarking might reveal that institutions pursuing a robust online education strategy tend to have better student outcomes, or vice versa. This could equip trustees and leaders with a key data point they can use when deciding whether to expand the suite of online offerings or not, and further, what areas to deemphasize.
- *Identify existing and emerging organizational strengths for selective investment.* With limited resources at their disposal, higher education institutional leaders are often making strategic decisions about disproportionate investment in certain programs to advance their strategic agenda. Data and analysis help organizational leaders adopt a fact-based approach to making such decisions. Doing so provides greater credibility to the results of the prioritization, increases buy-in from key stakeholders, and helps mitigate the "have–have not" problem. It also allows institutional leaders to focus their efforts on a critical few initiatives that could yield strong results.
- *Communication with internal and external stakeholder groups.* Trustees and senior leaders in higher education institutions are constantly communicating with internal and external stakeholders. These include faculty, staff, students, patients, consumers, elected officials, donors, and key community stakeholders. Using data and analysis helps bolster communication efforts and equips leaders with facts to highlight institutional impact and build greater advocacy.

Case Synopsis: The Ohio State University Wexner Medical Center's Program Prioritization Methodology

In the mid-2000s Ohio State's Wexner Medical Center (OSU) undertook a comprehensive planning process to develop a long-term strategic plan. A key element of the process was to identify programmatic priorities that the institution would disproportionately invest in to further its ambition of being one of the top academic medical centers in the country. At the start of the process, different stakeholders had different views about which programs would emerge as priorities.

The strategic planning team took the opportunity to develop a fact-based methodology to complement the opinions of key stakeholders. The first step in the process was to identify all the programs needing prioritization. In a complex academic medical center setting, these programs were in all three mission areas of clinical care, research, and education. In total, the team identified more than 100 programs needing prioritization.

Next, the team, in conjunction with senior leaders throughout OSU, identified key prioritization criteria on which all programs would be evaluated. The criteria the team landed on fell into the categories in table 5.1, reflecting a balanced approach to prioritization: leadership, national impact and reputation, sustainable competitive advantage, profitability, research funding potential, impact on other programs, and impact on the community. A number of metrics were identified for each of these categories; most were objective metrics and a few were subjective ones. Once the categories were developed, the team polled senior leaders to identify weights for each category.

The data analytics and planning teams then collected data for each program and for each objective metric. For the subjective metrics, the team administered surveys or conducted interviews and focus groups. Equipped with a large set of data points across all programs, the team developed detailed comparisons and created various scenarios including weights and was able to rank the 100+ programs in priority order. This provided trustees and senior leaders with a critical fact base that allowed them to bring in their experiences to eventually yield a set of

Table 5.1. Signature Program Selection Criteria

Criteria	Weight	Distribution of weight	
		Subjective	Objective
Ease of Execution/Time to market (EE)	5.0%	5.0%	0.0%
Impact on other programs and services (IMP)	10.0%	10.0%	0.0%
Leadership (L)	20.0%	20.0%	0.0%
Market demand (MD)	5.0%	0.0%	5.0%
National Impact/Reputation (NIR)	10.0%	2.5%	7.5%
Profitability/Return on Investment (ROI)	15.0%	0.0%	15.0%
Research funding potential—Applicable for Clinical Service prioritization (RES)	15.0%		15.0%
Resources required (RR)	0.0%	0.0%	0.0%
Sustainable competitive advantage (SCA)	15.0%	10.0%	5.0%
Trends (T)	5.0%	5.0%	0.0%
TOTAL	100.0%	52.5%	47.5%

Source: The Ohio State University Wexner Medical Center, 2019.

priority clinical, research, and education signature programs. This approach also helped create a foundation for subsequently measuring performance of the signature programs as their plans were developed and implemented.

Board and Senior Leadership Support Is Essential to Analytics Success

Senior leaders and trustees can play a significant role in creating a culture of data and analytics-based strategy and decision making. They must signal to the campus that using data analytics for informed decision making is an institutional priority. To do so, they must insist on key data and facts as part of their deliberation process for all strategic decisions. As institution leaders develop the institution's overall strategic plan, senior leaders and trustees should emphasize analytics as a key component plan emanating from the institutional plan.

One important tool for senior leaders as they seek to improve strategic and operational performance is the development of key performance metrics using a balanced scorecard approach. We believe that a balanced scorecard is an important strategy execution tool and is an informative way to measure performance across a series of dimensions.

Ideally, there would be a balanced scorecard at the institutional level and then multiple cascades down to individual units, and ultimately individuals. These performance scorecards should be reviewed at a predetermined frequency, preferably monthly, by the senior leadership team and by the board of trustees at each of its meetings.

For example, at Ohio State, a balanced scorecard has been developed for both the university and its Medical Center. In both instances, the scorecard is organized by key results areas (KRA), or strategic goals. For each KRA, or goal, there are multiple institutional objectives and metrics of performance. Targets are established for each metric, and actual performance is evaluated against targets. This presents a clear picture of whether the institution is achieving desired results, and from a performance management standpoint, it fosters conversations on gaps in performance and how to establish accountability and interventions to bridge the gaps.

The annual budgeting and financial planning processes are another key touchpoint and opportunity to embed analytics into institutional processes and decision making. Analytics can help simplify the complexity embedded in higher education funds-flow and budgeting processes. Where should scarce financial resources be disproportionately allocated? What areas require additional investment, and where should investments be scaled back? What is the return on investment on existing budgetary allocations? Which units are over- or underperforming relative to their budget and why? What key assumptions will or will not change each year? What financial scenarios need to be developed to pressure test a baseline budget? Is the budget aligned with overall institutional direction? What forecasts around different activity parameters (e.g., volumes in a medical center) drive revenue growth? Where are the greatest opportunities to obtain efficiencies and rationalize expenses?

These and many other financial planning and budgetary questions can be answered using data analytics, and trustees and senior leaders should insist on using data and insights generated by it to develop budgets and financial plans. Senior leaders and trustees should ask for data evidence and analytical insights to inform all major organizational decisions. The leaders of a university do not need to know the details about how the numbers are crunched, from where the data are assembled, or what software is used. Instead, they need to focus on guiding the development of data analytics strategies, reminding the data analytics community to address key institutional priorities, using data intelligence to help institutions better serve students, and sharpening their competitive edge by making better strategic decisions.

Building a robust analytics enterprise requires investments in many areas including analytics talent, data analysis software and tools, high-powered computing capabilities, purchase of large data sets, and hardware to store these data sets. Without these investments, institutions will be in a disadvantaged position to leverage the power of data to make organizational decisions.

However, even the most costly investment will not be effective if trustees and senior leaders are not using the insights gleaned from the data intelligence generation process. To become an analytics competitor, senior leaders and trustees of an organization must institute a deep belief and commitment to treat data as a core strategic asset of the organization and demand its use to improve operational and strategic decision making. In higher education, only a relative handful of standout organizations are using data in highly intentional, systematic ways to address strategic challenges and react to—and in many cases anticipate—sweeping changes in the markets they serve (Ross, Sebastian, and Beath 2017). The competitive advantage of having superior analytics capabilities and using them to support organizational growth and strategy execution are tantalizing goals that university leaders must pursue. Data analytics can improve their ability to innovate and give them a competitive advantage. Effective data strategy supports the systematic use of data in decision making and strategy throughout the organizations.

Using data analytics to drive decisions does not mean knowing all the details on how each piece of data is analyzed. Pelletier (2015) suggests that board members and senior leaders should consider data at a strategic level rather than at an operational level. They should focus on what actions the institution should be taking, given the data (e.g., what are the *actionable* insights from data findings?) College administrative leaders must play an active role in helping their board members develop that understanding. These leaders should make sure there is enough time for board members to understand the story behind the numbers. The effective use of data analytics pivots on whether a college or university has developed "a culture of inquiry" that is open to mining the full benefits of what data reveal (Pelletier 2015). Taking actions on the analytics insights is critically important, as shown in the next case synopsis.

Case Synopsis: Ohio State University's Strategic Conversation Sessions

In the 2015–16 academic year, the Ohio State University Wexner Medical Center embarked upon a multi-month process to develop its 5- to 10-year strategic plan. An oversight group was assembled comprised of select board members and key members of the management team. The process was facilitated by the strategy and planning team of the Medical Center.

At the outset, the team identified a set of key strategic questions and outlined a four-step strategic planning process. Transcending all these steps was a strong focus on data evidence that informed senior leaders about the Medical Center's current competitive positions and what lay ahead. Extensive data modules were developed for every area of operations and then reported back to senior leadership through a series of "strategic conversation" sessions. Each strategic conversation session was a data deep-dive on key strategy management questions. Analytics staff prepared months ahead of the sessions with a multitude of data tables and visualizations. The data points introduced in the strategic conversation sessions answered some of the critical planning questions:

- *How are we doing compared to leading practice institutions?* Ten key dimensions of excellence in leading academic medical centers were identified. These included items such as research excellence, clinical quality leadership, strong medical education programs, ranking and reputation, strong philanthropy, and so on. For each of the dimensions, the planning team collected trended internal data from multiple sources and also collected benchmarking data from "best-in-class" institutions. These data were then mapped to clearly illustrate Ohio State performance, how it compared to benchmarks, and where the gaps were.

- *Where should we focus our expansion efforts?* Data and analytics helped understand and answer key areas of focus associated with clinical, education, and research expansion. For example, reviewing detailed market and population data helped the Medical Center determine where new ambulatory facilities should be located, how large they needed to be, and what programs were best suited for each location. On the research side, it helped identify the number of faculty needed to grow research funding significantly.
- *What programs should be prioritized?* A robust program prioritization methodology was deployed to systematically identify which programs were best suited to further the strategic objectives. As was mentioned earlier in this chapter, a mix of subjective and objective criteria were used to evaluate programs, and eight areas of concentration were accordingly identified.
- *What would the impact be on the financial plan?* The planning and finance teams worked closely to flow strategic planning assumptions into the long-range financial plan. These included forecast volumes, staffing expenses, capital allocation, and so on and resulted in an iterative process to discuss trade-offs to eventually arrive at a viable financial model linked closely to the strategy.

Conclusion

Among the many critical factors that are important to the success of data analytics transformation, McShea, Oakley, and Mazzei (2016) identified the active management of senior leadership dynamics as the most important one. Every organization's senior leadership group maintains a delicate balance of power. When a new executive is assigned to oversee analytics, that executive will oversee a powerful pool of resources, and thus may command a sizeable budget and more time on the board agenda. "Simultaneously, other executives will not only experience a loss of influence but also feel vulnerable. This vulnerability frequently compels traditionalists to resist analytics" (McShea et al. 2016, 3). This resistance, coupled with the typical decentralized common structure of higher education institutions, often creates organizational roadblocks that need to be actively managed by the board and by the chief executives.

To ensure achievement in developing successful analytics capabilities, the board and the senior leadership must appoint the right leader for analytics transformation. Oftentimes, the right leader should be technically savvy and knowledgeable of the terminology of Big Data analytics. More importantly, analytics leaders should possess three distinct qualities: an ability to collaborate, to have his or her ideas shaped by others, and to champion the ideas of others; an understanding of how the enterprise currently operates and a vision for how analytics could drive the organization to become more agile based on analytical insights; and a hunger to create an environment of discovery, where the data are allowed to shape the future of the organization (McShea et al. 2016).

Higher education organizations have talented researchers and staff members who are well versed in the art and science of data discovery and data analysis. However, higher education organizations may be slower than other industries in leveraging analytics insights to drive strategy and operational decision making. In part, the systematic development of an analytics infrastructure requires time and resources to build organizational commitment. Officials from many higher education institutions that are constantly struggling with resource constraints and organizational dysfunctions may see analytics as hardly an organizational imperative. Consequently, they are hindered in compiling, classifying, and organizing data managed by different functional silos (Ross, Sebastian, and Beath 2017). Organizational leaders who want to use data analytics to support organizational development and strategy innovation must find a way to organize and manage its data resources in a coordinated manner with the goal of making data accessible for operational and strategic decision making. That means breaking down the data silos and democratizing the analytical assets, with appropriate security controls.

Boards and the senior administration also need to make a focused effort to build a data analytics community within institutions. Traditionally, presidents and provosts often look to their institutional research (IR) office for data and information. While IR officers have the knowledge and skills to produce the data, they often do not have the deep understanding of institutional operations and strategy to provide truly actionable insights. University leaders must intentionally cultivate and foster the development of a data analytics community on campus to include relevant staff who will produce, use, and analyze data in support of administrative decision making. Data analysts, data scientists, data engineers, data governance managers, data architects, and analytics leaders from admissions to student success, from finance to career development, and from student life to alumni relations, all have valuable insights to offer. Collectively, they are the basic building blocks of an analytics culture. Leaving these staff working in silos will not help the analytics cause. Leaders must find a way to foster a high level of collaboration and shared knowledge of analytical tools.

Strategy management is an executive function that requires the active involvement of boards and senior leadership. Data analytics in the Big Data age means that senior leaders need to treat data assets as a strategic asset and truly use it to inform critical decision-making processes with the goal of developing competitive advantages. While the massive failure in higher education institutional leaders that Clayton Christensen (in Lederman 2017) postulated may be an overblown prediction, institutions will create for themselves many benefits if they pay attention to how they organize their analytical resources, use data to inform decision making, and use data to track key performance indicators systematically. Data analytics alone will not guarantee success, but the lack of data analytics capabilities and maturity will definitely weaken institutional leaders' ability to act with strategic agility. Diligent use of data analytics will greatly help institutional leaders discern where the institution is positioned and how to achieve future success.

References

Alt-Simmons, R. 2016. *Agile by Design: An Implementation Guide to Analytic Lifecycle Management*. Hoboken, NJ: John Wiley & Sons Inc.

Association for Institutional Research. 2017. "Duties and Functions of Institutional Research." Accessed November 20, 2018. https://www.airweb.org/ir-data -professional-overview/duties-and-functions-of-institutional-research.

Bichsel, J. 2012. "Analytics in Higher Education: Benefits, Barriers, Progress, and Recommendations." Louisville, CO: EDUCAUSE Center for Applied Research. http://www.educause.edu/ecar.

Calof, J., G. Richards, and P. Santilli. 2017. "Integration of Business Intelligence with Corporate Strategic management." *Journal of Intelligence Studies in Business* 7, no. 3: 62–73.

Davenport, T. 2006a. "Executing an Analytics-Based Strategy: Executive Summaries of Selected Sessions." May 17–19, 2006. Cambridge, MA: Harvard Business School Publishing and Balanced Scorecard Collaborative.

Davenport, T. 2006b. "Competing on Analytics." *Harvard Business Review* (January): 99–107.

Faggella, D. 2019. "The AI Advantage of the Tech Giants: Amazon, Facebook, and Google." *Artificial Intelligence Research*. February 26, 2019. https://emerj.com/ai -executive-guides/ai-advantage-tech-giants-amazon-facebook-google/.

Hewage, T. J., M. N. Halgamuge, A. Syed, and G. Ekici. 2018. "Review: Big Data Techniques of Google, Amazon, Facebook and Twitter." *Journal of Communications* 13, no. 2: 94–100.

Kitchens, B., D. Dobolyi, J. Li, and A. Abbasi. 2018. "Advanced Customer Analytics: Strategic Value through Integration of Relationship-Oriented Big Data." *Journal of Management Information Systems* 35, no. 2: 540–574.

Lederman, D. 2017. "Clay Christensen, Doubling Down." *Inside Higher Education*. April 28, 2017. https://www.insidehighered.com/digital-learning/article/2017/04 /28/clay-christensen-sticks-predictions-massive-college-closures.

———. 2018. "Peril for Small Private Colleges: A Survey of Business Officers." *Inside Higher Education*. July 20, 2018. https://www.insidehighered.com/news /survey/peril-private-colleges-survey-business-officers.

Levenson, A. 2015. *Strategic Analytics*. Oakland, CA: Berrett-Koehler Publishers.

Mazzei, M. J., and D. Noble. 2017. "Big Data Dreams: A Framework for Corporate Strategy." *Business Horizon* 60: 405–414.

McShea, C., D. Oakley, and C. Mazzei. 2016. "How CEOs Can Keep Their Analytics Programs from Being a Waste of Time." *Harvard Business Review,* July 21, 2016.

Parthenon-Ernst and Young Education Practice. 2016. "Strength in Numbers: Strategies for Collaborating in a New Era for Higher Education." The Parthenon Group, LLC, Boston, MA. Accessed February 10, 2019. https://cdn.ey.com/parth enon/pdf/perspectives/P-EY_Strength-in-Numbers-Collaboration-Strategies_Paper _Final_082016.pdf.

Pelletier, S. G. 2015. "Taming 'Big Data': Using Data Analytics for Student Success and Institutional Intelligence." AGB *Trustees Magazine,* June 29, 2015.

Ross, J. W., I. M. Sebastian, and C. M. Beath. 2017. "How to Develop a Great Digital Strategy." MIT *Sloan Management Review* (Winter): 7–10.

Southekal, P. H. 2017. *Data for Business Performance: The Goal-Question-Metric (GQM) Model to Transform Business Data into an Enterprise Asset.* Basking Ridge, NJ: Technics Publications.

Vidgen, R., S. Shaw, and D. B. Grant. 2017. "Management Challenges in Creating Value from Business Analytics." *European Journal of Operational Research* 261: 626–639.

Vriens, M., and J. D. Brazell. 2013. "How Integrated Analytics Tools Help Researchers Make Smarter, Faster Decisions." *Marketing Insights* (Fall): 33–38.

[6]

Data Governance, Data Stewardship, and the Building of an Analytics Organizational Culture

Rana Glasgal and Valentina Nestor

AN AFRICAN proverb that is now well known says that "it takes a village to raise a child." This proverb suggests that a young entity who seeks to grow and mature requires the involvement of the whole community. It also applies to what is needed for a data analytics culture to take root in an organization. Such a culture requires a network of people from across the institution to participate in elements of data governance and build a foundational layer for a data-enabled business. Collectively, this network provides a wide base of knowledge and people who are invested in making a data-informed culture work. In this chapter, we will describe the construction of a data governance infrastructure and how it fosters a data-informed culture through the case study of a private research university. This chapter describes the facets of a data governance program that are useful whether introducing a new program or advancing an existing one. The chapter also describes a specific case study, discussing the challenges and successes in building a culture of analytics.

What Is Data Governance?

There are multiple definitions of data governance in use today. For example, the Data Governance Institute (n.d.) defines data governance as "a system of decision rights and accountabilities for information-related processes, executed according to agreed-upon models which describe who can take what actions with what information, and when, under what circumstances, using what methods" (1). According to IBM's Data Governance Council (2007), data governance is "a quality control discipline for adding new rigor and discipline to the process of managing, using, improving and protecting organizational information" (1). Finally, Forrester (in Pusing, 2019) states that data governance is "the process by which an organization formalizes the fiduciary duty for the management of data assets critical to its success."

Each of these definitions contributes to our understanding of data governance in higher education. However, we believe a good definition of data governance may seek to be even more inclusive. The governance roadmap needs to incorporate several characteristics for success. It should: be proactive to anticipate and resolve issues before they happen; be spread throughout the organization to get many points of view; enable the management and use of data; recognize that data is an asset; and align with the goals of the business. To incorporate these points, we believe a comprehensive definition of data governance is *a multifunctional organizational strategic initiative which enables, enforces, and formalizes the proactive management of its essential data assets to achieve the organization's business goals.* We will return to these principles several times in this chapter. In light of today's growing needs in higher education for data analytics, we assert that a program that pays attention to these principles is far more likely to be sustainable, applicable, and successful.

Throughout this chapter and in our day-to-day work, we use the term *business* to mean the academic and administrative functions that manage the university, such as enrollment and registration, human resources, finance, accreditation, research administration, and purchasing. Some colleagues in academia object to the use of the word *business* in the context of an institution of higher learning, but in the context of data governance and analytics this term helps us efficiently describe the process and decisions that keep our universities running.

Data Governance Goals

The goals for a data governance program may vary depending on the nature and culture of the business, its organizational priorities, the skill set of the organization's people, the resources available, the size of the organization, and the desired focus and scope of the program. Despite varying organizational goals, our synthesis of information from a variety of educational readings (see the references at the end of this chapter) identifies five universal goals that apply across all higher education operations and provide a strong foundation for a data governance program.

1. *Create an actionable, well-defined, sustainable, and adaptable data governance program.* As is the case with other major organizational projects, building a well-defined foundation and articulated plan that sets the direction for a data governance program is essential. To accomplish this, organizational representatives, typically a committee composed of strategically chosen campus colleagues, builds the program's framework and defines the key components of a data strategy that assesses people, processes, and technology in relation to data. In this way, a roadmap for action is built, starting small and incrementally embedding the program into the fiber of the organization. Another part of this goal is to ensure that accurately capturing, sharing, distributing, securing, and leveraging enterprise data will result in sound business improvements. The benefits of this goal will ensure that the organization will interpret data more accurately, share and reuse data faster, and address business challenges in a more consistent way through data-informed decision making.

2. *Emphasize, support, and strengthen decision making.* A second important goal seeks to empower data users to find answers to business questions with confidence. This enables organization leaders to find data insights and trends not only to support their decisions but also to drive their actions and achieve tangible business outcomes. Institutional executives can strengthen decision making by aligning data governance with business

processes, tailoring data users' behavior, and improving data quality and access.

3. *Build a culture of stewardship.* Data stewardship should permeate the college or university. A data governance program needs to identify clear accountability and unity that holds primary stewardship for enterprise data. This will help ensure that key businesspeople are responsible for data and will protect data stakeholders' interests. A culture of stewardship will play an essential role in supporting effective and efficient business processes within their domains and provide the confidence that the data are trustworthy and available to data providers and consumers. This includes thoroughly considered processes for getting access to data (through the data custodians), including specification of the prerequisites for such access and particular emphasis on a person's job responsibilities.

4. *Promote data quality.* A data quality program involves the ongoing implementation of business and technical metadata and robust dictionaries and data catalogs. Data quality issues should be handled via well-defined processes with the assistance of data audits. Providing education on data standards will help to strengthen and operationalize data quality initiatives. A data quality agenda is an essential piece of every data governance program to ensure effective business decisions and inspire trust in the data. By following these principles data governance will ensure that data consumers have access to high-quality, accurate, consistent, and relevant data.

5. *Build a business-driven and IT-supported collaborative program.* As a business initiative, data governance is essential not just to the information technology office (IT) but to the entire organization to provide necessary articulation of assigned responsibilities, knowledge of data definitions and processes, and to encourage participation. Although IT frequently is the first to recognize the need for this program because it sees the data, process, and technology issues, it may not have the appropriate resources to determine the problems that need to be solved, and of course, it

will need to work with others to gather the key business knowledge necessary to recognize problems and find appropriate solutions. In a best-practice model (Seiner 2009), data custodians, such as officials who work in the registrar, admissions, or finance office will work collaboratively with a chief data officer or data governance manager to perform the day-to-day oversight of the data governance program, while the IT unit manages the applications architecture and tools, provides technical infrastructure for data security, access, and storage, as well as data extract, transformation, and load (ETL) support. There are multiple guides available for data governance programs that can be used, including examples such as the McLaughlin, Howard, Balkan, and Blythe model (2004) or Seiner's (2009) noninvasive data governance operating model.

To fully benefit from the data governance program and its processes, it is critical to align the business and IT to drive data governance program accomplishments. Data governance must recognize the IT team as a valuable contributor and partner to this program by asking it to work collaboratively with people who have the business knowledge of the organizational business tasks. In this way, IT can provide the complementary skillset and technical resources to successfully fulfill the data governance agenda.

Key Principles and Pillars of Data Governance

Data governance principles are the critical elements and foundational blocks that drive a successful data governance program implementation. They are the commonly agreed-upon rules that direct the demeanor and application of the data governance initiative (Foster 2019; Pal 2019). Below are the pillars of core data governance that serve to nurture the program's sustainability. Ideally, these key principles and pillars will, over time, be ingrained into daily data governance undertakings.

- *Institutional data in all of its lifecycle stages will be managed as an enterprise foundational asset.* Data is pivotal in making business decisions. Institutional data has tangible and measurable value and must be treated the way that traditional organizational assets—money and people—get treated and recognized across multiple organizational layers. A data asset refers to the capacity of data to become a high-value, indispensable enterprise end product used to run, monitor, integrate, and improve the institution. A data asset has value from its initial state of creation and capture through its shared use in reporting and analysis, and thus why managing data as an enterprise asset is an important concept for those involved in data governance to understand and internalize.

- *The institution's data will become a shared enterprise resource and will be used collaboratively across all business domains.* Data belongs to the organization as a whole. As mentioned above, data is not owned by any specific unit of the organization. Rather, it is under custodianship (i.e., protecting, properly maintaining). For enterprise data to become a resource and be jointly used enterprise-wide, it is important that leaders build a sound and actionable data stewardship/custodianship program, with roles, responsibilities, and accountabilities around data and data-related business processes, allowing the institution's technologies to become appropriately aligned in response to the organization's needs. Campus users need to have a mutual understanding of data standards, guidelines and policies, and rules of access and use. Further, leaders must acknowledge and allow for strategies that enable employees to develop new habits and behaviors to rely on data. Data analytics users should be encouraged to share their knowledge with others and to have confidence in and apply shared decisions in their jobs.

- *Appropriate data and content will be available to authorized users in an efficient way to streamline operational processes and enable decision making.* This principle ensures that data will be available to the users when they need it, where they need it, and the way they need it. Access to data should be provided in a secure and protected manner by obtaining proper authorization.

Once authorized, personnel will access only the information required to do their jobs.

In the future, data will continue to become easily accessible, up to date, and in the format users need. Data governance is helpful in defining and clarifying the "what, why, and how" of data access and classification. It safeguards data by creating access guidelines, ensuring that these guidelines are understood and followed, and inserting related processes and roles enterprise-wide. This will not only help in standardizing and democratizing data access but also in operationalizing analytics.

- *Institutional data quality will be managed and measured consistently to ensure that data is "fit-for-purpose."* Data quality is an important aspect of a data governance initiative because it helps to achieve the desired business outcomes and is a critical factor in turning data into insight. As Ladley (2019) states, data quality means that numbers are more than just accurate. It also means that the data is appropriate for its intended purpose (appropriate for planned usage) and that the fit is multidimensional. It encompasses completeness, timeliness, integrity, and relevance, and it should be defined in terms of the goals of the organization, to fit the defined purpose of its stakeholders.

Attending to data quality becomes an integrated business practice that acts on well-defined and well-communicated data quality standards to detect, record, and report on data quality, resulting in decision making improvements. For example, instituting audits on student data with regard to gender and ethnicity improves the ability of diversity officers to track the institution's progress for this goal and fine-tune their programs. If the data is incomplete, late, or inaccurate, diversity programs could go off track and miss goals.

As with all aspects of data governance, a data quality program is driven by the institution's business needs, with shared roles and responsibilities between business and IT. The data stewardship program should be involved to approve and then enforce proposed data quality standards and encourage the implementation of these standards through built-in system audits and controls.

- *Institutional data will comply with laws, policies, regulations, and standards and be prepared thoroughly as if planning for an audit.* A number of key activities within the higher education institution will help to implement measures that reduce risk and ensure data confidentiality, integrity, and appropriate access. These include ensuring that institutional data inventory, data definitions, usage of data, and data related processes will be defined and documented; data access guidelines and processes are defined and implemented to become a part of day-to-day operations; data stewards, custodians, and IT servicers will be involved in defining the roles, responsibilities, accountability and data definitions needed to ensure the security and privacy of institutional data. It is important to ensure access to training and affirm that processes and controls are in place to create reliable and timely audit capabilities.

Which Data Needs to Be Governed?

Not all data within a university can be governed right away. Leaders overseeing a new data governance program should look at their data assets and prioritize. Below is a way to categorize your data assets to assist in determining what will be governed and when. The key enterprise master data clusters, defined below, ought to be considered as strong candidates for governance (Villar, Kushner, and Wells 2013).

Shared data is the same data used in multiple business processes across the institution where definitions, allowable values, format, and quality need to remain identical and agreed upon. Examples include citizenship, race and ethnicity—such as for IPEDS (Integrated Postsecondary Education Data System) reporting—and date of birth.

Critical data is that which maintains critical business functions. If these functions get interrupted, it materially affects financial results and could cause criminal or civil penalties. The loss of this data has serious adverse effects on the university's reputation, resources, services, or individuals. Examples: financial data, personally identifiable information (PII), and health insurance data.

Strategic data is that which surrounds strategic business operations. It is in-house data unique to the university, mostly created internally, and it provides competitive insights and advantages. Examples include student enrollment strategy data and student and employee retention data.

For example, colleagues at Northeastern University started by governing shared data. Officials believed this was the most important component when setting up a new set of integrated enterprise systems (student, human resources, and finance). Some of the components were designated as PII, so the shared data fell into the critical data category as well.

It is important to note that not every data attribute/data set within a college or university should be governed. There are some data sets that are internal to a specific department and will not be shared or exposed, such as a department tracking the number of times its department's advisor meets with students. This is helpful data for the department, but since it is not shared, joined with other types of data, or used to run a critical business function, it does not need central governance.

Which Features of Data Are Important to Govern?

Villar, Kushner, and Wells (2013) have identified several features of data that a data governance program should consider governing. In order to safeguard university data, it is suggested that some, if not all, aspects of data can be governed, including: data ownership and accountability; definition, use, and format of metadata; creation of the data architecture; data handling, storing, and auditing; and data reporting and analytics. With a full focus on quality of data, the above listed items are roughly in order of priority. However, your organization's needs and context should be the primary consideration of what features of your data need to be governed first.

Why Does Data Governance Matter?

As described earlier in this chapter, data governance encompasses the implementation and ongoing maintenance of the array of correlated enterprise data management–related programs such as data stewardship and data custodianship, master data management, data acquisition, data integration, data warehousing, and analytics. It provides support in instilling best practices in process standardization, contributes to data education and knowledge, empowers users to unlock data value, and enables collaboration among people involved in these programs.

There are many good reasons to employ data governance. It:

- enables an effective way to curate institutional data through a set of activities;
- creates a foundation for new initiatives that span multiple institutional departments and functions;
- is pivotal in providing decision makers with secure access to consistent and reliable information through data availability across and within multiple lines of business
- helps leaders at each institution to understand what data they have, how good it is, and where it is;
- helps facilitate appropriate data usage, and enforces its safeguarding through stated rights, accountabilities, and defined roles and responsibilities enterprise-wide;
- encourages desirable behavior around data by establishing guidelines, policies, and standards for privacy and confidentiality;
- improves data quality and improves trust in data.

All of these reasons to employ data governance are good and convincing reasons, but it would not be possible without cross-functional, collaborative teams of data stewards, data custodians, and business users. Colleges and universities contemplating starting or expanding a data governance program should think about the human resources needed to start up and maintain a data governance infrastructure.

Why Data Governance Is Needed in Higher Education

Now that we have explained the objectives, principles, scope, and value of data governance, the next step is to understand why higher education, as an industry, needs the tools and techniques involved in a data governance program.

Universities have a history of being internally siloed into academic departments and stand-alone colleges and administrative functions. Today, however, institutions are more interconnected, and expectations have changed; officials now expect that our colleges and department staffs will work together to create interdisciplinary research and academic programs and that they will cooperate on administrative tasks and achieve efficiencies. Data governance strategists also expect, in this age of Big Data, that deans, department chairs, and administrative unit leaders will make decisions that are informed by data. Therefore, we must provide the tools of connection, access, and data-informed decision making.

Consistent with principles of data-informed decision making (DIDM, discussed in chapter 1), data that may likely originate from many different parts of the institution is brought together to gain new insights. Various owners of these different strains of data may have concerns over privacy, data security, and incorrect use of complex information. Data governance can help in this regard by providing assurance that the data is well understood, secure, and available to those who need it to perform their jobs. It also, through good master data management (MDM), provides a way to combine disparate sets of data together to gain new insights.

Data governance can provide higher education organizations with a way to comply with regulatory and compliance requirements. The recent enactment of the General Data Protection Regulation (GDPR) in the European Union (EU) and the broader European Economic Area (EEA) and new privacy and data protection laws in the United States rely upon governance and privacy functions. FERPA has been a guiding principle in US higher education since the 1970s, causing registrars to heavily protect data internally, often to the point of creating a bottleneck. Data governance can provide data owners with a set of policies to use when provisioning data access while still complying with FERPA and similar concerns with HIPAA as relevant to higher education institutions.

A good data governance design and structure can create well-defined, trusted, and well-understood data, leading to clarity and transparency. It can cut down on back-channel access to data and shadow systems, because members of the organization feel that they can get the data they need through the proper channels, without waiting a long time for approval, or being denied access for unknown reasons. In short, a good data governance program builds trust.

How Data Governance Facilitates and Supports Analytics

We posit that data governance is a critical part of analytics in higher education. This is because, by its nature, it helps to build trust in the data and it is a campuswide effort, which promotes transparency and buy-in.

Building Trust

Returning to our theme of proverbs, let us add another one. "You can lead a horse to water but you can't make it drink." As applied to analytics in higher education, designated officials who already support the use of analytics can build the tools and data necessary to create great information, but without considering the human side of analytics, we cannot make anyone use it. One might ask: What is needed to get buy-in and make information part of the university's culture?

Great analytics rest on great data. Without great data, even the most sophisticated algorithms will mislead decision makers and will not earn their trust. Many end users will find ways to mistrust the insights that are derived from "black box" algorithms or based on data that are perceived to be faulty. To counteract these perceptions, data dictionaries, data quality assessment (or badging), and master data management should be used regularly and kept updated. In addition, clear documentation of algorithms is an important way to gain trust. Anyone basing a decision on a predictive or prescriptive algorithm would surely trust what they are seeing more completely if they understand its origin. After all, higher education is all about learning and understanding!

Campuswide Involvement

As discussed previously in this chapter, data governance is not necessarily about the data; it is about people and collaboration. Data governance should not be dictated in a top-down manner; it requires willing involvement from all parts of campus. In other words, everyone is a steward of data.

At its most mature level, data governance involves people throughout the organization taking their responsibilities for data seriously. To fix bad data, colleagues at all levels need to have an awareness of the downstream consequences of poor data, poor decisions, failed business intelligence (BI) and analytics efforts, and inefficient business processes. Those directly involved in data governance have common goals, a shared awareness of the value of data, and a collaborative spirit. All agree on the goal to implement quality and security of institutional data.

How does a campus get to a high level of data governance maturity? Here are some steps to consider:

1. *Start small, with a coalition of the willing.* Is there a new project happening on campus, such as a new student success system? If so, try to get involved early with an offer to help build good data quality, a data governance infrastructure, or just data definitions. Use the best knowledge of the climate and appetite for data governance to determine how to get involved. Enumerating the benefits can be very convincing!
2. *Publicize what you accomplish.* Word will get around and others will want to participate, widening and deepening the reach of data governance over time.
3. *Find a data steward for each line of business.* You can form a data stewardship council and then ask those data stewards to

add data custodians who serve as subject matter experts, approve access to data, and act as detail-level data overseers.

4. *Provide a reason for the data stewards and custodians to participate.* Here are some good reasons to give to data stewards and custodians to join your data governance effort:
   a. Information sharing is beneficial for everyone.
   b. Networking with others in the university enables one to talk over common problems and expand one's network of colleagues.
   c. A great practice provides a sense of accomplishment and praise for a job well done, as well as opportunities to celebrate achievements along the way.

5. *Get some quick wins.* Quick wins can provide not just their own accomplishments but also provide evidence of how effective data governance can be. For example, a helpful data dictionary for a new student system can be a quick win that will generate enthusiasm for data dictionaries in other subject areas.

6. *Establish lines of communication.* Sharing information, policies, definitions, meeting notes, and data governance concepts is helpful to all staff members who are involved. Information sharing doesn't need to be an expensive new tool; existing methods on your campus can be very effective, such as setting up an email listserv, creating an internal web site, or using a collaboration suite such as Confluence, Microsoft Teams, or a combination of these.

If institutional officials can initiate governance activities slowly and build over time, they can facilitate analytics and build the confidence to use the products of analysis. This occurs because those who have been involved in data governance will have trust in the data and will communicate this trust to others in their organization. As a result, the lines of communication across campus will be opened and these new relationships can be called upon to improve business intelligence and analytics.

Northeastern University Data Governance Case Study
History and Approach of Data Governance
at Northeastern University

Data governance was initiated at Northeastern University (hereafter called Northeastern) for the first time in 1999 through the creation of a data administration unit in the institutional research (IR) department. This came about due to the implementation of a new integrated system for employee, alumni, and student data (PeopleSoft). This was the first time that the key data providers formally started working in a group to address data issues within their lines of business and across them. They were addressing data quality issues related to shared data in order to implement a new integrated system. It was the initial step on our journey to data governance. Although this initiative lasted for only about a year, it created a kernel that later benefited the Northeastern data governance landscape.

The next attempt to reconvene this program was in 2010. The data administration unit, which was charged with managing data governance, was recreated. It was formed as an independent unit to ensure data was managed autonomously and to create common practices for sharing data across the university. As mentioned earlier in this chapter, we believe it is important that the data governance function is not an IT function and is not managed by a data provider such as the registrar's office. The IR office (now called University Decision Support) was a neutral location with interest in all kinds of data.

At this time, Northeastern was in the early stages of bringing data together in a warehouse and needed leadership in creating the initial shared data set, common data definitions, shared calculated data values, and ongoing governance on access, security, and data usage. The data administration office also served as the facilitator for ensuring data quality.

Soon thereafter, the office was utilized for a new strategic business initiative to implement a "hybrid" responsibility center budget model in which financial leaders in the colleges of Northeastern needed the ability to analyze and report on their revenues and expenses. Members of the data administration unit were called in to help the staff in the colleges understand how to use their data assets to make data-informed decisions. This unit also served as a neutral arbiter to ensure that no one college or business unit was biased in how it used or shared its data.

In addition, new reporting capabilities were given to a wide community of college data users. They were given access to the custom-built reporting funnel sourced from the first generation of the Northeastern data warehouse (called the Operational Data Store, or ODS). To facilitate the use of this data the university introduced a new reporting tool, Argos, which became the gateway for data access. The data administration unit created ongoing user training on data usage and the Argos reporting tool. Clearly, a new process for secure data provisioning was needed. This turned into an opportunity to expand the breadth of the data governance initiative among multiple business areas.

Shortly thereafter, it became evident that attention was needed to resolve prioritized data challenges. The challenges revolved around business processes gaps and the ensuing lack of data quality for shared data. To address those issues, user education and training was instituted, as were communication channels using SharePoint, metadata dictionaries, and multiple governance forums. To be transparent, materials such as shared data standards, data access standards, and other documentation were available to all on a SharePoint site.

The data governance program at Northeastern has been in existence for more than eight years. It is led by the provost and resides in the university decision support office. It has evolved into a mature program that has gained respect because of its proven record of delivering value in support of managing university data assets aligned with the university's vision, mission, and business directives. It is viewed as a collaborative effort between the business units and the IT units. Today, data governance is a key contributor and advocate mechanism to support university business intelligence and analytics needs. Data governance has become integral when new business initiatives are discussed, while building the enterprise data layer, data catalogs, or master data management program. Figure 6.1 shows the Northeastern data governance organization as it currently stands. Readers may wish to review

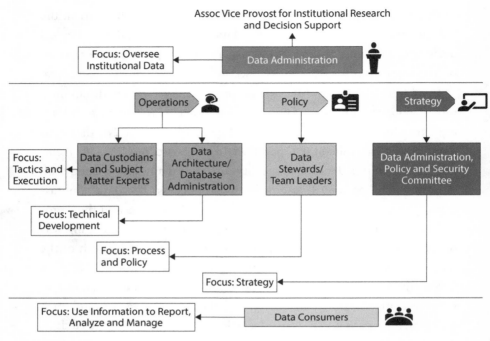

Figure 6.1. Northeastern University Data Governance Operating Model

Northeastern's web site for more detail: https://provost.northeastern.edu/uds/data-governance/.

The Challenges of Data Governance at Northeastern University

When starting an enterprise initiative or resuming one after a significant period of time, there are challenges to be faced. Our data governance voyage was no exception. Data governance is about changing organizational behavior around managing data resources. Challenges begin from the program kickoff and remain ongoing. They are unavoidable and sometimes unique to the institution. Typically, the organization's business and IT readiness, its leadership involvement and support, and its culture will determine how best to manage those challenges. Having survived these challenges to date, we share our experience and methods used to address them. These include enlisting executive sponsorship, choosing a data governance approach, and identifying data governing bodies and their roles and responsibilities, as well as managing all of the people involved and striving for longevity and sustainability.

Buy-in to the program approach and framework at the executive level is significant. At Northeastern, our executive sponsor, the provost, served as an initial communicator to announce the launching of our program, adding credibility and importance to the effort. In addition, staff members in the data administration unit worked with the provost to handpick a core team for the Data Stewardship Council (DSC), which was extremely helpful when navigating political subtleties.

Beginning our data governance program with a kickoff meeting provided a healthy start. The program facilitator at Northeastern enabled the success of this event by creating a detailed presentation delivered at the meeting. As a result, the DSC's members gained an understanding of the program's approach and framework as well as their role and commitment to it. This was pivotal because the data stewards are relied on to set the strategic direction for Northeastern's data governance program. In addition, one-on-one meetings with most members prior to the kickoff were important. This enabled us to identify (and convert) naysayers and find ways to balance the group dynamics from the beginning.

Initially, the DSC team members were wary about serving on the council due to the time they needed to allocate for this initiative. That skepticism was short-lived when they saw the value for their own business units through early results with shared data standards.

While the data governance program is overseen by the decision support unit, it is important to reiterate that it is business-driven and IT-supported. Data governance is not a technology problem; it is driven by business needs, though IT presence on the data stewardship council is important. Northeastern's IT contacts and participants became great partners along the way as our program matured. It was important to build that relationship from the beginning and incorporate IT as one of our biggest allies. At Northeastern, it was a key success factor for our program.

Data governance is all about people: people make data policies and standards, they generate metadata and auditing rules, and it is people who follow those standards and rules. People create and manage the supporting data governance processes and use the outcomes of them. People build and implement technological solutions for appropriate data access, usage, and better analysis and reporting. Gaining knowledge from involved staff members and, at the same time, educating and training staff is a critical and challenging task. Education, collaboration, change management, and development of a culture of quality, sharing, and trust is a critical activity on the data governance agenda. Therefore, we understood that building a data governance program at Northeastern would require strong people skills.

There is a considerable amount of evangelism and "selling" that brings people together around a common purpose, and a bit of patience and handholding comes into play as well. This process requires asking busy experts for their time and contributions. They need to know that what they are doing is important and valued, and this means that soft skills and emotional intelligence will be as important as technical and data knowledge. Leaders of the data governance effort at Northeastern led with enthusiasm and passion, and they moved ahead with a proven record of deliverables to make this journey an exciting experience.

Growth and Achievements of Data Governance at Northeastern University

The data governance apparatus around major reporting environments at Northeastern is a real strength, and there is enthusiasm and loyalty around the data governance initiative. It has widened and deepened over time as it has grown to include more institutional data domains. Currently, there are multiple data governance forums in place, both originally initiated and newly developed, which help to assure that new business priorities are on their agendas (see https://provost.northeastern .edu/uds/). Here are a few of them: Data Stewardship Council, Data Custodians groups, Business Concepts group, Data Classification group, Data Integrity group, College Liaisons, and Administrative Liaisons. Some of these forums are ongoing and some meet only as needed. These staff also provide knowledge and expertise in articulating data issues and business process gaps, and they play a key role in the issues-resolution process and data audits.

Members of these groups actively participate in the creation and maintenance of data standards and guidelines. As an illustration of the effectiveness of community participation, listed below are some of the key guidelines, policies, and standards that have been created and are in use as a result of this work:

- Shared Data Standards, created by the Data Integrity committee;
- Business Concepts, Terms, and Data Element Standards, created by the Business Concepts committee;
- Guidelines for access to data and an appeal process guide for access, created by the Data Security Workgroup; and
- Data Classification Guidelines, created by the Data Classification group.

Data governance is also ingrained in multiple business processes, a major one being the management of university person ID resolution (person ID de-duplication), which involves a variety of university systems, stewards, and custodians and allows the proactive management of person uniqueness at Northeastern. This was a foundational data governance achievement.

As of early 2019, data governance at Northeastern has evolved from a project-related governance body (related only to student reporting) into enterprise-wide initiatives over the course of eight years. It is worth mentioning four initiatives that were instrumental in classifying Northeastern data and managing risk and access.

- Data Classification guidelines were created to categorize data by its level of risk to the university. These guidelines and categories are presented in a custom-built web tool. This tool serves as a guide to categorize university data by the level of risk so that its confidentiality, integrity, and appropriate availability are maintained. It also provides rules for safeguarding data through its lifecycle from creation to disposal.

- The Unified Data Access dashboard is a new "One Stop Shop" used as a central, standardized, online repository for requesting access to major university systems and reporting tools.
- A workflow-supported electronic access request form for reporting environments was created with guidance and support from the data governance program. With this new workflow, Data Custodians can determine the appropriate access for their data domains and easily participate in the approval process.
- The Business Concepts workgroup is creating a mutual understanding of complex and often misunderstood key business concepts by bringing together subject matter experts. Some of the concepts defined by this group include online student, experiential education, faculty tenure status, and part-time employee. While these concepts do not seem complex at first, there are often shades of meaning associated with them, and those meanings are often not universal across multiple business units. The highly vetted and agreed-upon definitions are available to anyone at Northeastern via our DataCookbook application.

Current supporting programs or those in the pilot stage educate and train the university user community on appropriate data use and how to make better business decisions in support of business intelligence and analytics initiatives. Applicable governance forums are involved in all new business intelligence deliverables. These forums work in collaboration with IT to streamline development activities, user acceptance testing, and the release of new functionality to meet the needs of the business community. By the time the new functionality is released, the metadata is already defined and incorporated in the data dictionary through established governance entities and processes.

Drivers of Data Governance Success at Northeastern University

Northeastern's data governance program continues to grow and mature. As the overall portfolio expands, the maturity levels vary within the institution. What began as a targeted response to a specific business need is now evolving to an enterprise-wide program.

It is built for its longevity and sustainability due to its current success criteria:

- *Strong executive sponsorship.* An effective data governance program requires solid executive sponsorship. This includes continuous executive involvement to support program goals, champion initiatives, and enforce compliance. It is helpful to have executives who understand data management, pay attention to it, and get involved as necessary.
- *Governance must be aligned to business goals.* Although IT should be a key player involved in data governance, the driver of governance activities should be business partners. The reliance and support of IT is necessary to deploy and manage the enabling technology and tools and create a supportive partnership.
- *Ensure that collaborative efforts are supported by the data stewardship/data custodianship program.* We work together with data consumers and data providers as well as with compliance, security, and audit units on topics related to data privacy and security, such as the GDPR.
- *Have an incremental approach: start small and build.* The data governance program at Northeastern has been solidified over many years, but developers of the program never assume that a function or committee will be valuable forever. Regularly reevaluate the program's goals, objectives, and deliverables, as this will help ensure that these goals are reasonable, achievable, and align with business drivers and strategic priorities.
- *Include continuous education on data use and access.* In this agile world of business and technology, it is important to keep the community educated on data usage and access to data by keeping educational documentation up to date and providing all possible communication channels and training.
- *Recognize that people are the biggest asset.* Trained individuals use the data and create value from the data. They know when

the data is in good shape, when it isn't, and how to fix it. They make sure that rules governing data make sense. Ensuring that users are educated, knowledgeable, and powerful in decision making, and passionate about data are important success factors.

Northeastern University's data governance program continues to evolve and face challenges along the way. It is a big infrastructure to manage which requires effective delegation and a focus on prioritization. It demands switching focus from providing data to consuming data. Technology and end-user empowerment enable the work to be done quickly with fewer people in support, whether those people are business experts or IT professionals. To further enhance, widen, and build on the existing data governance program, Northeastern's leaders in data governance must remain vigilant in relation to regulatory reporting and data privacy needs. We also need to respond rapidly to the evolving demands of digital transformation in the data management landscape. Being able to respond rapidly and stay on top of new needs will not only expand the scope of data governance and strengthen university capabilities in the effective management of data, but it will also accelerate the process of alignment with the demanding needs of BI and analytics programs to make data-informed decisions faster.

Recent Developments in Analytics and Data Governance at Northeastern
The Analytics Center

The recently formed analytics center at Northeastern brings together those interested in or experienced with analytics into a central "virtual" organization to promote and establish analytics. As with our data governance infrastructure, the analytics center also utilizes a team approach, gathering input from across the university. The team, called the Analytics Center Committee (ACC), was formed to realize several of the goals from a strategic planning process: establish an analytics capability and provide the data necessary for next-generation analytics. The committee was formed with input and support from the senior leadership of the institution and is comprised of people involved with analytics in the areas of students, HR, finance, admissions, and institutional research.

Technology infrastructure is being established, including a data catalog as a first step to help analysts locate the data and understand it. Simultaneous to the implementation of this infrastructure, the ACC has been implementing pilot projects to demonstrate the value of analytics to Northeastern. These pilots have been chosen by the committee, with input from senior leadership. The criteria used to implement these projects are those that have a combination of urgency, a university-wide scope, alignment with the university's vision, and relative ease of implementation. This is the same approach as with data governance: start small, with a coalition of the willing.

The ACC's first pilot project was to create a detailed model to forecast undergraduate enrollment at the college level. While forecasting total university enrollment has been done for many years, the more detailed, college-level forecasts were not very accurate due to challenges around internal transfers among Northeastern's eight colleges. This inaccuracy led to poor revenue forecasts for each college and resulting budgetary woes. The undergraduate enrollment by college forecast took on those challenges, doing a forecast at the individual student level and improving the enrollment forecast by several percentage points.

Analytics Education, Culture, and Training

The analytics center is helping to create a culture of data and its use in decision making. As with data governance, the idea is to create a university that works with data to make decisions, and everyone should be involved. In fact, for many employees, being analytically competent is expected as part of one's job. While this is a new effort, we have many ideas on how to create a culture of analytics and educate people across campus about its value. Ideas include working with HR to put this requirement in job descriptions more explicitly, getting leaders in analytics to present their work to others who aren't quite there and therefore lead by example, and emphasizing that senior leadership expects the use of data in decision making.

We are also beginning to think seriously about how to address the ethics of analytics. In books such as *Weapons of Math Destruction* (O'Neil 2016), the bias present in algorithms based on historical data is discussed and documented. If the algorithms we build perpetuate the biases of the past, we will be doing our students an injustice. Our group will educate the campus on this danger because we believe it is within our purview and duty to do so.

Northeastern leaders have recently created an analytics interest group to get people together and talking about data and analytics. Such an interest group will be a member-driven avenue for creating ideas, sharing successes, and gathering a coalition to work on new projects. We hope this new group will help us build a culture of analytics from the ground up.

The Future of Data Governance at Northeastern University and in Higher Education Broadly

At Northeastern, we plan to expand data governance university-wide to include additional systems and databases, for example, Salesforce (salesforce.com). Because of our early successes with data, the data administration team is often asked to encompass more data areas, more systems, and more policy work. Overall, we want to continue to work toward a future where data governance is ingrained in our culture and operations.

Colleagues at other colleges and universities are taking this on as well. Because of data privacy and security concerns, there is an increasing need for well-governed and secured data, and the increasing use of analytics in higher education also calls for trusted data. A culture of analytics will continue to be emphasized through education on ethics in analytics, education on data-informed decision making, and the delivery of a data-informed message from senior leadership.

Future direction for data governance at Northeastern includes the expansion of master data management to more lines of business, such as employees. In addition, future initiatives will initiate profile-based security according to a person's function and role, enabling data access to more people who have received training, while retaining proper security. Currently, Northeastern's infrastructure does not support profile-based security, but with the right backing, timing, and a good pilot project, we can achieve this goal. Further, Northeastern is developing an enterprise-wide data access policy. This policy will elucidate our philosophy for responsible data use and provide usable guidelines when a request for data access is declined by the data owner. How broadly we implement data democratization across Northeastern will depend on the level at which senior leaders sign off on more data transparency and availability to facilitate decision making.

In today's world, with new privacy and data security regulations such as the GDPR (General Data Protection Regulation) in place, and privacy scandals such as Cambridge Analytica / Facebook making headlines, higher education officials must realize that the data we collect and how we use it will be scrutinized by data-savvy students and their parents, our alumni, and domestic and international watchdog groups. This should not be solely the purview of legal offices. By working across silos in institutions of higher education and using data governance techniques and best practices, we can put in place proper controls and reduce the risk of improper use of data.

As the editors of *The Analytics Revolution in Higher Education* (Gagliardi, Parnell, and Carpenter-Hubin 2018) have aptly stated, "realizing the value of the analytics revolution while mitigating the associated risks (e.g., cost, infrastructure, privacy and security, and perverse consequences) requires a unique blend of skills and competencies that are seldom found within one organizational or administrative unit" (xii). Indeed, it does take a village of committed and talented individuals in today's colleges and universities to make it happen.

References

Cole, Z. 2018. "Data Governance and GDPR: How the Most Comprehensive Data Regulation in the World Will Affect Your Business." Blog post. Accessed March 28, 2019. https://erwin.com/blog/data-governance-and-gdpr/.

Data Governance Institute. n.d. "The Basic Information." Data Governance Institute. http://www.datagovernance.com/the-basic-information/.

Fisher, T. 2009. *The Data Asset: Govern Your Data for Business Success*. Hoboken, NJ: Wiley & Sons.

Foster, J. 2019. "The Core Principles of Good Data Governance." Cynozure. Accessed February 4, 2019. https://www.cynozure.co.uk/insights/the-core-principles-of-good-data-governance/.

Gagliardi, J., A. Parnell, and J. Carpenter-Hubin. 2018. *The Analytics Revolution in Higher Education: Big Data, Organizational Learning, and Student Success.* Sterling, VA: Stylus Publishing, LLC.

Granville, K. 2018. "Facebook and Cambridge Analytica: What You Need to Know as Fallout Widens." *New York Times.* March 18, 2018. https://www.nytimes.com /2018/03/19/technology/facebook-cambridge-analytica-explained.html.

IBM Data Governance Council. 2007. "The IBM Data Governance Council Maturity Model: Building a Roadmap for Effective Data Governance." IBM Date Governance Council. https://www.scribd.com/doc/294669999/IBM-Data -Governance-Council-Maturity-Model.

Ladley, J. 2016. "Ensuring the Quality of 'Fit for Purpose' Data." *CIO Magazine.* October 17, 2016. https://www.cio.com/article/3124402/analytics/ensuring-the -quality-of-fit-for-purpose-data.html.

———. 2019. *Data Governance: How to Design, Deploy and Sustain an Effective Data Governance Program.* Waltham, MA: Elsevier Academic Press.

McLaughlin, G., R. Howard, L. Balkan, and E. Blythe. 2004. *People, Processes and Managing Data.* Resources in Institutional Research #15. Tallahassee, FL: AIR.

Nevala, K. 2016. "Selling the Value of Data Science, Governance or Analytics." Dataversity. April 20, 2016. https://www.dataversity.net/back-basics-selling-value -data-data-science-governance-analytics/.

O'Neal, K. 2011. "The Role of IT in Business-Led Data Governance." BeyeNetwork. May 19, 2011. http://www.b-eye-network.com/view/15165.

O'Neil, C. 2016. *Weapons of Math Destruction.* New York: Penguin Random House.

Pal, K. 2019. "What Are Some Core Principles of Data Governance?" Techopedia. Accessed February 3, 2019. https://www.techopedia.com/7/32187/enterprise /databases/what-are-some-core-principles-of-data-governance.

Pusing, A. 2019. "Governing Data with Control and Growth Mindset." *Business-World.* June 5, 2019. https://www.bworldonline.com/governing-data-with-control -and-growth-mindset/

Savage, M. 2008. "CIO Role Could Shift toward Data Quality, Says IBM Group." Search Security. July 9, 2008. https://searchsecurity.techtarget.com/news/1320563 /CIO-role-could-shift-toward-data-quality-says-IBM-group.

Seiner, R. 2009. "The 'Non-Invasive Data Governance'™ Operating Model." TDAN. December 1, 2009. http://tdan.com/the-non-invasive-data-governanceo-operating -model/12210.

Villar, M., T. Kushner, and D. Wells. 2013. "Data Governance Fundamentals." [online course] https://ecm.elearningcurve.com/Online_Data_Governance_Fundamentals _Course_p/dg-01-a.htm.

PART III. The Application of Analytics in Higher Education Decision Making: Case Studies

7

Data Analytics and Decision Making in Admissions and Enrollment Management

Tom Gutman and Brian P. Hinote

T HE FIELD of enrollment management is no stranger to data-informed decision making. Facing projected declines in the number of high school graduates and the increasing bureaucratization of federal student aid in the 1970s, institutions created administrative units specifically designed to achieve strategic enrollment and revenue objectives. This field—an amalgamation of admissions, marketing, student aid, student flow through the curriculum, and research on all of these facets—emerged because institutions could no longer assume that students would simply show up and enroll, and thereby continually fill and refill open seats and tuition coffers. Shortly thereafter, leaders in these newly created enrollment management units began analyzing data to predict students' decisions regarding where to attend and whether to stay or leave college (Hossler 1996). While the number of high school graduates decreased in the 1970s, college attendance rates among those graduates increased, so that overall college enrollment also increased (likely due to increased yield and/or longer time to degree), although enrollment grew more slowly than it had during the postwar baby boom (Coomes 2000). Since enrollment growth eventually slowed, institutions faced decreasing revenues alongside the need to ensure high-quality education. Amidst these new shifts, data-informed decision making occupied a prominent place in enrollment management since its inception.

Today, enrollment managers and admissions officers face an even more challenging landscape. Fueled in part by the Great Recession of 2008, demographers project another decline in the number of future high school graduates, which is already emerging in some regions of the country (Bransberger and Michelau 2016). However, economists predict that college attendance rates among those high school graduates will not increase, as was the case in the 1970s. In *Demographics and the Demand for Higher Education,* Nathan Grawe (2018) forecasted that demand among high school graduates for four-year degrees will decline precipitously after 2025. Though the decline in demand will not be uniform across the country or by segment of the marketplace, nearly every institution in the country will find smaller pools of students from which to recruit, enroll, and graduate, with the largest declines in the demand coming in 2026–2029. This means that enrollment managers and admissions officers will be forced to navigate an increasingly challenging landscape, with stakes that are remarkably high.

For example, the projected decline in the demand for higher education comes at a time when institutions are already struggling to meet their enrollment and revenue targets, and increasingly relying on enrollment-related revenue streams. More than half of respondents surveyed in *Inside Higher Ed's* 2018 Survey of College and University Admissions Directors did not meet enrollment goals by June 1, and 55% of respondents reported being very concerned about meeting new student enrollment goals (Jaschik and Lederman 2018). Most institutions also rely on enrollment-dependent revenue to operate, and partly due to stiffer competition for students institutions are increasing their discount rates (i.e., the share of unrealized tuition and fee revenue invested in institutional gift aid). The most recent NACUBO Discounting Study estimates the average discount rate for first-time, full-time freshmen at 48.2%, and the discount rate for all undergraduates rose to an estimated 44.8% in 2017–18. This is an all-time high (NACUBO 2018). As a result of rising discount rates, net tuition revenue is declining in inflation-adjusted terms. Increased discounting, whether the institution engages in the practice to remain competitive or to enhance students' ability to afford college, nonetheless stresses institutional budgets.

The combination of projected declines in demand for higher education, the increasing prevalence of discounting to attract new student enrollment, and the reality that many institutions face enrollment difficulties makes the use of data-informed decision making even more critical. Enrollment management as a field emerged from the demographic changes of the 1970s. Now, institutional leaders assign enrollment managers increasing responsibility for navigating these and other challenging circumstances, recognizing that their "input is critical to building institutional strategy and realizing the vision of the president" (College Board 2018, 65).

What might be surprising, then, is that while university leaders acknowledge the increasingly challenging landscape of American higher education, many do not prioritize the tools and methodologies that can facilitate institutional success. After all, admissions officers and enrollment managers have had access to data-informed decision support tools since the inception of the field in the 1970s; however, the extent to which these tools have been used is far from uniform across institutions. Grawe (2018) recounts firsthand that "[a]s never before, administrators and trustees understand that major decisions must be grounded in hard data," yet every administrator with whom he spoke admitted "that we are flying blind into a dangerous period for higher education" (4). Gagliardi, Parnell, and Carpenter-Hubin (2018) report that "when asked to choose growing areas of future importance to their successors, only 12% of college and university presidents identified using institutional research (IR) and/or evidence to inform decision making" (xi). This is particularly telling, since staff members in IR typically have access to abundant data and are positioned well to assist in informed decision making.

Since today we can easily store large volumes of data, most institutions probably have more data than they can possibly analyze, but leaders are limited in what they can do with raw data (Gagliardi 2018). To extract value, analyses must run deeper, and if carried out ethically, purposefully, and effectively, these analyses can yield remarkably useful and actionable insights. Such analyses are critical, since the decisions that we make today and in the coming years will help determine whether our institutions survive or flounder. With only a decade left before the demographics to which we refer above become actual enrollment trends, higher education leaders have yet to harness the increasingly indispensable power of analytics to translate what current trends and challenges mean for their specific institutions (Grawe 2018). In short, data analytics is, and will continue to be, a critical and essential strategic planning and decision-making tool in higher education, and there exists an urgent need for admissions officers and enrollment managers to rapidly accelerate their analytical capabilities to inform strategic decision-making processes.

Shifts in Higher Education and Enrollment Management

Big Data and the analytics revolution represent a small part of several broader, disruptive shifts in American higher education. Some critics (see Carlson 2019) purport that higher education today is "bloated and broken," while others (see Brint 2019a, 2019b) point out that American universities have never been stronger or more prominent in public life. Despite the current debates, we assert beyond doubt that higher education is in the midst of a major transformation. The Great Recession of 2008 represents a useful point of reference for thinking about transformations in higher education (see Ellis 2018), as this major economic event (and its aftermath) prompted renewed interest in novel educational, business, and delivery models (Grawe 2018; Mintz 2019b). This event also corresponds to a flood of books, articles, and commentary on higher education, most of which occupy a "reformist middle-ground" on the broader continuum of critique and analysis. As Mintz (2019b) notes: "On one end of the spectrum [are] the radical disruptors, like Clayton Christensen, who [views] digital technology, alternate credentials, the elimination of physical campuses, and unbundling of the faculty role as the answer to undergraduate education's purported inadequacies—especially its cost and disconnection from the job market. At the other end [are] defenders of the faith, like Jonathan Cole, who [offers] a ringing endorsement of the value of the top end of the nation's steep higher education hierarchy." What unites much of this recent work in these areas is the need for innovation, however defined, and the acknowledgment that colleges and universities must do something to address costs, access, inequalities, outcomes, and other real or perceived shortcomings (see Mintz 2019b).

Carlson (2019) uses the recent history of the newspaper industry as a cautionary tale of failing to embrace innovation amidst broader social, cultural, and market pressures. As readership decreased and audiences aged in the 1980s, journalists failed to recognize the need to modernize revenue streams or otherwise consider ways to innovate. Likewise, senior administrators and faculty came of age in a much more comfortable time, and many remain averse to meaningful change. In fact, mainstream institutions are already losing their historically monopolistic hold on academic credentials, and there is often a difference between how administrators and faculty view their jobs vis-à-vis what students want and need from higher education (i.e., credentials, skills, and meaningful, sustainable employment).

Grawe (2018) accurately notes that the dominant narrative amidst all of the pressures affecting higher education is one of fear, but the real questions in all of this pertain to how leaders' home institutions will experience and respond to larger demographic, economic, and enrollment trends. New funding models with a specific focus on outcomes (operationalized as persistence, retention, progression, graduation, and often postgraduate outcomes as well) now exert additional pressures on universities and higher education leaders to streamline personnel and processes on their campuses without significantly increasing costs. Responses to these pressures certainly reach into the domains of enrollment management and admissions, and especially the various operational areas comprising student success.

Gagliardi (2018) notes that university efforts to simultaneously maximize student success outcomes and contain costs have typically focused on "the large-scale adoption of programs, practices, and services designed to optimize remediation, shorten time to degree, reduce excess credits, and streamline credit transfer, all while enhancing teaching, learning, and advising in a cost-effective manner" (2). Lapovski (2013) adds pricing and discounting, increasing access and enrollments, increasing operational efficiencies, and improving student outcomes to this list of institutional responses. Many of these responses are particularly challenging in environments characterized by diminishing resources and increasingly competitive enrollment and admissions. All of this also unfolds within a context of dwindling public trust and support in higher education, likely exacerbated by public confusion about how higher education funding models work. Gardner (2019) reports that most Americans mistakenly think that government support for higher education has increased or remained the same since 2007, even though state support for public institutions overall (as of 2017) has decreased by about $9 billion since 2009, adjusted for inflation. Tuition has increased significantly as a result, up 62% from 2008 to 2018 for public institutions, and up 54% for private institutions. In short, colleges and universities have responded by experimenting with their business models and processes in order to promote financial sustainability (see Lapovski 2018).

Leadership at Middle Tennessee State University (MTSU), for example, responded in 2013 with the *Quest for Student Success,* which served as a comprehensive, strategic roadmap for improving retention and completion rates by focusing on recruiting, admissions, and enrollment, enhancing students' academic experiences, and embracing innovation and data-informed best practices. The initiatives and insights emerging from this document have yielded dramatic and transformative results across advising, learner support, course redesign, and the strategic deployment of data and technology to recruit, enroll, serve, and graduate students. While there is much left to do (as the next iteration of the *Quest for Student Success,* currently in revision, reflects), retention and graduation rates have significantly increased since implementation of *Quest* initiatives. Retention rates across multiple groups are the highest since such data have been collected at MTSU, while graduation rates among all students, Pell-eligible students, and students of color have also increased significantly. Whatever their approach, institutions should design and implement strategies with an eye toward return on investment (ROI) but also facilitating a return on education (ROE), which is defined as graduating more students, in less time, at a lower cost, with better postgraduate outcomes, and less student debt (see Hinote and Sluder 2018; Venit 2017a, 2017b, 2018). These approaches also directly connect to various recruiting, application, and admissions initiatives intended to boost enrollments during very challenging times (figures 7.1 and 7.2).

Recognizing that affordability issues contribute to difficulty in recruiting and retaining prospective and current students, an increasing

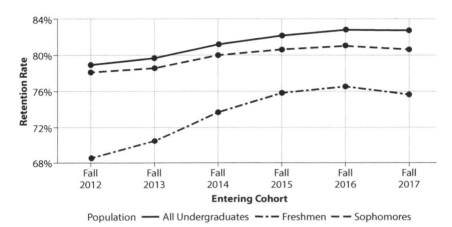

Figure 7.1. Fall-to-Fall Retention Rates for MTSU Freshmen and All Students, 2012–2017 Cohorts

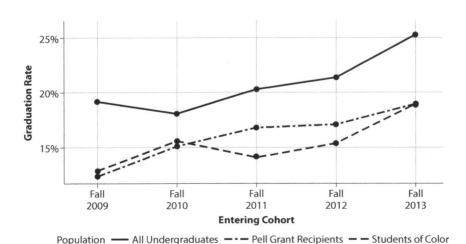

Figure 7.2. Four-Year Completion Rates for MTSU First-Time Freshmen, 2009–2013 Cohorts

number of institutions have committed themselves to meeting more admitted and enrolled students' demonstrated financial need. Institutional approaches to funding these initiatives vary. Some institutions have explicitly opted to make more need-aware admissions decisions—the practice of using student financial need to influence the choice of whom to admit—to limit the number of high-need students they must fund. Several institutions, like Vanderbilt University in 2008 and New York University in 2013, undertook massive fundraising efforts to enhance endowed resources for financial aid investment. These efforts underscore institutions' focus on using recruitment practices to improve student success, but choosing a particular approach is not an easy decision. If institutions cannot afford to meet the full demonstrated need of the students they admit, they must choose between packaging institutional and outside grant aid in a way that leaves a gap between students' need and cost of attendance on the one hand, and/or making need-aware admissions decisions on the other. There are positives and negatives to both approaches (see Brooks 2015 for further discussion).

Since higher education institutions are very large and structurally resistant to change, improvement for many colleges and universities has been slow and very challenging (Gagliardi 2018), and for others, nonexistent. Still, many are in the middle of reconsidering and reconfiguring their business and delivery models (see Fernandes 2019; Lapovski 2018; Lederman 2019; McKenzie 2018), and while they often use language to indicate that they are reinventing themselves in one way or another, most institution leaders are working on the margins to change the ways in which they operate in mission-critical areas (Lapovski 2013), either alone or in collaboration with external providers or other institutional partners. Still, there are at least two areas currently undergoing significant transformation amidst all of the developments only briefly described above—student success and enrollment management (not coincidentally the authors' respective domains of expertise). And this is largely due to the growing analytics capacities and methodologies available to forward-looking higher education leaders. It is also not coincidental that we choose to highlight these two domains, since both are critical elements of building an effective and integrated set of strategies to promote the overall well-being of an institution in an era of shifting higher education business models. In other words, enrollment management and degree completion are two ends of the same student success pipeline. The major reward associated with better leveraging the analytics revolution in these areas is student success (Gagliardi 2018), and by extension, the success of the respective institution. To be sure, this necessarily involves using analytics to connect these two critical institutional domains, both strategically and analytically. Since the focus of this chapter is enrollment management and admissions, however, we will now turn to analytics applications in strategic enrollment decision making.

Using Data Analytics in Strategic Decision Making

As noted above, the field of enrollment management is no stranger to using data to inform decision making, but with increasing expertise and computing power, the analytical capabilities employed to do so have certainly evolved over time. Lustig and colleagues (2010) distinguish three principal categories of business analytics: descriptive, predictive, and prescriptive. We will use this framework to explore the ways that enrollment management and admissions teams deploy analytical tools and processes to pursue enrollment goals and contribute to the operations and missions of their respective institutions. Enrollment teams can model very complex scenarios and decisions to inform discussions involving equity, access, and diversity, strategic finance, staffing and curriculum development, advancement, athletics, and more. For example, after estimating the relationship between the likelihood of enrollment and several possible predictors, such as academic quality, financial need, and distance from campus, analysts can assess how the institution may position itself to achieve multiple objectives by changing enrollment tactics, such as awarding financial aid. In his discussion of increasingly radical admissions proposals, Scott Jaschik (2019b) quotes Sue Cunningham of the Council for Advancement and Support of Education (CASE) to describe how enrollment decisions reflect complex sets of factors in play as institutions model incoming classes: "What prospective students are most likely to be successful? What students to whom an offer of admission is made will actually enroll, and at what tuition rate? What prospective students can pay more for their education (based on their estimated family contribution . . .), and in so doing underwrite part of the cost of admission and educating students whose EFC is much lower? What mix of students comprises a class that will take best advantage of the varied curricular offerings of the institution, that will after they graduate become both ambassadors for and supporters of the institution?"

Descriptive Analytics as Step One

One way that many such questions may be addressed involves the application of descriptive analytics. Though entirely backward-looking and post hoc in orientation, descriptive analytics represents the foundation of all analytical capabilities and is thus a powerful tool for understanding how business processes unfold. Tracking data longitudinally throughout the admissions cycle, including deposit counts and yield rates, is the quintessential example of descriptive analytics in enrollment management. Doing so can answer relatively basic questions pertaining to the current status of this year's applicant, admit, or deposit pool, how current numbers compare to previous years at the same point in time, and how current data compare to last year's cycle. At their best, analysts leverage their programming abilities and interpersonal skills to collaborate with key stakeholders to develop descriptive reports that are timely, comprehensive, informative, relevant, and insightful. Descriptive analytics is not limited to counting heads and calculating discount rates, however. Exploratory data analysis and data visualization are the backbone of any predictive and prescriptive analysis and are essential tools for telling compelling stories with data. Figure 7.3 displays enrollment plotted against standardized test scores for a subset of admitted students over a three-year period. Each point represents an individual student; students in the top of the plot enrolled, while students at the bottom of the plot did not. The smoother lines—one for each entry term—show the relationship between test scores and the likelihood of enrollment.

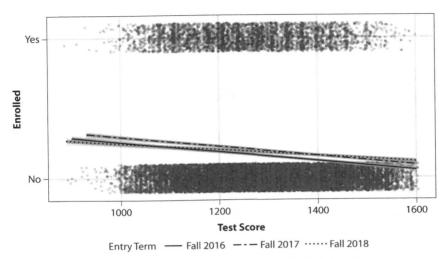

Figure 7.3. Using Descriptive Analytics to Estimate the Relationship between Test Scores and the Likelihood of Enrollment of a Subset of Drexel Admitted Freshmen, 2016–2018

In this example, students with lower test scores are more likely to enroll than those students with higher test scores, and this relationship has stayed consistent for each of the last three years.

Analysts employing these methods can identify, visualize, and interpret the relationship between multiple predictors and the likelihood of enrollment, including, but not limited to, additional academic indicators, traffic to institutional web sites, log-ins to admissions portals, interaction with emails, and financial aid data. If we extend these data to student success analytics, we can also examine students' likelihood to persist, progress, and graduate. Such data visualizations underlie any effective predictive model.

The Move to Predictive Analytics

While descriptive analytics examines data and scenarios that *did* occur, predictive analytics provides insight into potential outcomes that *could* occur. As a result, predictive modeling—provided by external consultants or internal analytics teams—is used extensively in the field of enroll-ment management. Each year, institutions set and pursue myriad en-rollment goals, and deciding who to admit and how much institutional aid to provide can influence whether or not institutions achieve those goals. At Drexel University, the Enrollment Analytics team develops many types of models, some of which are used to influence decisions prior to the release of admission offers, and some of which are deployed after offers are released to allow projections to change based on activ-ity realized throughout the cycle. The team deploys the former to set parameters to allocate financial aid subject to budget constraints, while the latter are essential to determine if leadership needs to change strat-egy quickly at this or that point in the enrollment cycle. For example, figure 7.4 displays hypothetical results from one of the Enrollment An-alytics team's models. Each of the points in the figure represents a sin-gle simulation of the model, which provides a headcount and discount rate projection. There are 2,000 separate simulations shown in this plot. The vertical line at 1,800 students represents a fictitious enrollment goal, while the horizontal line just above the 51% discount rate represents a fictitious discount rate target. The combination of a projected headcount

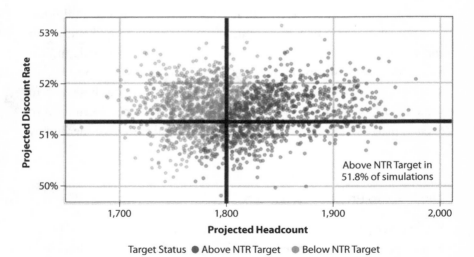

Figure 7.4. Summarized Discount Rate Projections Plotted against Summarized Headcount Projections for a Subset of Drexel Admitted Freshmen, 2016–2018

and discount rate allows one to calculate a projection for net tuition revenue (NTR); lighter points represent simulations with projected NTR below a hypothetical target, and darker points represent simulations with projected NTR above target. The Enrollment Analytics team uses visualizations similar to this to assess the uncertainty associated with its projections and to compare multiple aid-allocation scenarios.

Projections like this can be valuable, but predictive models must be developed carefully. Kuhn and Johnson (2016, 3) describe several common reasons why predictive models fail, including: (1) "inadequate preprocessing of the data," (2) "inadequate model validation," (3) "unjustified extrapolation (e.g., application of the model to data that reside in a space which the model has never seen)," or, most important, (4) "overfitting the model to the existing data."

Issues 1 and 2 refer to technical issues like poor data cleaning and poor processes used to build the model itself. In enrollment management, however, issues 3 and 4 are especially dangerous. Consider an institution that awards all prospective freshmen a financial aid award of $10,000. Changing strategies to award $30,000 to everyone is likely to result in behavior unanticipated by a predictive model, as there is no history to assess the effects of the proposed policy change. Models are entirely based on historical data and are incomplete snapshots of student behavior. Analysts simply cannot systematically capture the nuanced complexity of any given current or future event without data from comparable events. When using models to make decisions, analysts must therefore accurately acknowledge and specifically disclose their limitations, particularly the ubiquitous uncertainty (i.e., error) built into all statistical analyses, and leadership must recognize that models are not deterministic. Here it is important to remember that not all colleagues with whom you (or the authors) will come into contact will possess the requisite training in quantitative analysis and analytics methods to accurately and probabilistically interpret statistical results, so it is left to whomever leads the analytics team to recognize and skillfully navigate these limitations.

Using Prescriptive Analytics (Carefully) to Achieve Optimal Outcomes

Once an analytics team masters the art and science of predictive modeling, the opportunity exists to apply prescriptive analytics to identify and achieve best possible outcomes, given the constraints that institutions currently face. This process can proceed automatically or manually. The latter is the most effective method mathematically, but perhaps the least effective way to incorporate nuance. Identifying and mathematizing the constraints institutions face (e.g., budget limitations, test scores, expectations for diversity, etc.) allows leadership to strategically address those constraints in the future. But in enrollment management—and particularly in admissions—defining the best outcome is a difficult task. Institutions have multiple enrollment goals, some of which are exceedingly difficult to quantify (e.g., how does one accurately operationalize student "fit" with an institution?). To be successful, analysts should never perform this type of work in a vacuum; instead, this process should collaboratively engage institutional leadership in order to define best outcomes and to interpret results. Ideally, the analytics team is embedded within the enrollment management unit and actively participates in shaping the strategic vision of the institution. Regardless, employing prescriptive analytics to identify most desirable outcomes is a useful exercise for enrollment managers, as it forces the team to prioritize goals, identify potential strategies, and most important, assess whether proposed strategies align with the mission and vision of their institutions and are feasible given the market environment.

Using predictive and prescriptive analytics in admissions and financial aid is not like other, more well-known applications, however. Some of the most famous examples of data-driven optimization to realize best outcomes occur in the technology industry, particularly Google and Amazon. These industries have optimal outcomes that are easier to define, and nearly infinite iteratives, in that there are constant opportunities to test and refine approaches. Typical models like this from Google or Amazon explain significant proportions of variance, and each decision that is made is relatively low-stakes. For example, consider targeted advertising that appears while browsing the internet. These ads are essentially laboratory tests to see if potential customers will purchase the companies' products. These companies have millions of opportunities to find the best approach, and each testing opportunity is low-cost.

On the other hand, college admissions are very different. First, because best outcomes are difficult to define, analysts and enrollment managers alike risk proposing strategies devoid of necessary context and nuance, leading to outcomes with unintended second- and third-order effects that may harm the institution. For example, if an institution wishes to maximize its yield rate, one strategy is to deny admission to those students estimated as unlikely to attend. This strategy might be successful in the short term but may inflict long-term damage to the perceived value of the institution as students become wise to the admissions strategy and opt out of the process altogether.

Second, there are not many chances to assess models for efficacy. Each year, institutions have a small number of unique decision making opportunities that coalesce around the time that admissions decisions are released. Even institutions that use rolling admissions to enroll freshmen are faced with this issue, as there is almost always a delay between when admission offers are released and when students must accept those offers. Finally, enrollment managers make decisions with enormous implications, both for students and for the institution, and these decisions are not easily undone. For example, during the financial aid allocation process, institutions routinely anticipate that a significant proportion of students admitted will reject their offer, creating a need to offer more aid than budgeted to effectively invest the appropriate amount. As a result, choosing the correct amount to offer is a balancing act. Investing too much when offers are released can lead to overspending the financial aid budget, increasing the discount rate, and enrolling more students than targeted. Institutions risk significant damage to their reputations if they revoke financial aid dollars when they invest too much during the admissions process (Hoover 2018). Investing too little can lead to the exact opposite outcome, necessitating additional aid investment to boost headcount and net tuition revenue. Deciding to invest additional aid can damage the institution's reputation, and it diverts administrators' time away from other essential business when time is a scarce resource. Clearly, a sound analytics approach can empower an institution's capacity for strategic decision making amidst increasingly challenging current and future enrollment trends. But this is also about more than using the latest and greatest analytics tools to achieve objectives. An effective analytics strategy involves building data-informed decision tools and workflows into the bedrock of an institution's culture(s) and structure(s). We will briefly explore several practical elements of culture and team building below, but we must first acknowledge the ethical considerations typically involved in applying the power of data in enrollment management and admissions.

Analytics and Enrollment Management: Ethical Considerations

The expansion and analysis of personal data in business and institutional decision making have undoubtedly outpaced the ethical and regulatory frameworks to govern its use. The ubiquity of data is unlikely to change in the future, and due to far-reaching institutional implications, this is especially true in enrollment management. Using customer relations management (or CRM) systems, analysts can track students' navigation on institutional web pages, track log-ins into admissions portals, determine if student recipients opened institutional emails, and whether or not students clicked through URLs. Until the Department of Education ended the practice in 2015, the order in which students listed school on the FAFSA could be used to provide insight into the likelihood that they would enroll. The department ended the practice in part because, according to Stratford (2015), some colleges may have been denying admission and possibly reducing financial aid to students based on the FAFSA information. As increasingly personal data proliferate, potential for misuse increases, creating situations where institutions will have to address issues related to data governance, student privacy, and ethics as they find the balance between monitoring students' progress, informing students about how their information will be used, and appropriate decision making (Parnell 2018). This section briefly discusses several examples where misuse of data can lead to suboptimal and/or surprising outcomes, including the use of demonstrated interest in admissions decisions, the increasingly focused efforts to enroll Pell-eligible students, and the application of holistic admissions processes laid bare in the Harvard University admissions lawsuit.

The use of demonstrated interest in admissions is not new, but the personal information available to assess student interest has increased substantially. Some institutions track how long [students] spent on the institution's website, whether they opened emails and at what point in high school they started looking at the website, using this information to assist with admissions decision making (Belkin 2019). Enrollment managers must themselves determine the ethical boundaries that apply when using this information, as they may use such data to predict enrollments, to decide between borderline cases in admissions processes, or to materially influence entire admissions strategies or objectives. For instance, using direct indicators of interest, such as visits to campus or to off-campus information sessions, is quite different from tracking web activity or email activity, since students often do not know they are being tracked, or worse, assessed. Given that students often have no idea that they are being tracked in this way, there are serious privacy concerns to consider, regardless of how data are used. There are also reasons to suggest that these data may not always be valid, regardless. For example, some students may have no web activity because they are not interested in an institution, or they may (wisely) use an ad blocker to protect their privacy. As a practical consideration, the more visible these new practices become, the more likely that students, aware of such admission criteria, flood institutional web pages with tracked activity and open every email merely for the sake of doing so, rendering data useless for everyone.

As another example, the Department of Education, bond-ratings agencies, and news outlets have for decades used a set of basic measures to assess institutional quality, such as the distribution of test scores among first-time, full-time cohorts, retention and graduation rates of first-time, full-time cohorts, and salaries after graduation, among many others. In recent years, these same assessors have emphasized higher education's key role in promoting economic mobility and educational access, and have done so by focusing on the enrollment, retention, and graduation of Pell-eligible students and students in the lower quintile of the national income distribution (Hoxby and Turner 2019). Students are eligible to receive Pell grants from the federal government if they submit the FAFSA and have an estimated family contribution (EFC) calculated below a certain threshold—$5,576 for aid year 2019–20. Students with EFCs $1 above this threshold are ineligible to receive Pell grants, but these students still have substantial financial need. With heightened focus on Pell-eligible students and the ubiquitous emphasis on institutional rankings, many institutions responded by systematically attempting to increase enrollment among Pell-eligible students. On one hand, this is good news, as institutions invest financial aid dollars in the neediest population; on the other hand, this population already receives additional funding from the federal government and possibly other resources, depending on the state. Students whose EFCs are calculated just above the maximum threshold to receive Pell grants lose out on this source of funding, and since they are not part of a highly identifiable, easy-to-define group, they may not receive additional investment from the institution, despite need or merit (or potential contribution to the incoming cohort, or to the institution). In short, incentives to boost these metrics inevitably carry unintended consequences that enrollment managers must address if they truly wish to improve access to higher education (Hoxby and Turner 2019). In short, the way that enrollment leaders use personal information to further institutional goals carries great ethical responsibility, whether in the case of demonstrated interest or alternatively, in targeting specific student subpopulations. Put another way, leaders must constantly balance costs and benefits.

In a case with a slightly different twist, the Harvard University admissions lawsuit, from an ethics perspective, weighs holistic admissions against the ideal of academic meritocracy (see McNamee and Miller 2013). At issue is Harvard's application rating system and the role or influence played by race in its admissions process. This high-profile case follows other cases that have challenged considerations of race in admissions like *Regents of the University of California v. Bakke* (1978) and *Fisher v. University of Texas* (2016), but it is also different from these precedents in that lawyers for Students for Fair Admissions (or SFFA, a nonprofit that opposes affirmative action, also representing the plaintiffs) did not call a single witness who was also a rejected Harvard applicant (Jaschik 2019a). With both sides planning an appeal, the case is expected to reach the Supreme Court regardless of the pending decision, and is one of two current legal challenges to race-conscious admissions policies involving SFFA—the other comes from the University of North Carolina at Chapel Hill (Hoover 2019). Harvard's holistic admissions policy (similar to those used at other institutions where race, ethnicity, athletic ability, alumni status, and other qualities are considered) ranks students across multiple domains, of which academic ability is only one (Jaschik 2019a).

This case, which has reignited debate over affirmative action and the use of race in admissions, hinges upon questions of discrimination and the role of race in Harvard's applicant evaluation process, where Harvard stands accused of violating federal civil rights law in utilizing racial balancing to influence admissions in a way that discriminates against Asian American applicants (Hartocollis, Harmon, and Smith 2018; Hoover 2019). Specifically, SFFA used statistical evidence to demonstrate that Harvard admissions discriminated against Asian Americans through its use of a personal rating, where Asian American applicants scored lower on this measure than did applicants of any other racial category in the admissions process. SFFA contends that the most important question in this trial pertains to exactly why this happens—either because Asian Americans deserve lower ratings or because admissions officers hold an unconscious bias and/or fall victim to racial stereotyping (Hoover 2019).

Regardless, this case has opened up for public view many of the covert and obscure aspects of Harvard's admissions processes, which contain a number of hidden but internally explicit preferences for certain applicant characteristics. For instance, Harvard gives "tips," or advantages in admissions, to applicants in five groups: racial/ethnic minorities, legacies (i.e., the children of alumni), relatives of a Harvard donor, the children of staff or faculty, and recruited athletes. Alumni also try to increase their children's odds of admission by volunteering for Harvard. Applicants can help their chances by securing a spot on the "dean's interest list"—which includes candidates who are of particular interest to donors or have other connections to Harvard—or the "Z-list," which contains applicants who are borderline academically but whom Harvard wants to admit due to personal connections or some other justification. Whether or not Harvard administers a de facto penalty to Asian Americans (i.e., the effect of withholding a "tip") lies at the center of this litigation (Hartocollis 2018a, 2018b; Hartocollis et al. 2018).

Of course, attorneys representing Harvard University (and apparently the president of Princeton University as well—see Jaschik 2019a) defended the institution's holistic process, which incorporates race in admissions decisions. They argue that diversity in admissions is Harvard's goal and it is essential to its mission. They also concede that admissions officers consider race as one of many factors (in part because so many applicants have outstanding or perfect GPAs, test scores, and other academic credentials), yet they note that the racial composition of freshman classes fluctuates from year to year. They also argue that there are no viable race-neutral approaches as an alternative to its own process, and that admissions officers do not discriminate against any one of about 40,000 applicants (via a personal rating or otherwise) competing on a year-to-year basis for around 2,000 admissions and 1,600 seats in the Harvard freshman class (Hartocollis 2018a, 2018b, 2018c; Hoover 2019).

In addition to the sophisticated statistical analyses presented by both sides, attorneys for Harvard and SFFA also argued the legal standard that should govern the outcome of the case. Harvard contends that the plaintiff must prove intentional discrimination and show evidence of racial animus, while SFFA argues that Harvard must *dis*prove the claim of intentional discrimination, since statistical evidence demonstrates such a pattern. Hence, SFFA argued that there is no need to call any witnesses who were also denied admission, since the statistical evidence speaks for itself. As Judge Allison Burroughs summarizes: for SFFA, "[t]hey have a no-victim problem," in reference to the lack of direct testimony from a rejected Asian American applicant, which could help substantiate Harvard's discriminatory admissions. While for Harvard, Judge Burroughs notes, "You have a personal rating problem," referring to the part of the admissions process that considers personal qualities, and where the admissions probability of Asian Americans with perfect or near-perfect academic qualifications allegedly decreases (Hartocollis et al. 2018; Hoover 2019; Jaschik 2019a). A decision on this case is expected in summer or fall 2019, and the court's opinion certainly has the potential to shape admissions practices at many types of institutions across the country. What all of these examples share is the risk of unintended, negative consequences as the result of applying admissions decision algorithms (whether based on technology or human judgment) to achieve ostensibly laudable objectives (i.e., assessing student interest, estimating likelihood of attendance, increasing access, and/or maximizing diversity). Indeed, successfully harnessing the decision support capabilities of personal information and the methodologies to manage such data is one thing, but doing so ethically and responsibly is probably the much more difficult undertaking. Maintaining an ethical and responsible stance is particularly important, and sometimes difficult, because of the high stakes, pressure, and expectations closely tied to college and university admissions, even involving many of the same groups described above, like parents, athletes, donors, etc. (see Medina and Benner 2019).

Conclusion: A Culture of Data-Informed Decision Making

One frequent refrain in the Office of Student Success at MTSU is that "culture eats strategy for breakfast, and technology for lunch." In other words, no amount of technology or strategizing can overcome a failure to build data-informed decision making into the very bedrock of an institution's shared knowledge regarding how to get things done (i.e., culture). This shared knowledge relates directly to the structure of the organization but also the norms that govern behaviors within that organization. For example, institutions should consider embedding an enrollment/admissions analytics leader into the campus leadership team to bring the full power of these methods to enrollment and admissions strategies. Another related element of data-informed culture involves "de-siloing." We've all heard of the divisional "silos" that exist at nearly every college or university, but de-siloing refers to coordinated efforts to permeate those barriers with collaboration, thus producing new insights and approaches to our work. Strategies like these promote a data-informed culture, but they also can more specifically promote the integration of analytics with strategic planning and assessment. At MTSU, for instance, the president hosts a (tentatively) weekly gathering of university colleagues including the provost and key campus leaders from faculty, student success, enrollment management, admissions, marketing and communications, graduate studies, international education, and other offices to share insights, initiatives, and perhaps most important, the data and other essential information to help guide a large university in effectively serving its students and other stakeholders. In emphasizing people and relationships over the vast technologies and data stores on campus, we are more able to integrate people and information to produce actionable insights across multiple operational and strategic areas, including enrollment, admissions, and student success, and (where possible) to pursue jointly developed, and therefore shared, objectives in these and other key areas.

Successfully applying enrollment analytics is essential to effective decision making, especially given current and future enrollment trends. However, these tools must be carefully, thoughtfully, and purposefully deployed in order to mitigate risk of adverse outcomes attributable to methodology or misinterpretation. Embedding a data team within the enrollment management division/organization and involving the team in the strategic planning of the unit ensures that analyses are relevant, effective, and aligned with institutional vision. Further, staff on the data team must understand both the power and limitations of the analyses they perform. In addition to norms and leadership team composition, these insights obviously carry over into more routine personnel decisions, recruiting, and hiring, since the efficacy of an analytics team depends on the strengths of its constituent members, as well as its positioning in the institutional structure. For example, when hiring analytics professionals, the Enrollment Analytics team at Drexel University searches for individuals with technical proficiency in statistical techniques and programming, the ability to be creative and independent, the willingness to learn the broader context of how analytics fits into the strategic vision of the team, division, and university, and the desire and ability to form partnerships with colleagues to effect positive change using data. Based on searches conducted in the last several years, there are plenty of candidates with technical skills, but fewer candidates demonstrate proficiency in the latter three areas. We believe that these skills are important pieces of the hiring and team-building equation and should therefore be considered as part of these processes.

Without a doubt, the various changes affecting higher education in recent years have created great opportunities in the areas comprising data analytics, and enrollment management and admissions leaders should work to both accelerate and maximize their analytical capacities through a careful assessment of campus culture, key personnel, and institutional organization. Within these broader shifts, the "analytics revolution" makes these aspects of higher education leadership indispensable elements of strategic planning, assessment, adjustment, and reassessment (and so on, as part of an iterative data and planning process). Still, with great potential across multiple institutional domains comes a number of ethical considerations that, unacknowledged, can cause great harm to a strategic agenda or initiative, or an entire institution. Many institutions are already facing enrollment challenges. Those that are not will likely face such challenges in the near future. Data analytics, if deployed in ways that effectively balance the considerations outlined above, can help these institutions thrive amidst an increasingly challenging higher education landscape.

References

Belkin, D. 2019. "Colleges Mine Data on Their Applicants." *Wall Street Journal.* January 26, 2019. https://www.wsj.com/articles/the-data-colleges-collect-on -applicants-11548507602.

Bransberger, P., and D. Michelau. 2016. "Knocking at the College Door." Western Interstate Commission for Higher Education. Accessed January 26, 2019. https://static1.squarespace.com/static/57f269e19de4bb8a69b470ae/t /58d2eb93bf629a4a3878ef3e/1490217882794/Knocking2016FINALFORWEB -revised021717.pdf.

Brint, S. 2019a. *Two Cheers for Higher Education: Why American Universities Are Stronger than Ever—and How to Meet the Challenges They Face.* Princeton, NJ: Princeton University Press.

———. 2019b. "Is This Higher Education's Golden Age?" *Chronicle of Higher Education.* January 9, 2019. https://www.chronicle.com/interactives/golden-age.

Brooks, S. 2015. "Using Campus-Based Financial Aid Strategically." In *Handbook of Strategic Enrollment Management,* 213–227, edited by D. Hossler, B. Bontrager, and L. Tom. San Francisco, CA: Jossey-Bass.

Carlson, S. 2019. "What Higher Ed Can Learn from the Newspaper Industry." *Chronicle of Higher Education.* February 19, 2019. https://www.chronicle.com/article/What-Higher-Ed-Can-Learn-From/245723.

College Board. 2018. *The Future of Enrollment Leadership.* College Board. Accessed January 26, 2019. https://www.collegeboard.org/membership/all-access/counseling-admissions-financial-aid-academic/examining-future-enrollment.

Coomes, M. D. 2000. "The Historical Roots of Enrollment Management." *New Directions for Student Services* 89: 5–18.

Ellis, L. 2018. "How the Great Recession Reshaped American Higher Education." *Chronicle of Higher Education.* September 14, 2018. https://www.chronicle.com/article/How-the-Great-Recession/244527.

Fernandes, D. 2019. "UMass Plans National Online College Aimed at Adult Learners." *Boston Globe.* March 4, 2019. https://www.bostonglobe.com/metro/2019/03/04/umass-plans-national-online-collegeaimedadultlearners/2pthhOsSgwM5GOUFT0wUCO/story.html.

Gagliardi, J. S. 2018. "The Analytics Revolution in Higher Education." In *The Analytics Revolution in Higher Education: Big Data, Organizational Learning, and Student Success,* 1–14, edited by J. Gagliardi, A. Parnell, and J. Carpenter-Hubin. Sterling, VA: Stylus.

Gagliardi, J. S., A. Parnell, and J. Carpenter-Hubin. 2018. *The Analytics Revolution in Higher Education: Big Data, Organizational Learning, and Student Success.* Sterling, VA: Stylus.

Gardner, L. 2019. "Most Americans Think Government Support for Public Colleges Is Rising or Flat. They're Wrong." *Chronicle of Higher Education.* February 25, 2019. https://www.chronicle.com/article/Most-Americans-Think/245764.

Grawe, N. D. 2018. *Demographics and the Demand for Higher Education.* Baltimore, MD: Johns Hopkins University Press.

Hartocollis, A. 2018a. "Harvard's Admissions Process, Once Secret, Is Unveiled in Affirmative Action Trial." *New York Times.* October 19, 2018. https://www.nytimes.com/2018/10/19/us/harvard-admissions-affirmative-action.html.

———. 2018b. "Getting into Harvard Is Hard. Here Are Four Ways Applicants Get an Edge." *New York Times.* November 7, 2018. https://www.nytimes.com/2018/11/07/us/getting-into-harvard.html.

———. 2018c. "What Would Happen If Harvard Stopped Considering Race in Admissions?" *New York Times.* October 23, 2018. https://www.nytimes.com/2018/10/23/us/harvard-admissions-race.html.

Hartocollis, A., A. Harmon, and M. Smith. 2018. "'Lopping,' 'Tips' and the 'Z-List': Bias Lawsuit Explores Harvard's Admissions Secrets." *New York Times.* July 29,

2018. https://www.nytimes.com/2018/07/29/us/harvard-admissions-asian
-americans.html.

Hinote, B. P., and R. Sluder. 2018. "Generating Sustainable Innovations in Student
Success Management at MTSU." Paper presented at the National Student Success
Conference, Tampa, Florida, February 22, 2018.

Hoover, E. 2018. "U. of Texas System Apologizes for Revoking Nepali Students'
Scholarships." *Chronicle of Higher Education*. May 11, 2018. https://www
.chronicle.com/article/U-of-Texas-System-Apologizes/243402.

———. 2019. "At One Final Hearing, Harvard and Students for Fair Admissions
Squared Off. Here's What Happened." *Chronicle of Higher Education*. February 13,
2019. https://www.chronicle.com/article/At-One-Final-Hearing-Harvard/245695.

Hossler, D. 1996. "From Admission to Enrollment Management." In *Student Affairs
Practice in Higher Education*, 63–71, edited by A. Rentz. Springfield, IL: Thomas.

———. 2007. "Putting Students First in College Admissions and Enrollment
Management." In *Fostering Student Success in the Campus Community*, 101–119,
edited by G. Kramer. San Francisco, CA: Jossey-Bass.

Hoxby, C., and S. Turner. 2019. "Measuring Opportunity in US Higher Education."
Working Paper 25479. *National Bureau of Economic Research*. doi: 10.3386/
w25479.

Jaschik, S. 2019a. "Closing Arguments in the Harvard Case." *Inside Higher Ed.*
February 18, 2019. https://www.insidehighered.com/admissions/article/2019/02
/18/critics-and-defenders-affirmative-action-submit-their-closing-briefs.

———. 2019b. "Pushing for Radical Change in Admissions." *Inside Higher Ed.*
February 25, 2019. https://www.insidehighered.com/admissions/article/2019/02
/25/democratic-senators-urged-consider-radical-policies-college-admissions.

Jaschik S., and D. Lederman. 2018. "2018 Survey of College and University
Admissions Directors: A Study by Inside Higher Ed and Gallup." *Inside Higher
Ed.* https://www.insidehighered.com/booklet/2018-survey-college-and-university
-admissions-directors.

Kuhn M., and K. Johnson. 2016. *Applied Predictive Modeling*. New York: Springer.

Lapovski, L. 2013. "The Higher Education Business Model: Innovation and
Financial Sustainability." New York: TIAA-CREF Institute. November 2013.
https://www.tiaa.org/public/pdf/higher-education-business-model.pdf.

———. 2018. "The Changing Business Model for Colleges and Universities." *Forbes
Magazine*. February 6, 2018. https://www.forbes.com/sites/lucielapovsky/2018/02
/06/the-changing-business-model-for-colleges-and-universities/#30a14e425ed5.

Lederman, D. 2019. "A University Goes It (Mostly) Alone Online." *Inside Higher Ed.*
March 6, 2019. https://www.insidehighered.com/digital-learning/article/2019/03
/06/university-working-2-online-management-companies-now-plans-go-it.

Lustig, I., B. Dietrich, C. Johnson, and C. Dziekan. 2010. "The Analytics Journey."
Analytics Magazine (November/December). http://analytics-magazine.org/the
-analytics-journey/.

McKenzie, L. 2018. "Next for SNHU: Game-Based Learning and Digital Badges for
Middle Schoolers." *Inside Higher Ed.* October 19, 2018. https://www.insidehighered
.com/digital-learning/article/2018/10/19/acquisition-snhu-seeks-pathway-between
-k-12-college-and-work.

McNamee, S. J., and R. K. Miller. 2013. *The Meritocracy Myth* (3rd edition). Lanham, MD: Rowman & Littlefield.

Medina, J., and K. Benner. 2019. "College Admissions Scandal: Actresses, Business Leaders and Other Wealthy Parents Charged." *New York Times*. March 12, 2019. https://www.nytimes.com/2019/03/12/us/college-admissions-cheating-scandal .html.

Mintz, S. 2019a. "Higher Education Under the Microscope." *Inside Higher Ed*. February 12, 2019. https://www.insidehighered.com/blogs/higher-ed-gamma /higher-education-under-microscope.

———. 2019b. "A Worrisome Glimpse through a Spyglass." *Inside Higher Ed*. February 18, 2019. https://www.insidehighered.com/blogs/higher-ed-gamma /worrisome-glimpse-through-spyglass.

NACUBO. 2018. "Average Freshman Tuition Discount Rate Nears 50 Percent." NACUBO. April 30, 2018. https://www.nacubo.org/Press-Releases/2018/Average -Freshman-Tuition-Discount-Rate-Nears-50-Percent.

Parnell, A. 2018. "Data Analytics for Student Success." In *The Analytics Revolution in Higher Education: Big Data, Organizational Learning, and Student Success*, 43–54, edited by J. Gagliardi, A. Parnell, and J. Carpenter-Hubin. Sterling, VA: Stylus.

Stratford, M. 2015. "Ending the FAFSA List." *Inside Higher Ed*. August 14, 2015. https://www.insidehighered.com/news/2015/08/14/education-department-will -stop-giving-colleges-information-about-students%E2%80%99-choices.

Venit, E. 2017a. "The Emerging Discipline of Student Success Management." Day 1 Keynote, CONNECTED 2017. November 1, 2017. https://eab.com/technology /on-demand-webconference/student-success/the-emerging-discipline-of-student -success-management/.

———. 2017b. "Feeling Connected All Over Again: A Look Back at CON-NECTED17." EAB Student Success Insights Blog. November 1, 2017. https:// www.eab.com/blogs/student-success-insights/2017/10/staying-connected.

———. 2018. "The ROI of Student Success." Day 2 Keynote, CONNECTED 2018. https://eab.com/technology/on-demand-webconference/student-success/the-roi-of -student-success/.

8

Predictive Analytics, Academic Advising, Early Alerts, and Student Success

Timothy M. Renick

Georgia State is a perpetual laboratory of new ideas for using "big data" to improve higher education and to keep disadvantaged students on track toward a degree.   —*The Washington Post*, October 1, 2015

Georgia State has been reimagined, amid a moral awakening and a raft of data-driven experimentation, as one of the South's most innovative engines of social mobility.   —*The New York Times*, May 15, 2018

THIS CHAPTER offers a case study in the deployment of data and analytics to improve student outcomes at Georgia State University. Over the past 15 years, Georgia State has seen graduation rates improve by 23 percentage points even while doubling the number of low-income and non-White students it enrolls. This chapter will explore how predictive analytics and data-informed systems in advising, financial aid, and student-support services have contributed to these gains. It will outline conditions necessary for the implementation of data-based approaches to student success and lessons learned from Georgia State's implementation processes.

The National Challenge

When it comes to higher education, the vision of the United States as a land of equal opportunity is far from a reality. Today, it is eight times more likely that an individual in the top quartile of Americans by annual household income will hold a college degree than an individual in the lowest quartile (Calahan and Perna 2015). Nationally, White students graduate from college at rates more than 10 percentage points higher than Hispanic students and are more than twice as likely to graduate with a four-year college degree when compared to Black students (US Department of Education 2014, table 326.10). According to the US Department of Education, Pell-eligible students nationally have a six-year graduation rate of 39%, a rate that is 20 points lower than the national average (Horwich 2015; US Department of Education 2014).

In 2003, Georgia State University (GSU) was the embodiment of these national failings and a prime example of the devastating equity gaps that exist between students based on their race, ethnicity, and income level. The institutional graduation rate stood at 32%, and underserved populations were foundering. Graduation rates were 22% for Latinos, 25% for African Americans, and 18% for Black/African American males. Pell-eligible students—individuals who are categorized as low-income by federal standards and who qualify for federal Pell grants—were graduating at rates 10 percentage points lower than non-Pell students.

At the time, no one paid much attention to these numbers. GSU is a large, urban public university in downtown Atlanta, and its graduation rates were not unlike those found at similar urban postsecondary institutions in cities such as Boston, Detroit, and Cleveland. In each case, these universities enrolled a disproportionate number of low-income and non-White students and, not coincidentally, had graduation rates 30 to 40 percentage points lower than the flagship public universities in their states. That's just the way it was, or so the conventional wisdom held.

An Unlikely Transformation

By most outward indicators, GSU was an unlikely candidate to challenge the conventional wisdom. Located in Atlanta's urban core, the institution was a commuter school with limited resources and a modest endowment. Perhaps Georgia State's greatest claim to fame historically is its geography. Georgia State's campus is bisected by the National Park Service Historical District commemorating the life and work of the Rev. Martin Luther King, Jr. Only a few blocks from Georgia State's dormitories and classroom buildings are King's birthplace, the church at which the Rev. King was head pastor, and his gravesite. Millions of visitors make pilgrimages to the district annually.

For much of its history, though, Georgia State did not live up to this legacy. The institution was segregated into the 1960s. As recently as 2003, three of every four African American students coming to Georgia State with hopes and dreams of a brighter future dropped out with debt and nothing to show for it.

Complicating Georgia State's efforts to improve its graduation rates were rapidly shifting demographics. In the late 1980s, Georgia State's student body was more than 70% White; it is now more than 70% non-White. At the leading edge of demographic changes impacting the entire southeast, Georgia State became a minority-serving institution (MSI) a decade ago (federally designated as an institution that is more than 50% non-White), and it has become more diverse every year since. Having no majority population, Georgia State now enrolls more Black/African American, Hispanic, Asian American, first-generation, and Pell students than any college or university in Georgia (University System of Georgia 2019).

In addition, its students also have become less well-resourced financially. During a five-year period during the Great Recession, the institution almost doubled the number of Pell-eligible students it enrolls, moving from 32% of the student body in 2008 to 59% by 2013. For the 2018–2019 academic year, Georgia State enrolled a record 28,900 Pell-eligible students. As a comparison, the entire Ivy League enrolls 9,800 Pell students (University Innovation Alliance 2015). According to *US News and World Report,* Georgia State University is one of only two universities to rank in the top 15 in the nation for both its racial/ethnic diversity and the percentage of low-income students enrolled (*US News and World Report* 2017a, 2017b).

In part due to the radical changes in student demographics, in part due to conscious decisions made by its administration, Georgia State also became less selective from an admissions perspective over the period in question. The quickest and most reliable path to enhancing "outputs"—the number of students graduating from college—is to improve "inputs"—the academic qualifications, test scores, and financial resources of incoming students. As a rule, graduation rates increase with admissions selectivity. For the past twenty-plus years, two highly established public universities in Georgia, Georgia Tech and the University of Georgia, made dramatic moves up the national rankings, perhaps in part by becoming far more selective in their admissions. To serve students getting turned away by other universities in the state, Georgia State took a very different approach. It broadened its admissions criteria and, in 2012, began to admit all applicants meeting the state's minimum requirements for admissions. Over a seven-year period, Georgia State's average SAT scores for incoming freshmen declined by more than 30 points. Finally, Georgia State faced significant cuts in state appropriations over the past decade, losing more than $40 million annually in state funding during a five-year period during the Great Recession.

In summary, over the past 15 years, GSU has seen dramatic increases in its enrollment of students from underrepresented minorities, doubled the number of Pell-eligible students it enrolls, seen a significant drop in incoming SAT scores, and lost tens of millions of dollars in state appropriations. These are not the typical ingredients for institutional transformation—at least not for the type of transformation that includes significant improvements in student-success outcomes.

A National Outlier

Despite the demographic shifts that to many observers would predict declining graduation rates, Georgia State instead has become a national outlier when it comes to student success. The graduation rate for bachelor's degree–seeking students has improved by 23 percentage points since 2003. Equity gaps are gone or close to eliminated. Rates are up 35 points for Latinos (to 57%) and 29 points for African Americans (to 58%). Both groups now graduate at higher rates than White students. Pell-eligible students now graduate at a slightly higher rate than non-Pell students. In fact, over the past four years, Black/African American, Hispanic, and Pell-eligible students have, on average, all graduated from Georgia State at rates at or above the rate of the student body overall—making Georgia State one of the very few and perhaps the only national public university to attain this distinction.

Georgia State now awards more bachelor's degrees annually to Hispanic, first-generation, and Pell students than any other university in Georgia and more bachelor's degrees to African Americans than any other nonprofit college or university in the United States (*Diverse Issues in Higher Education* 2018). In 2016–2017, GSU became what is believed to be the first institution in US history to award more than 2,000 bachelor's degrees to African American students in a single year, a feat that was repeated in 2017–2018 (*Diverse Issues in Higher Education* 2018).

Just as important, students are succeeding in some of the most challenging majors at Georgia State. Over this period, the number of bachelor's degrees awarded in STEM fields has increased by 113% overall, 116% for Black/African American students, 153% for Black/African American males, and 275% for Hispanic students.

Because of Georgia State's unprecedented successes in supporting underserved students, in 2016 the University System of Georgia "consolidated" the university with the largest community college in Georgia, Georgia Perimeter College, creating one large university. Georgia Perimeter enrolls 20,000 associate's degree–seeking students on five campuses throughout metro Atlanta, and at the time the plan was announced it was struggling with large budget deficits and troublingly low graduation rates. The three-year graduation rate for associate's degree students at Georgia Perimeter was 6.5%. Upon consolidation in 2016, Georgia State systematically began to implement its data-based student-support programs at Perimeter College. Within three years (and with no increase in admissions criteria), Perimeter College's retention rate increased from 58% to 70%, while three-year graduation rates more than doubled, from 6.5% to 15%. The percentage of students who either graduate on time or who successfully enroll in a four-year institution improved from 41% prior to consolidation to 58% today, moving Perimeter College from well below to above the national average.

As with Georgia State's baccalaureate students, achievement gaps for the associate's degree students at Perimeter College quickly began to close. By 2018, the graduation rate for Hispanic students was above that of the student body overall, Pell-eligible students graduated at the same rate as non-Pell students, and Black/African American students graduated at rates only three percentage points behind the overall rate. The elimination of achievement gaps based on race, ethnicity, and income level has been a distinctive and much-studied accomplishment of Georgia State's bachelor's programs, and the rapid progress in this same area at Perimeter College has lent credence to the view that Georgia State's unique data-based and proactive approach to student success—an approach now being implemented at Perimeter—helps level the playing field for students from diverse backgrounds. Just as important, Georgia State's efforts with Georgia Perimeter College show that the model pioneered on its main campus is replicable in a very different context.

A Move to Big Data and Analytics

What did GSU do to bring about this unlikely transformation? A critical factor was the university's turn to data- and analytics-informed decision making more than a decade ago. Of course, Georgia State is far from alone among postsecondary institutions in turning to Big Data in recent years. According to a 2017 survey, 91% of colleges and universities are currently expanding their use of data and 89% are deploying predictive analytics at least in some capacity (Parnell et al. 2018). What distinguishes Georgia State is the timing and extent of its use of data to promote improved student outcomes. The university has consistently been at the leading edge nationally of the adoption of new data-based and technology-enhanced student-support initiatives, and it has implemented these systems at scale. It was among the very first institutions in the United States to deploy predictive analytics in academic advising and has now tracked every undergraduate student for more than 800 data-based risk factors every day for the past seven years. The program has resulted in more than 300,000 proactive interventions with students. Georgia State pioneered the use of predictive data in awarding financial aid with the launch of its microgrant program, Panther Retention Grants, in 2011. The program, which is aimed at keeping students with high probabilities of graduating from stopping out, has awarded more than 13,000 grants since its inception, with 85% of grant recipients going on to graduate. In 2016, Georgia State became one of the first universities in the nation to deploy artificial intelligence (AI) for student-success purposes by developing an AI-enhanced "chatbot"—an automatic texting platform—that answers students' questions about financial aid, registration, and other issues 24 hours a day, seven days a week. The chatbot answered more than 200,000 student questions in its first three months of operation.

Collectively, these and other initiatives have allowed Georgia State to accomplish a goal that was previously believed to be attainable only by small, elite institutions with low student to faculty/staff ratios: delivering personalized and timely support to students at scale. Rather than waiting for students to diagnose their own problems and to seek out help—a feat particularly challenging for low-income, first-generation college students who often lack the context to know when they have gone off path—these new data-based platforms are continuously analyzing student behaviors and, with the help of trained staff, proactively delivering personalized support. The results have been transformative.

The move to this model at Georgia State did not come easily. Three conditions had to be met, if only as a starting point for change. First, Georgia State's campus leaders and technology partners had to have access to clean, reliable data. At a large, decentralized institution such as Georgia State, multiple data systems managed by different stakeholders across campus can conspire to undermine data consistency. As an example, in 2008 Georgia State was unable reliably to report which bachelor's students were enrolled in which majors. The major field in Banner (the student information system deployed by Georgia State) is infinitely flexible. This means that staff members can enter any term into the field, and Banner will accept this entry as the student's major. In and of itself, this is not a problem. But if there has been no quality control over who enters the data into the major field and how they do so, problems follow. If a staff member transposes two letters in "Psychology" or abbreviates "Biological Sciences," the staff member has just created a new major. Any person pulling the list of majors in "Biological Sciences" will not find the student listed as "Biology" or "Bio. Sciences." In 2008, substantive campus discussions about the use of data with department chairs and faculty members quickly devolved into discussions about the quality of the data. The common refrain was: "These data cannot be correct because students X and Y are not listed here, and I *know* they are in my program."

An early part of Georgia State's transition to a data-driven institution was cleaning up the data. In the case of the major field in Banner, Georgia State introduced a gold standard for the terms that could appropriately be entered by staff and began to run nightly reports to kick out any terms entered into the major field during the previous 24 hours that did not adhere to the gold standard, enabling any discrepancies to be corrected immediately. It took time, but eventually the data became more reliable and the substantive discussions with chairs and faculty began to focus on the substantive topic of improving student outcomes rather than issues of data quality.

Second, multiple sources of data had to be united into a single platform. Fifteen years ago, various offices across Georgia State collected their own data on individual servers. Campus discussions often hinged on whose data was being cited, and this meant decisions were often difficult to come by or, worse, ill informed. In 2009, GSU's president Mark Becker drew a line in the sand by announcing at university meetings and for university decision making (such as budgeting) he would only consider data that were housed in the university's central data system. Others could run their own data systems; these data just would not be considered by him. Not surprisingly, deans, vice presidents, and others quickly began to collaborate with the institutional research office to ensure that their data were properly vetted and then centrally housed, and that any new data systems adopted would be compatible with the university platform. Today, Georgia State's data warehouse,

IPORT, offers 200 publicly accessible screens that pull from multiple data sources from across campus and that are updated nightly. IPORT has become the accepted data source of record.

The third and final ingredient that launched Georgia State's Big Data transformation was in many ways the most surprising and the most difficult. Georgia State had to move to a culture where it was acceptable, even lauded, to publicly talk about its failings. At many institutions, data are cited by campus leaders when they shine a light on accomplishments and highlight points of pride. Georgia State leaders intentionally began to use the data to identify what it was doing *wrong*. Every self-help program begins with the sober admission of failing. Georgia State officials began to admit there was a problem.

In fact, each of the significant data-based innovations implemented by the university over the past decade came not from a desire to innovate per se, but from the identification of a serious problem that was being created by Georgia State that demanded a solution. The data led the process.

Predictive Analytics in Advising

As recently as 2010, 5,700 students were dropping out of Georgia State every year. In preparation for the writing of the university's new strategic plan, President Becker requested an assessment of the impact of academic advising on combating dropout rates. While most individual students tended to leave advising sessions pleased with their advisors and advisors were working hard, the assessment drew a sobering picture of the impact of advising on graduation rates overall. With campuswide ratios of 800 students per advisor, advisors were mostly putting out fires by responding to the students who came for advising each day. These students fell into two basic categories: first, there were honors students who were conscientious in all issues related to their program, but the reality foretold that most of these students would graduate with or without the help they received from advisors. Second, there were failing students who, by academic policy, were forced to see advisors because their GPA had dipped below 2.0. These students were foundering and, while the advice from their advisors was appreciated, the data showed that the university was getting to them too late to turn most of their trajectories around. Despite the advice they received, most of these students still failed to graduate. Ironically, the students who advisors were *not* seeing at scale—B and C students who tend to fly under the radar screen at many universities and rarely raise their hands for attention—were precisely the students who, with the right advice at the right time, might be turned from college dropouts into college graduates.

Georgia State's move to predictive analytics started with a simple and practical question: What would an advising system look like that was designed to reach these students in the middle? The university set out to find indications that a student was going off track, not after the student's GPA had plummeted and the student was on probation with one foot already out the door, but at the first sign of a misstep. In the 2011–2012 academic year, Georgia State became one of the first partners with the Education Advisory Board (EAB) in a project that eventually became known as the Student Success Collaborative. With the help of EAB, the university used 10 years of its own data, 144,00 student records, and 2.5 million Georgia State grades in a Big Data project. The goal was simple: Can the university find identifiable academic behaviors by students that correlate in a statistically significant way to their dropping or flunking out of the university?

The projection was that the university might be able to identify a few dozen such behaviors. In fact, it found more than 800 identifiable student behaviors that correlated statistically to students dropping out or academically failing. For the last seven years, the university has been tracking every student every night for each of these 800 risk factors. (It also has been updating and adjusting the predictions based on the new data coming into the platform daily.)

Georgia State branded the resulting system GPS Advising. GPS in this context stands for Graduation and Progression Success, but it is also an intentional reference to the GPS in modern cars. The parallels are real. Prior to GPS in cars, drivers would make a wrong turn and did not realize their mistake for a while had a very difficult time getting back on path. Now with GPS, drivers are notified of their mistake instantly and can immediately take corrective measures. So, too, with GPS Advising: it used to be that students would get off path academically—they would sign up for the wrong course, struggle on a midterm, or underperform in a prerequisite class—and not realize the problem for months or even years. By the time they did, they may have gone far off path, wasting time, money, or worse, dropping out. With GPS Advising, students are notified the moment that they make a wrong turn and advisors can help them with the steps to get back on path again.

What kinds of things are being tracked by GPS Advising? Here are a few examples from among the 800 risk factors tracked.

- *Registration records.* College requirements can be complicated, and they differ by major. There is no easier way to get off path than for students to attempt a class for which they are unprepared, and there is no clearer waste of financial resources than to register and pay for the "wrong" course—a course that does not fit a student's program. If these mistakes are not caught up front, students too often end up with failing grades or are forced to withdraw from a class in the middle of the term. The data also reveal "toxic combinations" of courses. Students may pass calculus and physics at good rates if they take the two courses in different semesters, but when they take the courses at the same time, success rates plummet. Since the launch of GPS Advising, Georgia State advisors use the platform to track students' registration records and proactively reach out to thousands of students, helping to ensure students are in appropriate courses before the first day of class.
- *Class Attendance.* There is a strong correlation between class attendance and success, on the one hand, and students who do not attend class and those who struggle academically, on the other. Since it is nearly impossible to get thousands of faculty members to take class attendance daily, Georgia State is monitoring the electronic footprint students leave behind as a proxy for attendance. Are students not signing on to the campus wi-fi

system or the course's learning management platform? Advisors proactively reach out to students to help.

- *Early grades in the student's major.* The data show that the grades that students earn in the first course they take in their majors are highly predictive of their chances for success. As an example, at Georgia State political science students who earn an A or B in their first political science course graduate from Georgia State at a 75% rate. Those who receive a C in that first course graduate at a 25% rate. Georgia State historically had done nothing with the C students but to pass them on to upper-level (and more demanding) coursework where, for 75% of students, the C grades would turn to Ds and Fs. With GPS Advising, an advisor reaches out immediately upon the student receiving the C grade. The advisor and student meet. They may look at papers and exams from the semester to see if the student may need help in reading or writing. Perhaps the student is just working forty hours a week and is overwhelmed. The goal, though, is to address the problem while it still can be corrected—not after the student has collected a string of failing grades, has lost a scholarship, and is on academic probation.

- *Grades in Prerequisite Courses.* Two students can sit in the same course and earn the same grade, and yet one is at risk for dropping out while the other is not. For instance, if a student earns a C in College Algebra and is an English major, he or she may have a 90% chance of graduating; if the student earning the C grade in the same course is a neuroscience major, the chances of graduating may drop to 20%. The reason is simple: C-level math skills may be enough to get a student through the rest of the required courses for the English major, but they may be wholly inadequate to equip the student to tackle senior-level coursework in neuroscience. This is the reason that Georgia State has focused on delivering individualized outreach to students. One size does not fit all.

Georgia State launched GPS Advising in August 2012. Since then, there have been more than 300,000 one-on-one meetings between advisors and students that were prompted by alerts coming out of the platform. All 300,000 problems were not corrected upon being identified, but before the initiative the 300,000 problems had gone completely undiagnosed by the university. Students were signing up for the wrong courses, underperforming in prerequisites, and so forth, and no one was lifting a finger to help. The university was unrealistically expecting its students—the majority coming from underserved backgrounds—to have diagnostic powers that the university itself did not have. Now, Georgia State is (finally) providing students by the thousands with the information they need to make informed decisions.

The impacts have been dramatic. GSU is graduating 2,800 more students every year than it was before launching GPS Advising in 2012, and it has eliminated all equity gaps in graduation rates based on race, ethnicity, income level, and first-generation status. Surprisingly, the data that Georgia State is collecting about students is almost exactly the same now as it was before the launch. The university is *not* tracking students' personal habits such as who regularly goes to the library and who checks into their dorm rooms past 1:00 am. It is collecting data on student grades, majors, registration records, class attendance—all the data that universities have collected for generations. The difference is that Georgia State is finally using these data proactively to let students know what they need to do to succeed.

GPS Advising was intentionally designed to empower students, not to create new layers of confusion. At the launch of the program, all advisors on campus were provided with a second computer monitor in their offices so students could see the same information that they were seeing. GPS works only because there is no "black box." Advisors and students know exactly why an alert was triggered, and it is with this information in hand that the two discuss options, which the students are empowered to select or to reject.

While much attention has fallen on the novelty of Georgia State's introduction of predictive analytics in advising, the implementation of the GPS data platform and its accompanying alerts was accomplished in only six months. On the other hand, the university has taken years to develop the administrative and academic supports that allow the data to have a positive impact on students. Academic advising was totally redesigned by Georgia State to support the new, data-based approach. New job descriptions for advisors were approved by HR, new training processes were established, and a new centralized advising office representing all academic majors at Georgia State was opened. Forty-two additional advisors were hired. More than this, new support systems for students had to be developed. When the university was blind to the fact that hundreds of students were struggling in the first weeks of certain courses, it was not compelled to act on the issue. Once hundreds of alerts began to be triggered in the first weeks of courses such as Introduction to Accounting or Critical Thinking, university officials needed to act. Advisors not only had to let students know they were at risk for failing these courses; they had to offer some form of support. As a result, Georgia State has implemented perhaps one of the largest near-peer tutoring programs in the country. In the current academic year, the university will offer more than 1,000 undergraduate courses that have a near-peer tutor embedded in the course throughout the semester. Undergraduate students who excel in courses with high nonpass rates one term are hired back the next term to sit in all sessions of the same course, to get to know the students, and to offer group tutoring sessions. Advisors then can refer struggling students identified by the GPS system to these "supplemental instructors."

These efforts cost money, but they generate additional revenues as well. A recent independent study by the Boston Consulting Group looked specifically at Georgia State's GPS Advising initiative with attention to impacts and costs. It found that "the direct annual costs to advise students total about $3.2 million, or about $100 per student" (Bailey et al. 2018). This is about three times the costs to advise students before the initiative. Another $2.7 million has been invested by Georgia State in new academic supports, such as the near-peer tutoring program. But the return on investment of these programs has to be factored in as well. Each one-percentage-point increase in success rates at Georgia State generates more than $3 million in additional gross revenues to the university from tuition and fees. After all, students who stay enrolled continue to pay. Since the launch of GPS Advising, success rates have increased by seven percentage points. While the additional costs of the GPS program are close to $5 million, GPS Advising has helped the university to gross $21 million in additional revenues. The annual costs of the technology needed to generate the predictive analytics represent only about $200,000 of the $5 million total.

Microgrants and Chatbots

Other data-based initiatives at Georgia State have followed a similar pattern; a problem was identified via data analysis and new data-informed solutions were introduced to address the problem.

In 2010, Georgia State was dropping more than 1,000 students every semester because the students failed to pay their tuition and fees. By State of Georgia policy, students who have not covered the full cost of their tuition and fees by the end of the first week of classes every semester must be removed from the courses. From a student-success perspective, these are the last students one wants to lose; they are academically qualified, fully registered, and want to progress. They simply lack the funds to do so. In 2011, Georgia State conducted a detailed data analysis of the students it was dropping every term for nonpayment. It discovered that the largest single group of students being dropped were seniors—students who, by definition, were within two semesters of graduating. Further analysis revealed the cause of the problem: Students were running out of eligibility for aid before they graduated. With a student body constituted mostly of low-income students—many of whom had transferred from other institutions, eating up eligibility for aid before they arrived—and a state scholarship program that covered no more than four years of study, Georgia State had hundreds of qualified students running out of scholarship and grant funding only a few courses before they were scheduled to complete their degrees.

In the fall of 2011, Georgia State launched the Panther Retention Grant program. Students do not have to apply or self-identify for the program. The university identifies recipients via the data. Just before the scheduled drop of students each semester, Georgia State identifies students (typically seniors) who: (1) are close to graduating, (2) are likely to graduate based on predictive analytics, and (3) have balances below $1,500. It then simply puts the funds in the students' accounts so that they do not get dropped from their classes. Recipients do not have to be great scholars. In fact, the analytics show that seniors with even marginally passing grades who only have a few courses to complete are very good prospects for graduating.

In the fall of 2011, a dozen grants were awarded. Since then, more than 13,000 Panther Retention Grants have been given out, with an average grant of $900. More than 85 percent of these recipients have gone on to graduate when, in the past, the vast majority of these students would have stopped out and dropped out of Georgia State. The program is not merit-based, meaning that students with all levels of GPAs are equally eligible as long as they are on track to graduate.

A critical factor in the success of the program has been its accuracy in identifying good prospects for graduation, even among students with low GPAs. These decisions are based on some of the same predictive analytics that ground the GPS Advising platform. As is the case with GPS Advising, the program also produces a positive return on investment. Boston Consulting Group has analyzed the costs of the program and found that not only do the grant funds return to the university— they cover the gap in what the students owes Georgia State—additional revenues are generated as well (Boston Consulting Group 2018). The average bill of a student who receives a grant is more than $2,500, so the university also retains the funds that the students have already paid toward their semester bill. In addition, a subset of students then enroll for subsequent semesters, thus generating additional revenues in the process. According to the Boston Consulting Group, who completed the Panther Retention Analysis, the program has netted between $1 and $2 million dollars for the university since its inception.

Georgia State's use of data not only impacts students close to graduation; it also supports students who have yet to set foot on campus. In 2015, Georgia State had a growing problem with "summer melt"—the percentage of confirmed incoming freshmen who never show up for fall classes. This is a vexing challenge nationally, especially for students from underserved, urban backgrounds. Castleman and Page (2014) estimate that 20% to 25% of confirmed college freshmen from some urban school districts never make it to a single college class. They simply melt out of the college-going population in the summer between finishing high school and starting college.

Ten years ago, Georgia State's summer melt rate was about 10%. By 2015, with the large increase in low-income and first-generation high school students admitted to Georgia State, the number had almost doubled to 19%. Once again, Georgia State turned to data to understand the growing problem. Using National Student Clearinghouse data to track the students, the university found 278 students scheduled to start at Georgia State in the fall semester of 2015 who, one year later, had not attended a single day of postsecondary work anywhere across the United States. These students were 76% non-White and 71% low-income.

In preparation for the fall of 2016, Georgia State conducted an analysis of all of the bureaucratic steps it requires students to complete during the summer before their freshman year—a time when students are no longer in contact with high school counselors but not yet on college campuses—and documented the number of students who had been tripped up by each step. There were students who never completed the FAFSA, the federal application for financial aid. Others completed the FAFSA but did not comply with follow-up "verification" requests from the federal government for additional documentation. Still others were tripped up by requests for proof of immunization. In each case the data showed that the obstacles had been disproportionately harmful to low-income and first-generation students—students who typically lack parents and siblings who have previously navigated these bureaucratic processes and who can offer a helping hand (Georgia State University 2018).

With a better understanding of the problem, Georgia State partnered with a start-up technology company, Admit Hub (admithub.com), to deploy one of the first artificial intelligence (AI)–enhanced student support chatbots in the nation. What is a chatbot? It is an automatic texting platform. Using data from previous summers about the types of questions that had come from incoming freshmen, Georgia State developed a knowledge base of more than 2,000 text-based answers to commonly asked questions by incoming students—related to financial aid, registration, immunizations, housing, and so forth. Admit Hub placed this knowledge base on a smartphone texting platform so that students could text questions 24 hours a day, 7 days a week to the platform. The AI would determine if there was an appropriate answer to the question in the knowledge base or, alternately, whether the applicant's question needed to be directed to a staff member to write an answer and add it to the knowledge base. As such, the knowledge base would continue to grow. In addition, the AI would "learn" the semantic meaning of words in their contexts over time, understanding, for instance, that the question "When is orientation?" is synonymous with "Hey, I have a question: At what time is my new student orientation?"

The chatbot went live in May 2016 with projections that it might answer 5,000 questions for incoming students in the first months of operation. Between May and August 2016, the chatbot in fact sent out 200,000 text-based responses to incoming freshmen, with an average response time of seven seconds. Suddenly, the playing field when it came to access to information had been leveled. Students did not need to have access to someone with personal knowledge of college bureaucracies to get help; they just had to have access to the chatbot.

In the first year of the chatbot's use, summer melt at Georgia State declined by 19%. As the chatbot has been refined—the knowledge base now includes 3,000 answers and the bot's semantic learning continues daily—summer melt has dropped further and is now down 37% relative to the baseline year of 2015. Further, Page and Gehlbach (2018) conducted a random control trial of the implementation of the chatbot at Georgia State. The study not only confirmed the effectiveness of the chatbot in reducing summer melt but also showed that the positive benefits were disproportionately enjoyed by students from underserved backgrounds.

Lessons Learned

As senior vice president for Student Success at Georgia State for the past 11 years, I have overseen each of the initiatives outlined above as well as the general move to data and predictive analytics in the university's student-success efforts. What lessons have we learned from implementing these and similar projects at Georgia State?

First, when students' futures hang in the balance, one cannot sit on the sidelines and wait. The data are never perfect—but even imperfect data can provide the basis for improved decisions if current judgments are, in effect, based on no data at all. Often, the search for data and technology partners at Georgia State has not followed a traditional path of posting a Request for Proposals and then vetting responses. In the cases described above, we were trying to solve problems for which there were no established solutions. Instead, we leveraged our reputation for innovation and our network of contacts to identify partners who were working on next-stage solutions that had yet to hit market. There were no demos prior to our signing on. By being at the ground floor, we assumed some risk (what if the system did not function as promised?), but our pioneering position also afforded us the ability to be thought partners and to shape the platform as it was developed, thus increasing the chances that it would work in our setting.

Second, culture always trumps innovation. By design, the division of student success which I oversee has led the development and implementation of the new data-based approaches described in this chapter. We are the ones who best understand the problems and will be held accountable for the outcomes. The biggest challenge to adopting new data-based systems at a large institution such as Georgia State is not getting the data but creating a context in which faculty and staff actually *use* them. When we launched GPS Advising, we intentionally gave it a catchy title. We worked with our HR office to revise position descriptions for advisors to reflect the new responsibilities created by the technology. We asked our president to engage deans on the new model, and we moved the advising office to a new physical location at the center of campus. Why? To signal to everyone—including staff in the impacted offices—that this would not be business as usual. Something big was being initiated. Such advanced planning can make a critical difference in the adoption of new, data-based approaches (Alamuddin, Kurzweil, and Rossman 2018). More than 500 colleges and universities in the United States now deploy the analytics-driven advising platform that

Georgia State helped to develop, but not all have seen strong gains in student outcomes. In too many cases, the analytics have been activated, but the staff go about their business as if nothing has changed. If processes do not change, neither will student outcomes.

Third, well-chosen and carefully deployed data-based innovations pay for themselves. We all know that the economics of higher education are challenging. Georgia State has lost $40 million in state appropriations in recent years, and we have been required by stakeholders to freeze or to limit increases in tuition and fees. In times of dwindling funding for higher education and understandable public frustration with skyrocketing costs, how can institutions simultaneously cut costs and serve students better? The turn to data has been a critical part of the answer at Georgia State. GPS Advising has helped thousands of Georgia State students who previously were dropping out to stay enrolled. Every percentage point that Georgia State raises its retention rates is worth about $3 million in tuition and fee revenues. Imagine how much staff time was saved when the chatbot automatically answered 200,000 questions over a several-month period—questions that, in the past, were answered one by one by individual staff members. In both cases, students succeeded at higher rates *and* the institution delivered services more quickly and efficiently.

In recent decades, there has been a great deal of talk nationally about creating "college-ready" students. With the emergence of promising new data-based approaches to student success, institutions such as Georgia State University are finally beginning to focus on creating "student-ready" colleges.

References

Georgia State University institutional data are derived from the Georgia State University Office of Institutional Research. Please contact Timothy Renick, 2018, Georgia State University.

Alamuddin, R., M. Kurzweil, and D. Rossman. 2018. "What We've Learned from Scaling and Studying Proactive Advising Nationwide." Ithaka S + R. Accessed June 6, 2019. https://sr.ithaka.org/events/what-weve-learned-from-scaling -studying-proactive-advising-nationwide/.

Bailey, A., N. Vaduganathan, T. Henry, R. Laverdiere, and M. Jacobson. 2018. "Turning More Tassels." Boston Consulting Group. Accessed February 20, 2019.

http://image-src.bcg.com/Images/BCG-Turning-More-Tassels-Jan-2019_tcm9
-215186.pdf.

Boston Consulting Group. 2018. "ROI Analysis of Panther Retention Grants, 2018."
Boston Consulting Group. Accessed February 15, 2019. https://success.gsu.edu
/download/panther-retention-grant-roi-analysis-2018/?wpdmdl=6472129&refresh
=5c93a3992eb051553179545.

Calahan, M., and L. Perna. 2015. "Indicators of Higher Education Equity in the
United States: 45 Year Trend Report." The Pell Institute. Accessed March 3, 2018.
http://www.pellinstitute.org/downloads/publications-Indicators_of_Higher_Educ
ation_Equity_in_the_US_45_Year_Trend_Report.pdf.

Castleman, B. L., and L. C. Page. 2014. *Summer Melt: Supporting Low-Income
Students through the Transition to College.* Cambridge, MA: Harvard Education
Press.

Diverse Issues in Higher Education. 2018. "Top Bachelor's Degree Producers."
Diverse Issues in Higher Education. Accessed November 19, 2018. http://
diverseeducation.com/top100/pages/BachelorsDegreeProducers2017.php?dtsearch
=&dtrace=&dtmajor=&dtschool=Georgia State University&dtstate=&dtpage=0.

Georgia State University. 2018. *Complete College Georgia Report 2018.* Georgia
State University. Accessed January 30, 2019. https://success.gsu.edu/download
/2018-status-report-georgia-state-university-complete-college-georgia/?wpdmdl
=6472128&refresh=5ca78a604e5a31554483808.

Horwich, L. 2015. "Report on the Federal Pell Grant Program." NASFAA. Accessed
December 4, 2018. http://www.nasfaa.org/uploads/documents/Pe110212.pdf.

Page, L. C., and H. Gehlbach. 2018. "How Georgia State University Used an
Algorithm to Help Students Navigate the Road to College." *Harvard Business
Review.* January 16, 2018. https://www.bing.com/search?q=lindesy+page+harvard
+buisness+review+summer+melt&src=IE-SearchBox&FORM=IESR4S.

Parnell, A., D. Jones, A. Wesaw, and D. C. Brooks. 2018. "Data and Analytics for
Student Success." NASPA. Accessed March 1, 2018. https://www.naspa.org/rpi
/reports/data-and-analytics-for-student-success.

University Innovation Alliance. 2015. Accessed September 22, 2017. http://www
.theuia.org/.

University System of Georgia. 2019. *University System of Georgia Enrollment
Report, Fiscal Years 2017–2019.* Accessed June 5, 2019. https://www.usg.edu
/research/enrollment_reports.

US Department of Education. 2014. "Table 326.10: Selected Cohort Entry Years,
1996 through 2007." Institute of Education Sciences, National Center for
Education Statistics. Accessed August 15, 2017. https://nces.ed.gov/programs
/digest/d14/tables/dt14_326.10.asp.

US News & World Report. 2017a. "Economic Diversity: National Universities." *US
News & World Report.* Accessed August 15, 2017. http://colleges.usnews.rankings
andreviews.com/best-colleges/rankings/national-universities/economic-diversity.

———. 2017b. "Campus Ethnic Diversity: National Universities." *US News & World
Report.* Accessed August 15, 2017. http://colleges.usnews.rankingsandreviews.com
/best-colleges/rankings/national-universities/campus-ethnic-diversity.

[9]

Constituent Relationship Management and Student Engagement Lifecycle

Cathy A. O'Bryan, Chris Tompkins, and Carrie Hancock Marcinkevage

M ANY HIGHER education institutions are data rich and informa-tion poor. Institutions collect student data using enterprise man-agement systems like Banner or PeopleSoft, but the data are mostly locked behind security layers and not utilized for analytical processing. In respective functional areas, institutional programs track individuals who visited their institution's sites, who came for campus tours, and who submitted applications, but in most cases these data are not con-nected to predict and support their future success when admitted stu-dents arrive on campus. Institutions keep records of students who par-ticipated in various campus activities, but the data are usually scattered and not utilized to personalize and enhance students' learning experi-ence. University academic advisors meet with students regularly but may not be equipped with the right data to individualize their interactions. Officials likely have limited knowledge about graduates' career success and continuing engagement with their alma mater. While these issues may not have been major barriers to student success in the past, the abil-ity to improve retention, graduation, and lifelong engagement of uni-versity students depends on improving the "connectedness" with stu-dents, alumni, and other key stakeholders. Institutions need to start connecting the disparate data points to understand the full lifecycle of student engagements starting from the early date when they show interest in the university and throughout their life journeys before and after graduation. This chapter will address the connectedness by introducing the concept of customer relationship management in the context of higher education.

The Concept of Constituent Relationship Management

Constituent relationship management (CRM) technology is designed for managing an organization's relationships and interactions with current and potential constituents or customers. From a corporate perspective, CRM systems help companies stay connected to constituents, streamline processes, and improve profitability. Widely published researchers Payne and Frow (2005) define CRM as: "a strategic approach that is concerned with creating improved shareholder value through the development of appropriate relationships with key customers and customer segments. CRM unites the potential of relationship marketing strategies and IT to create profitable, long-term relationships with customers and other key stakeholders. CRM provides enhanced opportunities to use data and information to both understand customers and co-create value with them. This requires a cross-functional integration of processes, people, operations, and marketing capabilities that is enabled through information, technology, and applications" (Payne and Frow 2005, 168). Whereas *customer* relations management is the standard term leveraged for commercial sales-based CRM, the term *constituent* is more commonly used in the higher education context, therefore we will use constituent throughout this chapter. A CRM, in the simplest terms, is a relational database that tracks constituents, the pertinent relationships they have with the institution, and the interactions that occur between constituents and the institution.

According to Gartner (reported by Del Rowe 2019), CRM became the largest software market in 2017 with $39.5 billion in revenue. Although CRM is a digital strategy widely used to manage customer relationships in the business world, CRM is "still emerging in higher education" (McClure 2006, 47). Universities are developing increased business acumen as a result of highly competitive market forces, but the prevailing taboo has always been referring to students as "customers" (Dixon 2017; Guilbault 2018).

CRM strategy in higher education is often a response to an environment challenged by heightened competition, increasing student loan debt, and new expectations for universities' purposes and outcomes (Rigo et al. 2016; Trocchia, Finney, and Finney 2013; Vedder 2017). CRM strategy in higher education involves viewing all the university's constituents as connected to the institution and one another and building mutually beneficial, lifelong relationships. Business logic assumes that well-connected constituents create a stronger university. The concept of a "connected campus" envisions CRM software that has a highly integrated data collection and analytics system that captures students' campus interactions through their digital footprints. However, constituent engagement lifecycle management encompasses data and interactions captured from all institutional constituents, not just students. These constituencies include prospects, students, faculty, staff, affiliates, grant participants, research collaborators, employers, alumni, donors, and so on. Indeed, one of the key features of CRM systems is their ability to illustrate the interconnectedness of these relationships by capturing the higher education institution's relationships both internally and with other external organizations.

Within the higher education organization, a constituent can be defined by a multifaceted set of roles, relationships, and interactions. While these roles are distinct, they are all part of a single constituent's relationship to the institution. Each of these roles has related dimensions with accompanying interactions specific to that role. For example, a higher education constituent might simultaneously be an undergraduate alumnus, donor, graduate student, parent, and employer. For this alumnus with an undergraduate degree in business, the CRM captures information such as major, graduating class, sports interests, Greek affiliation, and a record of contributions to entrepreneurial scholarship programs. Today, that alumnus parent is working toward a master's in an online MBA program, and the CRM captures interactions that began with recruitment and continue through interactions as a second-year remote student. Additionally, this constituent's teenager is applying as an undergraduate, and the CRM connects this parent relationship to the applicant. As an employee of a large corporation, the constituent has sponsored and hired several interns, and these interactions are also tracked. From this example, one can see how this individual is simultaneously engaged with the university in multiple roles. "Higher education CRM is a good deal more than 'contact management' . . . It's all about tracking alumni and contributions, financial aid, HR, payroll, student records, and the campus community. A CRM in a higher education institution can be quite comprehensive" (Gaska 2003, 30).

CRM Development in Higher Education

Across the higher education landscape, the implementation and adoption of CRM is diverse and complex. As CRM evolved over the past decade or so, it often originated from a vast range of vertical functional silos across the institution. Particularly at large universities, CRM systems have typically been purchased, developed, and run by specific business units or colleges. Enrollment management often led the adoption of admissions-specific CRMs (Langston and Loreto 2017; Polona and Iztok 2018). Communication management systems were sometimes adopted by units with sizeable communication and marketing needs but limited to email marketing. Executive education units employed typical business to business CRMs. According to the 2014–2015 *State of CRM Use in Higher Education Report* by the American Association of Collegiate Registrars and Admissions Officers surveying over 600 educational institution professionals, 56% of the 600 surveyed respondents used CRM technology for recruiting and admissions, 34% for alumni and development, and less than 15% for other functions such as student support and advising (Kilgore 2014). This siloed landscape of multiple CRM and communication platforms both planted the seed for wider CRM deployment and created a set of historical obstacles that must be overcome in order for CRM to truly realize its potential for building institutional relationships. Indeed, in the early days of higher education

CRM, Fayerman (2002) asserted that the time is right for higher education institutions to further break down departmental barriers and work collaboratively to build stronger relationships with their constituents.

Higher education is evolving its capacity to leverage constituent relationship and engagement management strategy and technology. Somewhat similar to the more familiar notion of a "one-stop shop" strategy that may include student enrollment, payment of tuition or fees, parking passes, or other immediate needs, CRMs are collecting and utilizing larger volumes of data to connect and paint a more integrated view of individual constituents. Such a holistic view of engagement requires an enterprise CRM implementation instead of siloed solutions by units, departments, schools, and/or individuals (Hemsley-Brown and Oplatka 2006). An enterprise CRM is not only infinitely more useful to institutional decision making, it also provides operating efficiencies, potentially reduces vendor costs and maintenance expenditures by minimizing integration complexity, and contributes directly to meeting business unit goals. Institutions are maturing in their understanding and utilization of inherently data-rich CRM tools and are sharing their experiences through conferences and research. Today, higher education CRM has evolved to support many objectives, including:

- Organizing for strategic communication to all constituents, strengthening information sharing, collaboration, and relationships;
- Providing students, faculty, staff, alumni, and external partners with a more engaging and personalized experience;
- Increasing recruiting and enrollment through improved targeting of best-fit students, providing up-to-the-moment information on prospective students, marketing channel alignment, and increased personalization of interactions and communications, including enhanced reporting capability;
- Improving service to students and other constituents by leveraging immediate and up-to-date information to staff, faculty, and administrators, allowing service providers to spend more time on targeted, high-value interactions;

- Predicting and serving at-risk students through well-informed and multifaceted indicators that aggregate data on assignment/course completion, attendance, finances, health, and other indicators;
- Increasing the value of career services and employer relationships for improved graduate job placement;
- Providing data-driven insights to grow alumni engagement and donor giving;
- Understanding and leveraging strategic external organizational engagement;
- Optimizing employee productivity by replacing manual processes through system integration and business process automation;
- Enabling institutional leaders to leverage just-in-time, accurate, robust data for faster reporting, analysis, and decision making; and
- Developing 360-degree views and connecting students, parents, faculty, partners, alumni, employers/corporations, and additional institutional service providers such as human resources, facilities, and outreach officers.

For all their potential benefits, CRM projects are difficult to scope and successfully deliver due to their complexity. CRMs are often referred to by vendors as the nexus of existing source data systems. However, CRMs are seldom the system of record or "source of truth"; rather they rely on data from a multitude of systems (e.g., human resource, financial, academic, advising, student life, advancement, and alumni). CRMs both receive data from institutional systems and upload updated data back to the originating systems. Therefore, defining the CRM data model carefully and with strategic intent is critical to CRM value. All enterprise resource planning (ERP) projects are complex, but as CRMs typically combine elements from a variety of ERP systems, there is an additional level of intricacy. CRM implementation and adoption across higher education is an ongoing journey, not a destination. As a result, all CRM stakeholders, project executive sponsors, and users need to establish distinct objectives and milestones along the way.

Higher education institutions are complex organizations when considering the variation of business silos that engage with constituents. Unlike commercial entities with centralized marketing, sales, and service units, these activities are distributed across a university, and aspects of each can be found in each business vertical. For a CRM to be effective across the institution, it must accommodate the key business objectives of each area in an extensible and holistic manner while taking a larger view of the individual constituent's experience with the institution. When considering a truly enterprise CRM in higher education, it's necessary to look at the institution as a constituent would. Typically, those who engage with a university do not see it as a collection of loosely connected business silos but rather as a single unified organization. A student needing assistance does not seek help from department X located at campus Y or expect to be shuffled across departments to find the right solution. Instead, in most instances, students engage with "the university," and the experience they have with one area shapes their impression of the entire institution. Officials implementing a CRM system should strive to design a system that improves the constituent experience as a whole, regardless of the constituent's specific purpose. For example, students applying for an online course offered by a school or campus that is different from their campus of application should not have to reexplain their need for the course or any of their general academic or demographic information. The CRM will help individual units provide a unified university service to each constituent.

CRMs in Action at Higher Education Institutions with Multiple Campuses

At Indiana University (IU), CRM is a mission-critical technology that is used to manage the student lifecycle. IU was an early adopter of CRM in 2005. Many valuable lessons were learned from that nascent implementation, but its adoption was ultimately quite limited. In 2012, early sponsors including IU's communication and marketing, university information technology services, and the offices of enrollment management sponsored small targeted projects to replace a legacy CRM with one popular vendor that is widely available today, the Salesforce.org platform. A significant amount of skepticism among institutional users and leaders was evident. Indeed, for the first four years of CRM replacement, no enterprise initiative resulted from these siloed efforts. However, adoption across IU in the areas of communication/marketing and undergraduate recruitment catalyzed interest in graduate recruitment and human resource service requests. Total adoption began to increase rapidly, and an enterprise initiative began in January 2018. The value of enterprise or institution-wide adoption was quickly recognized as essential to achieving a 360-degree view of constituents across IU's nine campuses. Leaders in the Office of Online Education championed the critical need not to silo the data by campus, school, or department. It is important that a multifaceted and hence multi-informed view of a single constituent be possible. CRMs are designed to provide that holistic view by combining data about each constituent from a multitude of disparate institutional systems.*

At the Pennsylvania State University (PSU), CRM adoption followed a typical pattern of unit-to-unit adoption. PSU's work began in 2005 by implementing applicant constituent relationships using Embark and Hobsons enrollment management technologies (see hobsons.com) for residential and executive MBA programs in the business school. In 2009, Salesforce (salesforce.org) was selected with the intention to grow to managing multiple constituents. This extended CRM's use into executive education, academic programs, and research centers. The next phase of implementation grew the lifecycle and constituent base to include student and career advising, alumni engagement, and employer corporate partner relationships. The key objective for Penn State's CRM effort was growing both individual and organization-level relationships with the institution. This intention was critical to engaging and aligning all leaders and stakeholders. The strategy and design developed in the business school became the model for comprehensive CRM in other Penn State colleges and units.

*For more information about Indiana University's CRM efforts, please visit https://crm.iu.edu/index.html.

Key Applications of CRM in Higher Education

As CRM has grown throughout the higher education enterprise, it has become a critical component of meeting key objectives in academic and business units. In each area, CRM provides data to meet organizational goals, allows for tracking and analyzing trends over time, and enables innovation and growth as both the unit and the CRM mature. With proper data security, explicit policies that identify individuals or units responsible for specific tasks, and strong policies about release of data, a CRM can expedite data-informed decision making. Examples of key uses and metrics for today's CRM cross the entire enterprise and constituent engagement lifecycle. CRMs affect communications and marketing, student recruitment and admissions, enrolled student experience, career services and employer relations, alumni and donor relations, external relations, and institution employee services.

Communications and Marketing

Whether the institution manages mass communications through a centralized model with global oversight or a distributed model across the university, constituent messaging is approached very differently. Pairing an enterprise CRM with a mass digital communications tool provides the opportunity to establish powerful, personalized, and efficient communications strategies. Catherine Burdt, senior analyst for Education Technology at Eduventures, explains that "CRM is driven by a compelling need to consolidate and control communications" (McClure 2006, 47). Strategies include:

- *Branding awareness:* Having university communicators in a single solution allows for consistent branding of institutional messages so that official university standards may be established and maintained. By employing shared assets, such as official university headers and color palettes, the central marking department can leverage professional branding campaigns in a distributed communication landscape. The result is a significant increase in global brand awareness for all constituent populations.

- *Message consistency and reduced oversaturation:* A major complaint of constituent groups regarding university communications is the rampant message saturation that they experience. Constituents often receive multiple communications in a single day that contain repetitive and occasionally conflicting messages. An enterprise CRM that maintains single contact records can establish global communications calendars to significantly reduce oversaturation (Langston and Loreto 2017; Tapp, Hicks, and Stone 2004).

- *Targeted communication and associated content:* University communicators are often not trained marketing strategists, and they approach messaging in a more tactical fashion. Outdated distribution lists to large recipient populations and blanket distribution of content are standard practices. With an enterprise CRM in conjunction with an effective communication strategy, institutions can tailor content to the right recipients and more effectively achieve communication objectives.

- *Holistic communication strategy:* CRMs capture interaction histories of engaged community members along with their relationships to the organization and each other. Long-term email, web, and social media analytics include delivery and click-through rates, opens, unsubscribes, page view tracking, referral referencing, social media mentions, and positivity ratings. These data contribute to improved messaging and successful engagement. Tracking analytics provides data-informed decisions essential for developing a holistic and effective university communication strategy.

Student Admissions and Recruiting

With increasing competition for student applications, the need to remain competitive continues to increase (Vedder 2017). Student recruitment staff strive to improve the experience of the prospective student while reducing administrative overhead. Having an enterprise CRM that provides robust information and engagement capabilities offers dramatic improvements to recruiting strategies and execution. Below are examples of how CRM can improve processes related to admissions and recruiting:

- *Institutional awareness and outreach:* The first step for any recruitment process is making prospective students aware of the institution. The enterprise CRM provides an effective means of filling the "top of the funnel" at the pre-applicant level through advertising and acquired lists, and it allows for lead scoring, targeted communications, and other recruiting campaigns to establish awareness for future prospective classes.
- *Targeted engagement to meet enrollment goals:* A CRM enables recruiters to assemble information about distinct subsets of prospective students to determine if their interests, achievements, and future goals align well with the institution's offerings. Using that subset of information, recruiters can personalize the messages and communications sent to prospects to pique their interest in applying.
- *Recruiting funnel management:* Successful student recruitment is based on the ability to accurately identify and manage prospective students as they progress through the recruiting funnel. Effective engagement based on funnel stage can ensure that the prospective student journey is driven to the desired outcome of enrollment. CRM recruiting funnel management coupled with data integrations to university application and student information systems provides recruiters essential information and automation.
- *Personalized prospective student experience:* The more information maintained in the CRM, the more recruiters can create a positive, personalized experience for prospects. In 2006, Abilene Christian University went live with a CRM that enabled "any admission officer who communicated with a prospective student to access the database to see previous information . . . allowing for customized communications, providing tools to measure the

effectiveness of marketing campaigns, facilitating communications between divisions such as admissions and development, enhancing reporting capability, and creating a seamless way for the constituents to communicate with the institution" ("Strategic Planning" 2007, 4).

- *Reduction of administrative barriers to admission:* A CRM can provide a single source of information on each prospective student, thus preventing recruitment officers at various schools or campuses from asking for redundant applicant information. A CRM can be used by recruitment officers to construct a communication campaign that nudges students with reminders on due dates and missing application items. A CRM can enable applicants to choose the type of communication channels they prefer, such as texts rather than email. It also provides faster communication of important dates, events, and required actions critical for the admissions process.

Enrolled Student Experience

The student experience has become the focus of many conversations about maintaining a competitive edge in higher education today. Students expect a modern experience that reduces the burden on them and provides real-time service to support their needs. "Students are showing up on campus, whether it's an online campus or in real life, with these expectations that generations before didn't have. You can't look like and feel like the DMV anymore" (Marcinkevage 2017a, 13). Although most universities have distributed service models for housing, financial aid, registration, and so on, leveraging an enterprise CRM makes it possible to provide a holistic, one-stop service approach and more personalized experience.

- *Student services one-stop:* The days of forcing students to hand deliver forms and walk from building to building are gone. The emergence of the enrolled student "one-stop" has become the new norm and a standard student expectation. When leaders in a higher education institution employ an enterprise CRM for this purpose, all related data can be aggregated and accessible to student service staff to provide a streamlined and informed experience when students seek help. Information related to housing, financial aid, registrar, bursar, and so on can be accessed from a central service desk to provide single point support. Arizona State University and the University of California–San Diego have implemented student service one-stops, with ASU solving over 1,000,000 student cases by 2018 (De Luca and Glassman 2014; Mainland 2018).

- *Holistic student view:* A siloed view of students consistently shows itself to be problematic when trying to provide effective service and support for student needs. Only when student service agents can see the current, holistic picture of a student can effective service be provided. Having pertinent data aggregated or virtualized in a single view removes administrative barriers, streamlines processes, and removes the risk of incorrect guidance due to missing or conflicting information.

- *Student success and retention:* A CRM aggregating information across traditional silos provides an early warning system that allows advisors to predict and proactively support students through a variety of situations that may endanger their graduation. Administrators and faculty can connect across departments to collectively aid student success. At Central Queensland University in Australia, the CRM-enabled campus portal gave learning advisors "a breadth of integrated information" to then "see the student's level of class-attendance, their patterns of submission of assignments as well as their academic results, allowing them to tailor the support provided" (Pember, Owens, and Yaghi 2014, 121–122). At Ivy Tech Community College in central Indiana, the admissions and advising departments use a Microsoft Dynamics CRM system to track at-risk students throughout their campus careers. A staff member reports that the system "addresses the relationship with the student" and "we don't allow them to fall through the cracks" (McClure 2006, 47).

Career Services and Employer Relations

Universities are increasingly evaluated not only on educational outcomes but also on graduate employment outcomes. CRMs allow effective management of both individual student career coaching as well as aggregate employer engagement.

- *Career coaching and services:* In addition to academic advising, CRMs can manage and track individual career coaching and resources. Career coaches can create predictive analytics for scoring students on employment readiness, develop coaching recommendations individually and in aggregate across groups, rate and improve career resource usage, and track employment metrics. Penn State and the University of Colorado at Boulder both improved career outcomes through CRM-enhanced career coaching and employment services including meeting scheduling, activity tracking, and aggregate reporting and analytics (Ayoubi and Marcinkevage 2015; Conner 2017).
- *Employer relationship management:* Universities benefit not only from their individual constituent relationships, but also from strong relationships with the companies who hire their graduates. Hiring companies often increase their relationships with universities to attract more top graduates by becoming corporate partners and sponsoring projects and research. CRMs allow employer relations specialists to track company engagement across units and develop strategies for growing relationships with their students' preferred companies.
- *Strategic employer engagement:* Despite the increasing focus on graduate employment, universities have limited resources to devote to career development and employment needs. Employer activity and relationships (i.e., the degree to which a particular employer engages with the university to attract its students) aggregated across the university can direct attention to relationships that cost too much staff time for their value versus those that can grow to become the most fruitful for the institution. Staff can create strategic employer plans for culling outdated or

nonvaluable relationships and investing in those that will offer their students and faculty the most benefit. Tulane University created an extremely strategic approach to targeting key New Orleans employers using analytics from its CRM data (Ayoubi and Marcinkevage 2015).

Alumni and Donor Engagement

Both public and private institutions rely on alumni referrals and engagement as well as donor contributions for endowments and scholarships. These are increasingly important relationships as universities seek to achieve their educational missions while facing tuition and funding source challenges.

- *Increased advancement and support:* While many institutions have established alumni and advancement systems, they are often disconnected from any other systems. An enterprise CRM allows the institution to create and maintain information about a constituent from first contact throughout a lifetime engagement. Targeted, timely, and consistent communication helps increase alumni and donor engagement and support. Application of CRMs to advancement "enhances the interaction with alumni and donors during all phases and activities of fundraising, stewardship and alumni relations by applying customized and targeted information to the constituent through appropriate contact mechanisms" (Fayerman 2002, 59).
- *Personalized experience:* With individual contact and interaction information stored over time in the CRM, each communication with an alumnus or donor can be personalized. This could involve targeted mass communications based upon particular contact attributes or interests, or it could be individualized relationship management with a single contact. The result is the alumnus or donor feeling that the institution genuinely knows them and cares about their interests and support.

- *Donor funnel management:* Advancement professionals identify stages of life situations and donor capacity. From predicting donor giving potential to creating automated travel routes, CRMs can help maintain and develop these relationships throughout the stages while optimizing advancement professionals' time.
- *Nurturing the relationship with alumni:* CRMs can track student organizations, leadership roles, most frequented dining halls, housing history, favorite professors, and many other student interactions. These data allow alumni relations and advancement professionals to create extremely personal relationships with alumni and donors. Alumni can connect based on what they care about and what will make them feel most engaged and supportive of their institution.
- *Alumni communities of interest:* The best alumni engagement comes from alumni establishing relationships among themselves in affinity groups and communities of common interest. CRMs provide information to share and connect alumni with one another. The institution can utilize CRM communication technology to facilitate those relationships, and the alumni themselves can facilitate their own communities and engagement. Columbia University and the University of Colorado have developed CRM-powered alumni communities for communication and engagement that have "unified communication strategies and solutions, all the while increasing staff efficiency" (Egan, Mossaidis, and Morris 2015).

External Organization Relationships

Although the initial focus of most higher education CRMs is on the individual constituent, there is an emerging focus on the relationships and interactions between the university and external organizations. These organizations range from commercial for-profit, not-for-profit, and government agencies, to other institutions of higher education. All the benefits of the 360-degree view of individual constituents apply equally to organizations. Having a comprehensive organizational view of an organization in a CRM dramatically reduces the effort spent to aggregate data from multiple sources and provides a greatly improved and informed experience when engaging organizations.

- *Holistic organizational visualization:* By building out a relational data structure for an organization similar to that of a person, a single view of all pertinent information is possible. Everything from the various forms of financial support (gifts, sponsored projects, etc.) to campus visits and hiring history, to any form of collaboration can be managed and visualized for the purposes of informed future interactions. As more data are contributed over time, the information about and view of the organization become increasingly useful. The university can now strategically approach its interactions with those organizations to increase engagement in desired areas.

- *Visible network of organizations and individuals:* When the CRM manages both individual and organization constituents, the system can tie them together for new capability and insights. Not only will university representatives have a comprehensive view of all the relationships they have with an organization, but they will have that same view of the people they are engaging with at that organization. By expanding the ties further and relating people to each other, a network of engagement knowledge is created. The university representative can meet with any constituent and know all financial transactions, all collaborations, who they're meeting with, who else has met with them, any relationships that person has to the university, and if the person has relationships to any other person related to the university. For example, when calling on a corporation, an advancement officer will benefit from a proactive understanding of what members of the corporation are alumni, have hired alumni, have sponsored student internships, sit on grant boards, have sponsored collaborative research, and so on. These provide not only talking points in order to build a relationship, but they also create opportunities for future engagement.

- *Institutional engagement awareness:* A common problem universities face is a lack of awareness about how various university departments are engaged with the same external organizations. By collectively managing the projects, scheduling, contacts, and related information with each organization, university officials can reduce conflicting solicitations and establish a more strategic approach to those engagements.

Resources and Critical Factors for CRM Success

Whether an organization is embarking on an institution-wide CRM or building on an existing unit-based CRM, some considerations and resources will help set the initiative up for success. A good first step is to assess what areas of the institution's business are most in need of CRM-related functionality. Having identified the top three needs, sponsorship and leadership must be aligned so that the accompanying change management plans and proportionate resources are available. Studies show that successful CRM relies on a combination of people, processes, and technologies operating in concert with strategy (Chen and Popovich 2003; Payne and Frow 2005; Rahimi and Berman 2009; Rigo et al. 2016; Sin, Tse, and Yim 2005). CRM is not for the faint-of-heart, as higher education institutions have traditionally operated in silos of leadership, processes, and resources, with a "myriad of locally negotiated practices and interactions" (Pollock and Cornford 2004, 36). Hence the locus of control for many of the needed assets, including data, money, and business process evolution, are often of limited unit perspective. Ideally, over-arching executive-level support is needed to nudge, prod, and encourage the reluctant.

The ongoing success of a CRM project across any higher education institution is dependent upon a variety of resources that must enable and sustain the project at all levels. The availability of the following resources and critical factors can either constrain or empower the project:

- *Executive support:* Change in business processes both within and across siloed institutional units is a common and critical part of a CRM project. Top-down incentives and influence are important. This is a critical success factor across all stakeholder groups and throughout all stages of CRM implementation and is supported in both corporate and higher education CRM research (Lawson-Body et al. 2011; Mendoza, Marius, Pérez, and Grimán 2007; Payne and Frow 2005; Rahimi and Berman 2009; Sin et al. 2005).

- *Financial resources:* On a project-by-project basis, resources are needed for consultants, specialized applications, features, builds, data integration, and service charges in order to start and continuously improve CRM functionalities. Additionally, the CRM will have foundational pieces including the establishment, upgrading, and maintenance of data integration, de-duplication, archiving, training, and simple maintenance. These foundational resources will also be needed to add new communication channels such as chat, social media linkage and subscriptions, specialized authentication, and cloud or on-premise storage, as well as other linkages to third-party add-ons and system integrations. Even if a coalition of sponsors can be found for specific business areas of functionality (e.g., recruitment, marketing, and student services), these foundational pieces will need creation and sustenance as the CRM grows and matures.

- *Staffing:* Appropriate talent and time must be provided to plan the project and address technical, functional, and strategic challenges.
    - Technical staff enable both the functional project builds within the CRM and maintain a keen eye on the overarching institutional current and future. Ideally, large platform-based CRM implementation tools such as Salesforce.org or Microsoft Dynamics require a dedicated architect who is both an expert in the platform and understands the overarching goals of the institutional CRM mission. The architect must wisely assess the CRM's internal resources and limits in order to meet current goals and objectives as well as ensure that future goals are implemented.

o Staff members within each of the business units support users and nurture their ability to master the new CRM tool in their context. For example, digital marketing strategy is quite different from traditional digital branding and communication strategies. In order to leverage email as part of a personalized constituent journey, expertise must be available and shared across the many "communication" users of the CRM. This requires expertise, training, and ongoing, systemic coordination across the silos and IT within the institution.

o Strategic coordinators of CRM people, process, and technology are required to continuously focus on high-level, collective objectives and deliverables for all of the individual CRM project streams. It is easy to become enamored with a single department's goals and therefore lost in the incredible potential of CRM applications. Staying attuned to enterprise-wide goals and senior leadership needs requires staff who are tied to business unit objectives and align CRM with overall organizational objectives. These individuals monitor progress, adoption, collaboration, and the overall success of the CRM strategy.

- *Data and data modeling:* At the heart of any CRM is a well-organized, carefully selected, and highly leveraged collection of data on the institution's constituents and their relationships to the institution and each other. Careful attention must be given to capturing the data that matter and maintaining the consistency and usability of that information. Automation is essential to handle the volume of information, but governance and even manual intervention are needed to systemically manage the data. The success of the CRM project depends highly upon its reputation and usefulness to its users. Much of the data captured in the CRM originate in other institutional systems of record. However, a rather significant percentage of the data is dependent upon users' willingness to utilize the CRM for communication and interactions so that these can be captured and retained in constituents' records. A CRM with desirable data will garner more data and more usefulness and attract more willing users.

There are many data models currently deployed in CRMs across higher education with varying degrees of success. When considering which data model to choose, a few key factors must be considered. First and foremost is the ability to *scale,* a common IT term referring to the system's extensibility as the capacity of solving the same need across multiple units. It is impossible to have a comprehensive picture of a constituent population without having a unique representation of each individual person or entity. The single-person record is the anchor that all other data will be tied to and provides the coveted 360-degree view. Having this unique record is not without challenges that require the removal of traditional barriers. For all relationship and interaction information to be tied to a person, all users of the enterprise CRM must have access to and accurately utilize the same person record. This means that data about constituents are not controlled by individual employees or areas of the college or university, rather they are to be seen as a single-source resource used by all members of the institution as needed. This is a significant departure from the traditional siloed mentality. All verified users must have access to all data as needed regardless of the constituent population. It also necessitates the design of that person's record to be accessible to all the authorized users when needed.

In addition, collaboration at the institutional level is an integral component to CRM success. Leaders of functional business silos must be willing to align their business processes, coordinate their data management, share customer information, and contribute to the greater organizational benefit of more holistic customer relationship management. Leaders must be willing to share overall objectives as well as data and accountability, truly putting the customer at the center of CRM.

Along with collaboration, CRM success requires vision and a culture that supports change. Higher education institutions have longstanding traditions that translate to their overall business operations. Concepts such as customer ownership, limited access to institutional data, exclusive control of functional development, and death by committee are all common aspects of the institutional culture, and all contribute to failure of an enterprise CRM. We are in a new era, where the culture of higher education must evolve and embrace new concepts to remain competitive in an increasingly demanding world. However, changing the institutional culture is one of the greatest challenges facing higher education today.

The process of cultural change is often slow and unresponsive to the pace set by current technology and customer expectations. When confronted by this barrier, two methodologies have proven effective: revolution or evolution (Marcinkevage 2017a). In the revolution model, there is a top-down mandate based on a global strategic vision. This provides both the resources and endorsement needed to effect rapid change across the institution. It requires that the highest levels of leadership have both the vision and commitment to escalate the level of experience for university customers and the funding to provide the necessary resources to effectively execute that vision. This revolutionary approach is traditionally uncommon in universities and is sometimes caused by a seismic market or leadership challenge. One study indicated that "the presence of a major goal shift, financial pressure, or local scandal can have a significant effect on overall leadership response when they are 'faced with a crazy operational or business problem' and 'the problem is life or death for the institution'" (Marcinkevage 2017a, 13). The merits of the revolutionary approach can be seen at institutions such as Arizona State University, where the investment by the institution's leadership has paid off significantly, or in Maryville University's president-led focus on overall industry change and student engagement (Johal 2017; Marcinkevage 2017a).

The alternative is an evolutionary, not revolutionary, approach. Evolution is gradual and takes significant time to reach the goal of cultural change. Although it may have less impact, both the positive and negative, the institution can slowly warm to the concepts of an enterprise CRM while gaining momentum through consistent, albeit slow, successes. A number of institutions have used this approach to grow their CRM focus across units and constituent groups, using the CRM's successes to create momentum (Britt 2018). Both approaches require long-term vision and strategy, however, the evolutionary approach requires this to be done without institutional endorsement or backing and is significantly more difficult to remain true to the end goal of an enterprise-wide, constituent-centric vision.

Although management of IT projects in higher education is a challenging endeavor, it is important for successful CRM. However, the added complexity of diverse user groups, competing priorities, and lack of established CRM blueprints make the challenges even greater. Traditional models of project management need to evolve and expand just as the culture and technology must. Having a well-established project management process is imperative. An effective management model can be seen at Indiana University, where multiple efforts to establish new CRM user populations, while expanding on currently adopted capabilities, are standard. This project management approach relies on many key components, including:

- *Separation of implementation and adoption roadmaps:* When considering the scale of enterprise CRM adoption, it is beneficial to start with exclusive roadmaps for both technical implementation and user adoption. To streamline processes and provide functionality to those ready to use it, the institution can rapidly deploy capabilities and then allow units to adopt in sequence based on resource availability, business cycles, and overall readiness.

- *Sequential project phasing:* To implement a full CRM platform at once would be like attempting to boil the ocean. Setting a maximum duration for each project with clearly defined and achievable objectives in conjunction with executing sequential project phases provides several benefits. It offers quick, visible wins that increase leadership support and user adoption, immediate positive impact on established goals, and CRM success stories that can fuel new CRM interest and participation.

- *Documented project charter of scope:* The poison for any successful project can often be found in the dreaded "scope creep," where the project expands in features and timeline due to stakeholders' requests or developers' ambitions. To combat this, the most helpful tool is a clearly defined and approved project scope that is established in a manageable execution timeline.

- *Clearly defined project team roles and responsibilities:* Correct composition and clear roles within a dedicated project team are essential. Project teams should stay small to remain nimble but have membership of both technical and functional experts who work in collaborative partnership.

- *Management and oversight of task completion and delivery:* A single project management point of oversight to all tasks, timelines, assignments, and deliveries should be established. A lead project manager should be responsible for all project resources (technical, functional, and third party) to ensure successful delivery and completion of the scope. Since these projects are specific to technical implementations with separate adoption processes, it reduces the variables that need to be managed and streamlines progress.

- *Incremental deployment of completed objectives:* Combining the traditional "waterfall" with current "agile" project methodologies provides a highly effective delivery model. The total project may be broken down into delivery cycles where each objective flows through requirement gathering, design/development, acceptance testing, and implementation. Approaching the project in this fashion will provide usable functionality to those adopters who gain value immediately while allowing other adopters the option to wait until more features are available.

- *Communication:* Good communication is a critical component of any successful effort and exponentially more important in the realm of CRM projects. Well-established communication plans include global, executive, and stakeholder progress reports, dashboards, and significant milestones.

- *Metrics and milestones:* Fatigue can be inherent in this long, ongoing project. As the institution's CRM project continues, the initiative's success is dependent upon a series of smaller, but ever important, milestones that span business areas. Key metrics and milestones are essential to both momentum and morale. Identifying those metrics and milestones will vary by project type. Admissions may begin with general CRM adoption to obtain the next incoming class and will ultimately mature to analyzing yield by student journey type. Marketing and communication may first measure CRM template use for brand alignment and progress to measuring campaign effectiveness through interactivity, timing, cost, and personalization. To measure success, the data captured within the CRM must be input or created by CRM-based activity and then processed, organized, categorized, merged, and aggregated in meaningful dashboards and reports for monitoring. Users must see immediate benefit as well as a path to increased performance over time.

- *Governance and ownership:* Governance and ownership of an enterprise CRM are challenging. By its basic nature, an enterprise CRM is not "owned" by any one specific university business vertical such as a student or finance system. Instead, it is the consolidation of all university constituents and interactions that aggregate to the holistic view of a person or organization. Competing priorities, demands, and perspectives can easily skew the path to CRM success by focusing exclusively on one aspect of the multifaceted CRM platform. Due to the complexity of architecture and need for ongoing development and support, it is essential that a business-agnostic group of highly skilled technologists own the technology stack. By having the CRM platform owned by central IT, it ensures that the CRM remains architecturally extensible for both short-term objectives and long-term strategic goals. However, the oversight and governance of project prioritization and business process redesign should always be functionally driven and therefore governed by the representative leadership of the organizational business areas (i.e., enrollment, admissions, finance, HR, IT, marketing). This introduces a situation that must be carefully navigated, since each business area naturally focuses on its own strategic goals and may not necessarily sacrifice them for the institutional vision. Overall strategic governance is achieved by having a small executive oversight body at an organizational leadership level high enough to focus on university objectives. This body approves and prioritizes the future projects of each self-governed business vertical to ensure an effective holistic governance methodology and achievement of the overarching organizational CRM vision.

- *Service centers for business area support:* The majority of CRM users are those institutional employees who directly engage with constituents and require access to the conversational management and operational relationship data maintained in the enterprise CRM. Their contribution of robust data and the value of applying those data to constituent interactions is essential. However, some complex and high-risk capabilities offered in modern CRM platforms require a highly trained user with intimate knowledge of both the strategic business objectives and advanced CRM functionality to achieve those objectives. To maximize this value at scale, it is necessary to establish and maintain centralized service centers staffed by these advanced CRM users who facilitate and accelerate CRM usage for each university business vertical. Where the central IT organization is suited to administer the CRM technology stack to ensure a scalable and sustainable architecture, it is equally important that these CRM service centers be managed and maintained within the functional areas of business to ensure the university's strategic objectives are met.

- *Focus on constituent benefits and ethics:* To adapt a common phrase—with great data comes great responsibility. The more data that are gathered and transparent across the institution, the higher the risk of misuse or simple inattentiveness to the constituent. The CRM leadership team can help ensure that the CRM project priorities focus on how they benefit the constituents and their relationships with the institution. Additionally, they can encourage and ensure ethical use of constituent information and prevent intentional or accidental "dark side" CRM activity such as information misuse, privacy invasion, choice or financial manipulation, or the newest potential ethical consideration, bias in artificial intelligence algorithms and predictive modeling (Frow et al. 2011; Marcinkevage 2017b). Having data aggregated in one platform allows for more effective security of data as a single model, as opposed to multiple engagement systems requiring duplicative administration. Data compliance that may include FERPA (https://www2.ed.gov/policy/gen/guid/fpco/ferpa/index.html), HIPAA (https://www.hhs.gov/hipaa/index.html), and GDPR (https://eugdpr.org/) can be administered centrally to diverse user populations to ensure only users with a legitimate business need for the data would have access to them. This can be driven by security design that can be governed by designated CRM leadership instead of distributed management with departmental applications. Along with this overarching access administration, the CRM can also manage who has the ability to access, export, and implement decisions based upon sensitive university data. Lastly, the organization can form collaborative teams to ensure that automation and artificial intelligence applications are as bias-free as possible. These factors, along with transparent audit capabilities, significantly increase accountability and ethical use of constituent information.

Conclusion

Today's higher education landscape includes an increasingly competitive market. Some entrepreneurially minded institutions have developed corporate-inspired business models and processes, and they typically leverage mature CRM-based technologies that enable personalized service from recruitment to degree. It is not unusual for students to complete their application, be admitted, obtain financial aid, and complete registration in a matter of hours rather than the days, or more likely months, that it takes at some less forward-thinking institutions. And all this is done through a smooth, personalized process with Amazon-like service. Tolerance for redundant forms, long delays in application response, and daytime, on-site-only service is minimal. Applicants gravitate to easy-to-use, personalized, always-on, self-guiding services and those institutions that provide a digitally enabled enrollment process. Students and alumni benefit from this connected campus system. These institutions benefit from the data to tailor future interactions, not just with students, but beyond as alumni, donors, and parents and through a lifetime of engagement.

To compete in this marketplace, more colleges and universities must build a deeply connected experience with all their constituents. Only personalized communication that is meaningful, relevant, and timely will position higher education leaders to nurture these relationships within their institution. By leveraging a CRM with all constituent engagements with the institution, technology can automate and enable engagement regardless of place or time. This nurturing of data and affiliation creates lasting relationships across individuals and organizations. It builds the lifelong ties upon which the institution's success is built.

References

Ayoubi, A., and C. Marcinkevage. 2015. "Get the Job Done: Put Students and Employers at the Center of Career Services." Online Video. https://www.salesforce.com/video/194653/.

Britt, P. 2018. "Colleges Can't Cling to Old CRM Technology." Destination CRM. Accessed April 27, 2019. https://www.destinationcrm.com/Articles/ReadArticle.aspx?ArticleID=127678.

Chen, I. J., and K. Popovich. 2003. "Understanding Customer Relationship Management (CRM): People, Process and Technology." *Business Process Management 9*, no. 5: 672–688. https://doi.org/10.1108/14637150310496758.

Conner, K. 2017. "Leveraging Salesforce to Drive Career Center Success." Youtube Video. https://www.youtube.com/watch?v=W3_-2XBNqWM.

De Luca, A., and J. Glassman. 2014. "Building a One-Stop Shop for Exceptional Constituent Service." Online Video. Accessed April 23, 2019. https://www.salesforce.org/events/hesummit-day-one-breakout-1/building-one-stop-shop-exceptional-constituent-service/.

Del Rowe, S. 2019. "The State of Customer Relationship Management 2019." *EContent Magazine*. February 6, 2019. http://www.econtentmag.com/Articles/Editorial/Feature/The-State-of-Customer-Relationship-Management-2019-129249.htm.

Dixon, A. 2017. "The Business Strategy of a CRM in Higher Education Is a Student Support Decision." The Evolllution. June 28, 2017. https://evolllution.com/attracting-students/customer_service/the-business-strategy-of-a-crm-in-higher-education-is-a-student-support-decision/.

Egan, K., D. Mossaidis, and E. Morris. 2015. "Alumni Communication and Community." Online Video. https://www.salesforce.org/alumni-communication-and-community/.

Fayerman, M. 2002. "Customer Relationship Management." In *Knowledge Management. New Directions for Institutional Research* no. 113 (Spring): 57–67. https://doi.org/10.1002/ir.37.

Frow, P., A. Payne, I. F. Wilkinson, and L. Young. 2011. "Customer Management and CRM: Addressing the Dark Side." *Journal of Services Marketing* 25, no. 2: 79–89. https://doi.org/10.1108/08876041111119804.

Gaska, C. L. 2003. "CRM Hits the Campus." *University Business Magazine* 6: 28–32.

Gholami, H., M. Zameri Mat Saman, A. Mardani, D. Streimikiene, S. Sharif, and N. Zakuan. 2018. "Proposed Analytic Framework for Student Relationship Management Based on a Systematic Review of CRM Systems Literature." *Sustainability* 10, no. 4: 1–20. https://doi.org/10.3390/su10041237.

Guilbault, M. 2018. "Students as Customers in Higher Education: The (Controversial) Debate Needs to End." *Journal of Retailing and Consumer Services* 40: 295–298. https://doi.org/10.1016/j.jretconser.2017.03.006.

Hemsley-Brown, J., and I. Oplatka. 2006. "Universities in a Competitive Global Marketplace: A Systematic Review of the Literature on Higher Education Marketing." *International Journal of Public Sector Management* 19, no. 4: 316–338. https://doi.org/10.1108/09513550610669176.

Johal, N. 2017. "Positioning Enterprise-Wide CRM as a Strategic Asset Delivers Long-Term Value to Institutions: The Way Forward to Transform the Student Experience and Enable Student Success." *Ovum TMT Intelligence* (February): 1–11.

Kilgore, W. 2014. "CRM Usage Gap in Higher Education." The American Association of Collegiate Registrars and Admissions Officers. Accessed June 30, 2018. https://www.aacrao.org/resources/newsletters-blogs/aacrao-connect/article/aacrao-study--crm-usage-gap-in-higher-education.

Korasiga, V. R., and Y. Kiranmayi. 2013. "Innovation in Educational Institutions." *International Journal of Applied Services Marketing Perspectives* 2, no. 4: 587–597.

Langston, R., and D. Loreto. 2017. "Seamless Integration of Predictive Analytics and CRM within an Undergraduate Admissions Recruitment and Marketing Plan." *Strategic Enrollment Management Quarterly* 4, no. 4: 161–172. https://doi.org/10.1002/sem3.20095.

Lawson-Body, A., L. Willoughby, L. Mukankusi, and K. Logossah. 2011. "The Critical Success Factors for Public Sector CRM Implementation." *Journal of Computer Information Systems* 52, no. 2 (Winter): 42–50. https://doi.org/10.1080/08874417.2011.11645539.

Mainland, N. 2018. "Our Journey to Education Cloud for Higher Ed." Salesforce. Accessed April 23, 2019. https://www.salesforce.org/our-journey-to-education-cloud-for-higher-ed/.

Marcinkevage, C. 2017a. "Dear Old State! An Exploratory Study of Constituent Engagement Strategy Evolution in Higher Education." Manuscript submitted for publication.

———. 2017b. "Ethical Issues in Higher Education Customer Relationship Management (CRM)." Unpublished manuscript.

McClure, A. 2006. "Retention Intentions." *University Business Magazine* 9 (August): 45–49.

Mendoza, L. E., A. Marius, M. Pérez, and A. C. Grimán. 2007. "Critical Success Factors for a Customer Relationship Management Strategy." *Information and*

Software Technology 49, no. 8: 913–945. https://doi.org/10.1016/j.infsof.2006.10
.003.

Payne, A. F., and P. Frow. 2005. "A Strategic Framework for Customer Relationship
Management." *Journal of Marketing* 69, no. 4: 167–176. https://doi.org/10.1509
/jmkg.2005.69.4.167.

Pember, E. R., A. Owens, and S. Yaghi. 2014. "Customer Relationship Management:
A Case Study from a Metropolitan Campus of a Regional University." *Journal of
Higher Education Policy and Management* 36, no. 2: 117–128. https://doi.org/10
.1080/1360080X.2013.861056.

Pollock, N., and J. Cornford. 2004. "ERP Systems and the University as a 'Unique'
Organisation." *Information Technology & People* 17, no. 1: 31–52. https://doi
.org/10.1108/09593840410522161.

Polona, S., and P. Iztok. 2018. "The Concept of Customer Relationship Management
(CRM) in Higher Education." In *27th International Scientific Conference on
Economic and Social Development*, 1–7. Rome, Italy: VADEA.

Rahimi, I. D., and U. Berman. 2009. "Building a CSF Framework for CRM Implementation." *Journal of Database Marketing & Customer Strategy Management*
16, no. 4: 253–265. https://doi.org/10.1057/dbm.2009.29.

Rigo, G.-E., C. D. Pedron, M. Caldeira, and C. C. Silva de Araújo. 2016. "CRM
Adoption in a Higher Education Institution." *Journal of Information Systems and
Technology Management* 13, no. 1: 45–60. https://doi.org/10.4301/S1807
-17752016000100003.

Sin, L. Y. M., A. C. B. Tse, and F. H. K. Yim. 2005. "CRM: Conceptualization and
Scale Development." *European Journal of Marketing* 39, no. 11–12: 1264–1290.
https://doi.org/10.1108/03090560510623253.

"Strategic Planning." 2007. *Enrollment Management* 10 (August): 1–12.

Tapp, A., K. Hicks, and M. Stone. 2004. "Direct and Database Marketing and
Customer Relationship Management in Recruiting Students for Higher Education." *International Journal of Nonprofit and Voluntary Sector Marketing* 9,
no. 4: 335–345. https://doi.org/10.1002/nvsm.258.

Trocchia, P. J., R. Z. Finney, and T. G. Finney. 2013. "Effectiveness of Relationship
Marketing Tactics in a University Setting." *Journal of College Teaching &
Learning* 10, no. 1: 29–38. https://doi.org/10.19030/tlc.v10i1.7528.

Vedder, R. 2017. "Seven Challenges Facing Higher Education." *Forbes Magazine.*
August 29, 2017. https://www.forbes.com/sites/ccap/2017/08/29/seven-challenges
-facing-higher-education/#526f16db3180.

Wang, M.-L., and F. F. Yang. 2010. "How Does CRM Create Better Customer
Outcomes for Small Educational Institutions?" *African Journal of Business
Management* 4, no. 16: 3541–3549. https://doi.org/10.5897/AJBM.

Learning Analytics for Learning Assessment

Complexities in Efficacy, Implementation, and Broad Use

Carrie Klein, Jaime Lester, Huzefa Rangwala, and Aditya Johri

THE RISE of educational technology in academia is transforming teaching and learning. Among the educational technologies in use in academia today are learning management systems (LMS), early alert or early warning advising systems (EWS), and other tools that provide information on and management of student performance, course retention, and degree progress. At the same time, the capacity to harvest, store, and analyze large data sets, via data mining, analytics, and machine learning technologies, has also expanded (Ferguson and Clow 2017; Peña-Ayala 2018). As a result, educational technologies are increasingly employing learning analytics–based tools to make meaning of the vast amounts of data produced by higher education organizations and their members.

Learning analytics are educational Big Data that govern "the measurement, collection, analysis and reporting of data about learners and their contexts, for the purposes of understanding and optimizing learning and the environments in which it occurs" (Siemens 2013, 3). These educational Big Data, which are inclusive of student demographic, performance, and location data and that span curricular and co-curricular interactions, can illuminate trends that may not be visible via smaller data sets (Long and Siemens 2011). Defined by their volume, variety, and velocity of delivery, learning analytics data provide organizations with the potential to rapidly respond to complex organizational demands. The real-time, personalized, and actionable feedback provided by learning analytics can support decision making for administrators, faculty, and students alike. Through dashboards (i.e., tool interfaces) that visualize learning analytics data into easily digestible graphics and interventions, opportunities are created for administrators to assess trends in student retention and completion rates, for faculty to assess pedagogical approaches and course designs based on student performance and interactions, and for students to assess their learning behaviors based on their effort, performance, and outcomes (Macfadyen and Dawson 2012; Norris and Baer 2013; Peña-Ayala 2018).

As their popularity in higher education organizations grows, research on the development and use of learning analytics to assess teaching and learning is also burgeoning. At the Learning Analytics and Knowledge (LAK) conference (arguably the foremost conference in the field of learning analytics) more than 1,400 papers related to learning analytics have been presented between 2012 and 2018, and that pace is likely to continue (Viberg et al. 2018). Even with a vast and rapidly expanding cache of learning analytics literature (and associated tools) to pull from, the majority of the literature has focused primarily on smaller exploratory and experimental tools and has been evaluative and descriptive in nature (Ferguson and Clow 2017; Viberg et al. 2018). Missing is a broader understanding of how learning analytics tools are conceptualized, adopted, and used in practice by higher education organizational members.

This gap in the literature is narrowing as researchers, technologists, and technology users are acknowledging the importance of empirically understanding the interactions, outcomes, and implications for higher education organizations and individuals using learning analytics tools. This shift in focus is welcome, as issues related to scaling learning analytic tools to broader use within and between higher education organizations have emerged, including tool efficacy and alignment, organizational capacity and readiness, ethics and privacy concerns, and user interests and needs (Arnold, Lonn, and Pistilli 2014; Klein et al. 2019a, 2019b; Lester et al. 2017; Norris and Baer 2013; Prinsloo and Slade 2013, 2015; Rubel and Jones 2016; Slade and Prinsloo 2013).

The purpose of this chapter is to add to the growing body of literature focused on providing a sociological understanding of learning analytics used to assess teaching and learning. Pulling from the extant literature and from our own recent work on a National Science Foundation—funded exploratory study on learning analytics (IIS-1447489), we have divided this chapter into three parts. In the first part of the chapter, we provide examples of current learning analytics tools and research projects focused on learning assessments and an overview of the value, potential opportunities, and effectiveness of learning analytics tools. Because successful implementation and scaling of any innovation is dependent upon the context in which it is deployed, in the second part of the chapter, we review some of the technological, organizational, ethical, and individual constraints and concerns that work against scaling learning analytics. The chapter concludes with implications and recommendations for higher education stakeholders, who may be thinking about implementing or improving learning analytics tool use at their institutions.

Scope, Value, and Efficacy

Learning analytics is now in its adolescence, having emerged in the mid-2000s alongside the development and growth in capacity for data mining and machine learning (Ferguson and Clow 2017; Peña-Ayala 2018; Viberg et al. 2018). Developed as a result of technological advances in the late 1990s that allowed institutions to gather large data sets from their learning management systems (LMS), like Blackboard and Moodle, by 2003, these tools had evolved from data collection and analysis resources to more "socially and pedagogically driven" (Ferguson 2012, 5) tools that provided users (e.g., faculty, advisors, and students) with opportunities to make meaning and take action based on visualized learning analytics data (Siemens 2013). Learning analytics tools incorporate various aspects of learning measurement and support, including monitoring, analyzing, and predicting student performance, providing adaptions, advising, assessment, and feedback to personalize learning, aligning student performance with degree pathways, and alerting students via interventions to encourage reflection and to change learning behaviors (de los Santos and Milliron 2015; Ferguson and Clow 2017).

Importantly, while there is general agreement on what learning analytics is (i.e., the definition given earlier in this chapter), what data comprise learning analytics still remain relatively broad and dependent upon technological and organizational context and interest. For instance, Van Barneveld, Arnold, and Campbell (2012) have noted in their review of the literature that, despite their nuanced differences, academic, business, learning, and predictive analytics terms have often been conflated by data scientists, developers, and users of learning analytics tools. Viberg et al. (2018) also note the closely related nature of academic analytics, learning analytics, and educational data mining and the potential for overlap not just of terminology but of data within these varied analytics (i.e., "automated discovery" of student learning, 98).

Despite the conflation of nearly related terms and concepts, Van Barneveld, Arnold, and Campbell's (2012) recommended typologies for analytics have generally been accepted and in use since 2012. They argued that the term *academic analytics* should operate at the institutional or organizational level and should include business analytics and encompass any data that support "operation and financial decision making"; the term *learning analytics* should operate at the department or learner level and should support "resources to support the achievement of specific learning goals"; and *predictive analytics* should exist at all levels and should be used to "uncover relationships and patterns within large volumes of data that can be used to predict behavior and events" (Van Barneveld, Arnold, and Campbell 2012, 8). Viberg et al. provide further conceptions of learning analytics and educational data mining as mechanisms that support student learning through "research and practice" and that "reflect the emergence of data-intensive approaches to education" (Siemens and Baker 2012; Viberg et al. 2018, 98). They also point out the difference between the two, noting that learning analytics relies on human interaction and works to understand educational and social complexities, while educational data mining is automated and often works to create simplified correlations of complex data sets (Viberg et al. 2018, 99).

Understanding the differences between the various types of analytics data in use on higher education campuses is important for a few reasons. First, while data scientists often differentiate academic, learning, and predictive analytics, users of these data often do not. For instance, in our study of faculty and advisor users of learning analytics tools in higher education, we found that users did not always differentiate between analytic data types or even between analytics-based data and non-analytics-based data—rather, they viewed data simply as data (Klein et al. 2019a, 2019b). Further, because faculty engaged in learning assessment can also act as advisors to their students (as is often the case in engineering disciplines), they will likely use the breadth of learning and academic analytics data available to them to assess student learning and development.

Regardless of how *learning analytics* is defined, its presence has expanded dramatically in the last decade. From four-year research institutions to two-year community colleges and technical schools, higher education organizations are purchasing and implementing learning analytics–based technologies to assess and support student learning and to leverage organizational performance (de los Santos and Milliron 2015; Long and Siemens 2011). These tools and their data are being leveraged at an exponential rate to better measure, analyze, report, and predict data related to course design, major selection, and student learning, engagement, retention, and completion rates (Arnold and Pistilli 2012; Bichsel 2012; Dahlstrom, Brooks, and Bichsel 2014; Ferguson and Clow 2017; Macfadyen and Dawson 2012; Peña-Ayala 2014, 2018). Numbers vary slightly; the global education and learning analytics technology market is expected to grow from $2.6 billion in 2018 to between $7.1 billion and $8.3 billion by 2023 (Markets and Markets 2019; Market Research Future 2019). Although this is inclusive of P-12 technologies, the point is that the demand for these tools will increase by more than 25% in the next five years.

Use and Potential

Many of the tools developed in the last decade have been course-focused and rely on data visualizations and interventions based on large data sets from a variety of sources to alert users to student performance. Course Signals (CS), developed at Purdue, was one of the first learning analytics tools developed to monitor and assess course performance. Relying on demographic and academic variables, CS would assess student performance at the six-week mark and alert faculty to students who were at risk of failing the course with red, yellow, and green "traffic signals" via a dashboard interface. Faculty could then send email interventions to students, encouraging their successful completion of the course. Although successful within targeted classes—faculty using CS experienced uptick in student engagement and communication, and students reported feeling more connected to their courses and instructors (Arnold and Pistilli 2012)—CS had difficulty scaling to use across the university and is no longer in use.

The initial success of CS has led to newer learning analytics tools leveraging the ability to mine student and institutional data to provide learning and organizational assessment based on predictive modeling (Rubel and Jones 2016). Beyond providing real-time, visualized feedback to learners, learning analytics dashboards and the data underlying them have also been used to predict and communicate the likelihood of a student successfully passing courses, successful course sequencing for students, and identification of successful academic pathways (Arnold and Pistilli 2012; Irvin and Longmire 2016; Verbert et al. 2013). For example, the computer scientists on our team developed an algorithm (i.e., the formula underlying learning analytics technologies) that could successfully predict next-term grades for computer sciences and information technology students, within a plus or minus, based on prior performance of students and their peers (Sweeney, Lester, and Rangwala 2015). Our researchers were also able to identify course-taking patterns that resulted in successful or unsuccessful student pathways, with lower performers putting off difficult courses or taking combinations of courses that their successful counterparts avoided (Almatrafi et al. 2016) and to predict specific time periods when students are more at risk of dropping out (Chen, Johri, and Rangwala 2018).

While predictive tools like this can assess and illuminate individual performance to inform the individual learner, they can also alert organizations to ways they can better scaffold and support student learning. However, as the nursing school at Georgia State University (GSU) found, these predictions and alerts must be interpreted by informed faculty. Their predictive model indicated that students who had done poorly in an introductory nursing course were less likely to graduate. Although this was useful information, experienced faculty questioned the predictive data, finding that students who had earned a C in a preceding introductory math course were less likely to perform well in the subsequent introductory nursing course and successfully graduate (Treaster 2017). Digging into the predictive learning analytics data this way allowed the nursing faculty to more effectively target students who were struggling and to ultimately improve outcomes. Predictive learning analytics data can be used to help students make better academic choices and to help faculty and advisors support their progress to completion, but they must be integrated into a holistic student and organizational assessment process (e.g., one that is not driven by data but informed by data) and is paired with thoughtful and relevant interventions.

The potential of these tools is evolving beyond prediction toward personalizing the students' experience as they move through their coursework. Known as "intelligent curriculum," these tools will provide "each learner with resources, relevant to his or her profile, learning goals and the knowledge domain the learner is attempting to master" (Long and Siemens 2011, 38; Ferguson 2012). For students, the incorporation of learning analytics data into course and performance feedback can help make learning relevant, personalized, and more meaningful for students so that they can "make better and informed choices" (Slade and Prinsloo 2013, 6; Long and Siemens 2011). In turn, the use of learning analytics to provide personalized, immediate, and predictive feedback gives students and their faculty and advisors a greater understanding of their academic performance and potential. As a result, learning analytics research spans technological, organizational, and individual factors related to its use and efficacy.

Evidence of Efficacy

Learning analytics research and technologies are pushing learning measurement, design, and feedback into new areas. The potential of learning analytics tools to support personalized and interactive learning for students throughout their tenure at a college or university could transform how we think about learning and human development. The ability to identify successful course pathways and the use of tools like EAB's Student Success Collaborative are showing great progress for advising students toward better academic choices and alerting higher education organizations to students' needs. The work at Georgia State University, as discussed in chapter 8 of this volume, is a testament to that success. Further, analytics is increasingly being used to inform admissions and enrollment management, as discussed in chapter 7 in this book. Examples of these recruitment and enrollment tools are Intersect, from Starfish by Hobsons (hobsons.com), which touts the ability for institutions to "increase awareness and connect with best-fit students" (Hobsons 2019, 1) and Salesforce, which promotes its recruiting and admissions tool as being able to help institutions "reach, engage, and enroll the right students" (Salesforce 2019, 1). Notions of fit and "rightness" come with their own ethical issues, as we discuss later in this chapter, and are just part of the complexity that comes with analytics use to predict outcomes and inform choices. Further, use of analytics to support student learning beyond identification of pathways or predictions of performance—true learning analytics—is as complex as the learning process itself. As a result, although the potential for a learning revolution exists, actual evidence of learning analytics effectiveness in improving student learning outcomes is limited.

As learning analytics has developed, so too has a framework for reporting evidence of its efficacy and use. Ferguson and Clow (2017), in their review of literature within the Learning Analytics Community Exchange (LACE) knowledge hub, argue learning analytics research, data, and tools need to be designed, studied, and evaluated with four evidence-producing propositions in mind, namely, that learning analytics must: (1) improve learning outcomes, (2) improve learning support and teaching, (3) be adopted and widely used and deployed at scale, and (4) be ethically used (59). Evidence of improved learning outcomes in the literature is limited, and the focus of evidence and use to improve learning outcomes has focused more on potential than results (Viberg et al. 2018). However, in their review of learning analytics tool efficacy, Viberg, et al. (2018) state that there is some evidence that learning analytics use has improved *knowledge acquisition* (e.g., Guarcello et al. 2017; Mangaroska et al. 2018; Tempelaar et al. 2013; Whitelock et al. 2015), *skill development* (e.g., Kwong, Wong, and Yue 2017; Ochoa et al. 2018; Tabuenca et al. 2015; Worsley 2018), and *cognitive gains* (e.g,, Gašević, Mirriahi, and Dawson 2014; Chiu and Fujita 2014).

Viberg et al. (2018) found stronger evidence that learning analytics is effectively addressing Ferguson and Clow's (2017) second proposition—*improve learning support and teaching.* For example, evidence exists that student interaction with analytics dashboards and their feedback can result in better performance and outcomes in a course. For example, Brown, DeMonbrun, and Teasley (2017) found that students who incorporated feedback from learning dashboards early in their semester or before facing difficulty in a course were more likely to be successful, indicating that feedback can spur increased interest in successful course completion. Additional focus of evidence in this area has been on *student retention* via prediction and faculty and advisor interventions (e.g., Chen, Johri, and Rangwala 2018; Junco and Clem 2015; Rienties, Toetenel, and Bryan 2015) and on *learning design* via faculty and advisor support (e.g., Echeverria et al. 2018; Rienties, Toetenel, and Bryan 2015; Tempelaar, Rienties, and Nguyen 2017; Worsley and Blikstein 2015). Notably, for proposition three, *learning analytics being taken up and used widely,* according to Viberg et al. (2018), 94% of the papers they reviewed provided evidence that learning analytics data and tools would not "scale to entire institutions or other institutions" and only 18% of analytics papers address ethical use of learning analytics data (107). The limited mention of ethics and lack of evidence of improved learning outcomes and scalable solutions are problematic and speak to the limitations and concerns associated with learning analytics use in higher education.

Conditions Influencing Scalability

No matter how innovative a technology is, it is only useful to organizations and its members if its intended users choose to adopt and employ that technology into their practices. Otherwise, the ability to scale these technologies beyond local use is hampered. For learning analytics users, decisions to adopt and regularly use these tools rely on several conditions that span technological, organizational, and ethical concerns. Moreover, individual socialization, beliefs, routines, and capacity to incorporate these tools often lead to limited use and broad scale of these tools across an organization.

Technological Factors

Technological constraints exist on multiple levels, including a lack of appropriate infrastructure, adequate support and technical staff, adequate levels of data, and lack of alignment and integration of learning analytics tool data into already existing technologies that impact tool efficacy (Arnold, Lonn, and Pistilli 2014; Bichsel 2012; Klein et al. 2019b; Norris and Baer 2013). Research indicates that the ability to gain trusted, accurate, visually understandable, and relevant data that align with students' needs are key factors related to adoption (Aguilar 2018; Ali et al. 2012; Dawson, McWilliam, and Tan 2008; Klein et al. 2019a, 2019b; Lester et al. 2017). Of the studies focused on faculty use of learning analytics tools, the majority of work concentrates on the barriers to adoption of these tools, namely, a lack of clearly visualized, relevant, timely, personalized, or trustworthy data (Aguilar, Lonn, and Teasley 2014; Dahlstrom, Brooks, and Bichsel 2014; Dawson, McWilliam, and Tan 2008; Hora, Bouwma-Gearheart, and Park 2017; Lester et al. 2017; Lockyer, Heathcote, and Dawson 2013).

In our work, we found that, while learning analytics technologies were often met with interest by faculty and advisors to assist with learning assessment, they were also poorly integrated with other campus technologies and often misaligned with faculty and advisor needs, interests, and institutional reward structures (Klein et al. 2019b). As a result of these realities, the efficacy of learning analytics tools to assess teaching and learning was limited because faculty, staff, and students had limited interest in using tools with misaligned, incorrect, or useless data. In our study of student use of learning analytics dashboard interventions (Lester et al. 2017), we found similar results, including student frustration by learning analytics data that were incorrect, poorly visualized, and not tied to students' comprehensive academic records (see also Aguilar 2018). Inaccurate and misaligned learning analytics data are often not trusted by users, which can limit faculty's, advisors', and students' belief in the assessments they receive through these systems.

Organizational Factors

Institutional structures, commitment, resources, readiness, and capacity, and a lack of incentives and rewards, are some of the organizational factors that influence learning analytics use (Arnold, Lonn, and Pistilli 2014; Bichsel 2012; Klein et al. 2019a; Macfadyen and Dawson 2012; Norris and Baer 2013). Norris and Baer (2013), Arnold, Lonn, and Pistilli (2014), and Oster, Lonn, Pistilli, and Brown (2016) have noted that a lack of proper infrastructure, resources, personnel, and culture of learning analytics readiness can negatively impact the deployment of these tools on campus. Issues of capacity and readiness create an environment that informs individual use and perception of analytics tools.

In our work, we found that, in addition to infrastructure and resources, context specific issues impacted learning analytics use by advisors and faculty (Klein et al. 2019a). This included different tools used by different colleges and departments within the same organization, which effectively siloed student learning assessments to one part of the organization. Limited communication across departments and colleges extended to limited communication as to how federal and organizational policies governed use of those data. Lack of inclusion led to frustration from users who did not see alignment between learning analytics tools and their work. Unclear or outdated policies created concern for faculty and advisors over approved or appropriate practices for using these data. In fact, learning analytics scholars have called for more policies, guidelines, and practices for learning analytics use (Tsai and Gašević 2017; Tsai et al. 2018). While those are emerging, few have been universally agreed upon by scholars or adopted within academic organizations. However, given the increasing ethical concerns related to use of these data, more attention to privacy and data protection policy is needed.

Ethical Concerns

Researchers are only now beginning to understand ethics, power, and privacy implications related to learning analytics. Recent scholarly papers and studies have focused on issues of surveillance and power (Andrejevic 2011; Knox 2010; Lyon 2007; Selwyn 2015); privacy protections (Coll, Glassey, and Balleys 2011; Kraemer, Van Overveld, and Peterson 2011; Prinsloo and Slade 2013, 2015; Slade and Prinsloo 2013); algorithmic bias and opacity in black-box proprietary systems (Hajian, Bonchi, and Castillo 2016; Selwyn 2015; Zeide 2017); and ethical and socially just use of data (Johnson 2014; Pardo and Siemens 2014; Slade and Prinsloo 2013; Taylor 2017). Additionally, issues related to how data are created, conceptualized, collected, secured, and controlled have also come to the fore (Pardo and Siemens 2014; Slade and Prinsloo 2013; Steiner, Kickmeier-Rust, and Albert 2016). Attention to ethical issues like these is paramount in analytics use for learning assessment, as there is often a tendency in Big Data systems, like learning analytics, for the predicted outcome to become the decision (Selwyn 2015). In this case, assumptions about fit and "rightness" could easily move from well-intentioned data gathering and analysis toward discriminatory and biased outcomes through tracking and classifying students and their data (Selwyn 2015; Slade and Prinsloo 2015; Zeide 2017).

As a result of these concerns, federal and state agencies are paying more attention to the policies that govern learning analytics for educational assessment. Yet, the United States has lagged behind the EU in reassessing its privacy policies related to analytics data use. The European Union (EU) has been at the fore of this work, recently developing the General Data Protection Regulation (GDPR). The GDPR requires secure data protection process (including consent) and protocol for data (General Data Protection Regulation [GDPR] 2019). While the recent regulations process negotiated by the Department of Education focused on privacy protections for online learning data and both the Health Insurance Portability and Accountability Act of 1996 (HIPAA) and Family Educational Rights and Privacy Act of 1974 (FERPA) have provided some oversight over analytics data use and protection, as Brown and Klein (2019) recently argued, these policies are fairly limited in scope and not reflective of the advances in data mining, storage, and analysis that are possible with learning analytics technologies, especially those that are proprietary, black-box systems.

Notably, the proprietary nature of many of the learning analytics tools on the market has resulted in a movement to more transparent, open-source, adaptive learning technologies, like Smart Sparrow. These tools leverage the power of open, transparent technologies that are controlled by the needs and interests of faculty to aid in learning assessment. For instance, Smart Sparrow is a teacher-centered platform that is directly accessible to faculty and their departments and allows faculty to share course designs, best practices, and assessments (Blumenstyk 2016). The accessibility and relevance of these tools to course design and learning assessment may change the ways that faculty interact with adaptive learning analytics platforms. However, even when tools are transparent and open, the issue that remains is scaling them to broader use, as Smart Sparrow's creator attests: "Actually getting it to be used at scale, that's the hard part" (Blumenstyk 2016).

Individual Factors

Despite the presence and proliferation of learning analytics and the potential its data offer, like other educational technologies, their adoption by faculty is not universal (Bichsel 2012; Brown, Dehoney, and Millichap 2015). For example, although a majority of faculty are familiar with and access LMS tools (arguably the most ubiquitous technology in education), only about half use these tools regularly, and a majority do not use them to their full potential to assess learning (Brown, Dehoney, and Millichap 2015; Dahlstrom, Brooks, and Bichsel 2014). Individual decisions by faculty and advisors to use or refuse pedagogical innovations often hinge upon their disciplinary socialization. Socialization plays a strong role in establishing and locking-in professional beliefs, including the adoption of new technologies (Amey 1999; Austin 2003, 2011; Bichsel 2012; Dahlstrom, Brooks, and Bichsel 2014; Fairweather 2002, 2008; Locke 1995; Norris and Baer 2013; Tagg 2012). Faculty disciplinary difference and acculturation can have a large impact on whether faculty adopt or reject new approaches to teaching pedagogy, course design, and student advising as it informs both professional beliefs related to these tools and the subsequent behaviors that govern their adoption and use (Austin 2011; Brownell and Tanner 2012; Fairweather 2008).

Professional Beliefs

The decision to adopt a pedagogical innovation is deeply tied to faculty professional beliefs, which inform subsequent behaviors (Hora and Holden 2013; Kagan 1992; Liu 2011; Ottenbreit-Leftwich et al. 2010). Professional beliefs are comprised of attitudes and values that are acknowledged to be "unconsciously held assumptions about students, classrooms and the academic material to be taught" (Kagan 1992, 65; Ottenbreit-Leftwich et al. 2010). The belief (or lack thereof) in the value of a technology supersedes experience in decisions to use a technology (Ertmer et al. 2012; Ertmer 2005; Hora and Holden 2013; Liu 2011). As Liu (2011) notes, "even when teachers have sufficient successful experiences with technology, teachers do not necessarily integrate technology into instruction" (1012). Faculty must believe that an innovation or technology is useful, applicable, capable, and flexible to their needs and desires and that their organizations have the organizational capacity in place to ensure the efficient and effective implementation and use of these tools (Hora and Holden 2013; Norris and Baer 2013; Venkatesh and Bala 2008). To change behavior, technology users must see an alignment between the proposed technology and their beliefs in its value, ability, and capacity to improve teaching and learning (Ertmer 2005; Ertmer et al. 2012; Hora and Holden 2013; Liu 2011; Ottenbreit-Leftwich et al. 2010).

Professional Behaviors

Because professional beliefs are core to subsequent professional practice and decision making, it is necessary to understand the factors that influence faculty behaviors. Johri (2018) argues that diffusion of analytics technology among faculty is tied to individual absorptive capacity and routines. Absorptive capacity is a generative form of learning in which an organization relies on prior knowledge "to recognize, assimilate, and apply new information in innovative ways" (Johri 2018, 7; Cohen and Levinthal 1990; Lane, Koka, and Pathak 2006). Tied to beliefs and socialization, absorptive capacity has been extended to explain how individual faculty use prior knowledge from their organizations to make sense of their environments (Da Silva and Davis 2011; Zahra and George 2002). This sense-making could include decisions to use analytics to assess learning and teaching. Johri argues that faculty who are proficient with LMS and have had positive experiences with the tool are more likely to incorporate that prior knowledge use of LMS and their data to support students in their learning and assess their teaching and course design.

However, prior socialization, beliefs, knowledge, and experience to support analytics use may not be enough to overcome individual routines and organizational pressures. Routines are the standardized habits, norms, and day-to-day activities that govern professional behaviors (Cyert and March 1963; Johri 2018; Lewin, Massini, and Peeters 2011; Pentland and Feldman 2005). Johri (2018) and Lewin et al. (2011) have argued that absorptive capacity and routines intersect at the knowledge-action point, meaning that individual absorptive capacity informs legitimate changes to routine. An example of this interaction is the role that available time and organizational incentives play in informing faculty decisions to employ analytics technology.

Fairweather (2008) notes that faculty will often reject a pedagogical innovation, despite evidence of effectiveness, because the time required to change current behaviors and learn new ways of being is considered too great. Across the literature, researchers note that faculty often resist, and are incentivized against, change (Amey 1999; Austin 2003, 2011; Fairweather 2002, 2008; Locke 1995; Tagg 2012). The time necessary to change a behavior or to adopt a new practice is a pull that faculty (especially new faculty) can ill afford, as their priorities often lie in time spent writing for publication, not learning a new technology (Austin 2011; Zellweger 2007). This is especially true in organizations that are research-focused, wherein faculty time is constrained by reward systems that privilege research over pedagogical professional development (Fairweather and Beach 2002). Regardless of type, institutions rarely provide individuals with the training and professional development opportunities necessary to encourage changes in pedagogical practice by expanding their absorptive capacity related to analytics use and inform subsequent routines (Austin 2011; Johri 2018; Zellweger 2007).

Beliefs and Behaviors in Practice

In our work, we have found that faculty and advisors were more likely to use learning analytics tools when those tools aligned with their professional beliefs, supported their valued behaviors, and were relevant to their roles (Lester et al. 2017). Both faculty and advisors in the study noted that a student-centered model informs their philosophical perspectives on teaching and advising. One faculty member noted that his belief is based on "recognizing the student as a whole person." Advisors shared similar pedagogical beliefs, saying that their work with students was predicated upon "recognizing that every person comes with some individual needs . . . so you have to take each person individually and support each person differently because some people won't need my help at all and some people will need my help a lot." Ideally, the personalized nature of learning analytics tools meant to support student learning would align well with the beliefs of these faculty and advisors. Yet, the connections between the two were often not obvious to faculty and advisors, who were often worried about the risks versus rewards of integrating learning analytics tools into their assessments of students.

Among the concerns that faculty and advisors expressed was a belief that use of learning analytics data would create bias, by giving them too much or irrelevant information about their students. Bias was, in fact, the biggest concern related to using learning analytics tools. Participants worried that access to information, especially predictive information, might negatively bias their interactions with a student or be "risky," in that they might make decisions based on a student's potential outcome versus current performance. For instance, if faculty members knew a student's grades in other courses in a major, they might assume that the student should receive a similar grade in their course. Advisors worried that predictive data might steer a student away from an area of interest (or might steer their advising of that student), rather than using that information to help encourage student progress.

Despite some of the concerns about access to learning analytics data, many participants also acknowledged that additional information could help them improve teaching and learning. The ability to use learning analytics tools to improve teaching that aligns with faculty beliefs and engages student learning was viewed as valuable, especially if it contained a feedback mechanism, as many of the newer learning analytics–based tools do. A tenured faculty member explained, "So, this . . . all the technology, learning sciences research that is going on right now— that's a huge help. How we approach students and how we approach teaching and particularly learning. So, feedback is absolutely critical." This feedback creates a record from which faculty can learn, consider, and reconsider their teaching beliefs and behaviors. As a result, it refocuses faculty concerns toward learning analytics benefits, making adoption more likely. The benefit of learning analytics feedback also extends to advisors in the study, who are able to find more meaning and see trends across the 200–500 students on their individual workloads. As one advisor explained, she used learning analytics tools "to notice patterns and notice different types of students and problems, and use certain, um, databases . . . to proactively reach out to my students." This advisor values the feedback and information learning analytics provides as a means to quickly get to know students and to see patterns among those students. Having timely and time-saving feedback allows the rest of the session to be focused on valued appreciative advising practices—again, an example of informational concerns being addressed by the capability of adopted technologies.

An important finding from our work was that faculty and staff mull through the complexities of decision making related to learning analytics adoption by balancing the perceived benefits of tool use with the perceived barriers, namely: whether a tool aligns with their professional beliefs, whether a tool can be trusted, whether it can improve or enhance their current practices, and whether their concerns about using technologies are addressed. This finding is in keeping with the literature on faculty behavior change, wherein users must be able to see both the usefulness of a tool to their work and the connection of that tool to their social and professional norms, time constraints, and rewards systems (Austin 2011; Fairweather 2008; Hall 1979; Hora and Holden 2013). To overcome the ingrained nature of internal beliefs, learning analytics tools must be "proven" to be effective and relevant for faculty or advisor participants to decide to adopt this technology. An advisor in our study explained that she needed to see how they can benefit from using new technologies; "what would get me to want to use it is if you could show me something that it was going to do that I can't see for myself already." When learning analytics tools enhance the goals of an individual user's beliefs by supporting or improving his or her time-tested behaviors, that user is more likely to employ that particular tool. As Fairweather (2008) and Venkatesh et al. (2003) have argued in their work on innovation diffusion and adoption, proof of concept and efficacy are important factors, beyond socialization's impact, on decisions by users to adopt. When learning analytics tools meet these standards, user concerns or resistance that emerge in the adoption process are addressed and the likelihood of tool adoption increases.

The importance of understanding faculty and advisor beliefs and subsequent behaviors related to pedagogical innovation adoption cannot be overstated. Regardless of the potential that learning analytics technologies possess to enhance the assessment of teaching and learning, that potential will not be realized if faculty and advisors cannot see the need, relevance, or efficacy of these tools and, as a result, choose not to adopt them. Learning assessment through learning analytics is dependent upon faculty and advisor absorptive capacity to understand the relevance of these tools to their work and subsequently incorporate these tools into their routines. Further, the interventions and alerts sent to students to notify them of performance and progress are not and should not be generated in a technological vacuum. Rather, they are dependent upon faculty and advisors' interpretations and decisions to use these data. The need for learning analytics data to be contextualized in this way underscores the importance of addressing related technological, organizational, and ethical concerns, so that learning analytics can be scaled to broader use and greater effect. The following recommendations for successful learning analytics use are informed from this perspective.

Recommendations for Successful Learning Analytics Assessment

Learning analytics technologies have the potential to improve student outcomes and organizational metrics. These tools are rapidly evolving, and while colleges and universities can benefit from these advancements, officials must also ensure efficacious and equitable use of these tools to assess student learning. Further, successful implementation and use of these tools can be limited when faculty users do not see or experience an alignment between analytics technologies and their professional needs, beliefs, priorities, and practices. The following implications and recommendations for senior organizational leaders to improve use in higher education at scale by laying the groundwork for improved user absorptive capacity and by better aligning these technologies with user perspectives and routines, are considerations of relevancy, context, and transparency.

Relevance Is Key

To ensure relevance of learning analytics tools to those who will be using these tools, consideration of context, goals, and priorities should include the perspectives of faculty, advisor, and student users. As reported in another paper from this project, when analytics tool vendors create tools with educators in mind, they often do so without deep knowledge or understanding of the professional norms, desires, experiences, and practices of their users (Klein et al. 2019a). This lack of awareness by learning analytics developers limits the tools' applicability to users. Further, these tools are often purchased by administrators, who, despite being well intentioned, are not always attuned to particularities of teaching and advising practices (Klein et al. 2019a). Consequently, learning analytics tools, like other technologies, are often unevenly used and poorly adopted (Ertmer 2005; Hora and Holden 2013; Klein et al. 2019a; Ottenbreit-Leftwich et al. 2010).

Establishing learning analytics councils that are inclusive of faculty, students, and staff, in addition to institutional research and technology professionals and other administrators, can help organizations to leverage the knowledge and expertise of faculty and advisors and to improve the relevancy, training, support, and outcomes of learning analytics tools for all stakeholders. In their recent work, Knight et al. (2018) found that inclusion of students and faculty in analytics tool design creates more relevant and useful end products. Consequently, tool designers should incorporate users into the design process, administrators should include users in the implementation process, and faculty and advisors should actively seek to participate in these processes to ensure their perspectives are included, concerns are addressed, and needs are met.

Context Matters

Leaders must consider the unique contexts of their organizations and the relevance of learning analytics tools not just to the organization but also its members. As described in a recent work (Palmer 2018), not all learning analytics tools work for all institutional types or interests and what works well in one environment may not translate well to another. To ensure relevancy of learning analytics assessments, before tools are purchased or implemented, leaders must outline their organizational priorities and goals and consider their organizational culture, resources, and readiness for learning analytics, per Norris and Baer (2013) and Arnold, Lonn, and Pistilli (2014). The Learning Analytics Readiness Instrument (LARI) was developed by Arnold, Lonn, and Pistilli (2014) and tested by Oster, Lonn, Pistilli, and Brown (2016) at more than 24 two- and four-year institutions through surveys with more than 560 campus stakeholders and campus leaders to help organizations assess their readiness to deploy learning analytics technologies. The LARI provides a mechanism to help organizations take stock of their organizational strengths and areas for improvement (specifically, structures, expertise, resources, communication, and culture) as it relates to analytics implementation and adoption. Because the LARI incorporates measures that focus on a culture of analytics readiness, an audit of this nature can help to identify faculty and advisors' beliefs and conceptions related to use of these tools. Contextualizing users' perceptions prior to implementation can help broaden later adoption.

Transparency Aids Process

Beyond including faculty and advisors in the implementation of these tools, organizations must be transparent about how they are going to use the data generated from these tools to assess student learning. As with other forms of assessment, faculty and advisors can be deeply skeptical about how data about their teaching and student learning will be used by the administration (Beattie, Woodley, and Souter 2014; Carless 2009; Klein and Hess 2018). Working collaboratively (through inclusion) to establish transparent organizational objectives can help to establish trust, shift perspectives, and lay the groundwork for relevant, ethical, and broad data use. The development of inclusive data governance councils is one way to get at inclusive and transparent collaboration. RioSalado Community College and the University of Michigan have such groups in place, which rely on the involvement not just of data professionals but also faculty, advisor, and student members.

Also necessary is relevant and tailored communication about the purpose, potential, and limitations of learning analytics tools as a means of reducing resistance and encouraging adoption. Numerous studies have noted that socialization of faculty and their professional identities act as significant barriers to pedagogical change (Austin 2011; Brownell and Tanner 2012; Ertmer 2005; Fairweather 2008; Hora and Holden 2013). Locke (1995) and Tagg (2012) argue that these barriers are more likely to be surmounted when resistance is lessened. By creating messaging, policies, and other communications that align with the professional norms and that speak to professional needs, practices, and concerns, tool developers and campus administrators can mitigate barriers by allaying concerns, changing behaviors, and reorienting beliefs of faculty and advisors. In turn, the potential to scale learning analytics use broadly may increase.

Finally, transparency should extend to learning analytics technologies themselves. Given that many of the learning analytics tools on the market are "black-box" proprietary technologies, little is understood about them. What data are collected, how those data are weighted within algorithms, and how those algorithms produce predictions and interventions are areas that need more understanding and attention by relevant university officials. Transparency can also allow for better insight into the efficacy and accuracy of these tools. Because learning analytics data are prone to bias and misalignment, researchers and users of black-box technologies need to be able to understand and evaluate their learning assessment approaches and predictions. This transparency can help to improve the ethical use of data in higher education (Selwyn 2015), by giving faculty and advisor users a better understanding of how learning analytics data are being used and analyzed to support their students' learning.

Conclusion

Learning analytics is becoming more prevalent in higher education as a means to assess teaching and learning. It is creating environmental forces that are influencing course design, pedagogy, advising, and learning. These tools can be used to inform practice, but only if individuals choose to adopt them. Professional beliefs and behaviors, in addition to issues of technological misalignment, organizational readiness, and ethical concerns, can act to constrain broad use of these tools. With an understanding of the professional beliefs and socialized ways of being of faculty and advisors, development of these tools can be improved to better speak to users' needs and perspectives and to be leveraged for broader-scale use across higher education organizations.

Acknowledgments

This research was supported in part by a grant from the National Science Foundation under grant IIS-1447489.

References

Aguilar, S. J., 2018. "Learning Analytics: At the Nexus of Big Data, Digital Innovation, and Social Justice in Education." *TechTrends* 62, no. 1: 37–45.

Aguilar S., S. Lonn, and S. D. Teasley. 2014. "Perceptions and Use of an Early Warning System during a Higher Education Transition Program." In *Proceedings of the Fourth International Conference on Learning Analytics and Knowledge,* 113–117. New York, NY: Association of Computing Machinery.

Ali, L., M. Hatala, D. Gašević, and J. Jovanovi. 2012. "A Qualitative Evaluation of Evolution of a Learning Analytics Tool." *Computers & Education* 58, no. 1: 1470–1489.

Almatrafi, O., H. Rangwala, J. Aditya, and J. Lester. 2016. "Using Learning Analytics to Trace Academic Trajectories of CS and IT Students to Better Understanding Successful Pathways to Graduation." In *Proceedings of the 47th ACM Technical Symposium on Computing Science Education,* 691. New York, NY: Association of Computing Machinery.

Amey, M. J. 1999. "Faculty Culture and College Life: Reshaping Incentives Toward Student Outcomes." *New Directions for Higher Education* 105: 59–69.

Andrejevic, M. 2011. "Social Network Exploitation." *A Networked Self: Identity, Community, and Culture on Social Network Sites,* 82–101, edited by Z. Papacharissi. New York, NY: Routledge.

Arnold, K. E., S. Lonn, and M. D. Pistilli. 2014. "An Exercise in Institutional Reflection: The Learning Analytics Readiness Instrument (LARI)." In *Proceedings of the Fourth International Conference on Learning Analytics and Knowledge,* 163–167. New York, NY: Association of Computing Machinery.

Arnold, K. E., and M. D. Pistilli. 2012. "Course Signals at Purdue: Using Learning Analytics to Increase Student Success." In *Proceedings of the 2nd International Conference on Learning Analytics and Knowledge,* 267–270. New York, NY: Association of Computing Machinery.

Austin, A. E. 2003. "Creating a Bridge to the Future: Preparing New Faculty to Face Changing Expectations in a Shifting Context." *Review of Higher Education* 26: 119–144.

————. 2011. *Promoting Evidence-Based Change in Undergraduate Science Education*. National Research Council. Washington, DC: National Academies. https://sites.nationalacademies.org/cs/groups/dbassesite/documents/webpage/dbasse_072578.pdf.

Austin, A. E., and M. D. Sorcinelli. 2013. "The Future of Faculty Development: Where Are We Going?" *New Directions for Teaching and Learning* 133: 85–97.

Baker, R. S., and K. Yacef. 2009. "The State of Educational Data Mining in 2009: A Review and Future Visions." *JEDM—Journal of Educational Data Mining* 1, no. 1: 3–17.

Beattie S., C. Woodley, and K. Souter. 2014. "Creepy Analytics and Learner Data Rights." In *Rhetoric and Reality: Critical Perspectives on Educational Technology from the Proceedings of the 31st Annual Conference of the Australasian Society for Computers in Learning in Tertiary Education (ASCILITE 2014)*, 421–425.

Beer C., R. Tickner, and D. Jones. 2014. "Three Paths for Learning Analytics and Beyond: Moving from Rhetoric to Reality." In *Proceedings of the 31st Annual Conference of the Australasian Society for Computers in Learning in Tertiary Education (ASCILITE 2014)*, 242–250.

Ben-Naim, D., M. Bain, and N. Marcus. 2009. "A User-Driven and Data-Driven Approach for Supporting Teachers in Reflection and Adaptation of Adaptive Tutorials." International Working Group on Educational Data Mining. http://www.educationaldatamining.org/EDM2009/uploads/proceedings/benNaim.pdf.

Bichsel J. 2012. *Analytics in Higher Education: Benefits, Barriers, Progress, and Recommendations*. Louisville, CO: EDUCAUSE Center for Applied Research. http://net.EDUCAUSE.edu/ir/library/pdf/ERS1207/ers1207.pdf.

Blumenstyk, G. 2016. "Dror Ben-Naim Puts Digital Power in Professors' Hands." *Chronicle of Higher Education*. April 10, 2016. https://www.chronicle.com/article/Dror-Ben-Naim-Puts-Digital/235998.

Brown, M., J. Dehoney, and N. Millichap. 2015. *The Next Generation Digital Learning Environment*. EDUCAUSE Learning Initiative. Louisville, CO: EDUCAUSE.

Brown, M. G., R. M. DeMonbrun, and S. D. Teasley. 2017. "Don't Call It a Comeback: Academic Recovery and the Timing of Educational Technology Adoption." In *Proceedings of the Seventh International Learning Analytics & Knowledge Conference*, 489–493. New York, NY: Association of Computing Machinery.

Brown, M., and C. Klein. 2019. "Whose Data? Which Rights? Whose Power? A Policy Discourse Analysis of Student Privacy Policy Documents." Paper presented at the annual conference of the American Educational Research Association (AERA), Toronto, Canada, April 2019.

Brownell, S. E., and K. D. Tanner. 2012. "Barriers to Faculty Pedagogical Change: Lack of Training, Time, Incentives, and Tensions with Professional Identity?" *CBE—Life Sciences Education* 11: 339–346.

Carless, D. 2009. "Trust, Distrust and Their Impact on Assessment Reform." *Assessment & Evaluation in Higher Education* 34, no. 1: 79–89.

Chen, Y., A. Johri, and H. Rangwala. 2018. "Running out of STEM: A Comparative Study Across STEM Majors of College Students At-Risk of Dropping Out Early." In *Proceedings of the Eighth International Conference on Learning Analytics and Knowledge*, 270–279. New York, NY: Association of Computing Machinery.

Chiu, M. M., and N. Fujita. 2014. "Statistical Discourse Analysis of Online Discussions: Informal Cognition, Social Metacognition and Knowledge Creation." In *Proceedings of the Fourth International Conference on Learning Analytics and Knowledge*, 217–225. New York, NY: Association of Computing Machinery.

Cohen, W. M., and D. A. Levinthal. 1990. "Absorptive Capacity: A New Perspective on Learning and Innovation." *Administrative Science Quarterly* 35, no. 1: 128–152.

Coll S., O. Glassey, and C. Balleys. 2011. "Building Social Networks Ethics Beyond 'Privacy': A Sociological Perspective." *International Review of Information Ethics* 16, no. 12: 47–53.

Crookston, B. B. 1994. "A Developmental View of Academic Advising as Teaching." *NACADA Journal* 14, no. 2: 5–9.

Cyert, R. M., and J. G. March. 1963. "A Behavioral Theory of the Firm." Englewood Cliffs, NJ: Prentice Hall, Inc.

Da Silva, N., and A. R. Davis. 2011. "Absorptive Capacity at the Individual Level: Linking Creativity to Innovation in Academia." *Review of Higher Education* 34, no. 3: 355–379.

Dahlstrom, E., D. C. Brooks, and J. Bichsel. 2014. *The Current Ecosystem of Learning Management Systems in Higher Education: Student, Faculty, and IT Perspectives*. Louisville, CO: EDUCAUSE. http://www.educause.edu/ecar.

Dawson, S., E. McWilliam, and J. P. L. Tan. 2008. "Teaching Smarter: How Mining ICT Data Can Inform and Improve Learning and Teaching Practice." In *Hello! Where Are You in the Landscape of Educational Technology? Proceedings ASCILITE*, Melbourne, Australia, 2008. http://www.ascilite.org.au/conferences /melbourne08/procs/dawson.pdf.

de los Santos, G., and M. Milliron. 2015. *League for Innovation Trends Report*. Chandler, AZ: League for Innovation in the Community College.

Diakopoulos, N. 2015. "Algorithmic Accountability: Journalistic Investigation of Computational Power Structures." *Digital Journalism* 3, no. 3: 398–415.

Drachsler, H., and W. Greller. 2012. "Confidence in Learning Analytics." In *Proceedings of the Second International Conference on Learning Analytics & Knowledge*, 89–98. New York, NY: Association for Computing Machinery.

———. 2016. "Privacy and Analytics—It's a DELICATE Issue: A Checklist for Trusted Learning Analytics." In *Proceedings of the Sixth International Conference on Learning Analytics & Knowledge*, 89–98. New York, NY: Association for Computing Machinery.

Duval, E. 2011. "Attention Please!: Learning Analytics for Visualization and Recommendation." In *Proceedings of the First International Conference on Learning Analytics and Knowledge*, 9–17. New York, NY: Association of Computing Machinery.

EAB. 2019. "About the Student Success Collaborative." EAB. Accessed January 16, 2019. https://www.eab.com/technology/student-success-collaborative/about-the -student-success-collaborative.

Echeverria, V., R. Martinez-Maldonado, R. Granda, K. Chiluiza, C. Conati, and S. B. Shum. 2018. "Driving Data Storytelling from Learning Design." In *Proceedings of the Eighth International Conference on Learning Analytics and Knowledge*, 131–140. New York, NY: Association of Computing Machinery.

Ertmer, P. A. 2005. "Teacher Pedagogical Beliefs: The Final Frontier in Our Quest for Technology Integration?" *Educational Technology Research and Development* 53, no. 4: 25–39.

Ertmer, P. A., and A. T. Ottenbreit-Leftwich. 2010. "Teacher Technology Change: How Knowledge, Confidence, Beliefs, and Culture Intersect." *Journal of Research on Technology in Education* 42: 255–284.

Ertmer, P. A., A. T. Ottenbreit-Leftwich, O. Sadik, E. Sendurur, and P. Sendurur. 2012. "Teacher Beliefs and Technology Integration Practices: A Critical Relationship." *Computers & Education* 59: 423–435.

Fairweather, J. S. 2002. "The Mythologies of Faculty Productivity: Implications for Institutional Policy and Decision Making." *Journal of Higher Education* 73: 26–48.

———. 2008. *Linking Evidence and Promising Practices in Science, Technology, Engineering, and Mathematics (STEM) Undergraduate Education.* Board of Science Education, National Research Council. Washington, DC: The National Academies.

Fairweather, J. S., and A. L. Beach. 2002. "Variations in Faculty Work at Research Universities: Implications for State and Institutional Policy." *Review of Higher Education* 26, no. 1: 97–115.

Ferguson, R. 2012. "Learning Analytics: Drivers, Developments and Challenges." *International Journal of Technology Enhanced Learning* 4, no. 5–6: 304–317.

Ferguson, R., and D. Clow. 2017. "Where Is the Evidence?: A Call to Action for Learning Analytics." In *Proceedings of the Seventh International Learning Analytics & Knowledge Conference,* 56–65. New York, NY: Association of Computing Machinery.

Gašević, D., N. Mirriahi, and S. Dawson. 2014. "Analytics of the Effects of Video Use and Instruction to Support Reflective Learning." In *Proceedings of the Fourth International Conference on Learning Analytics and Knowledge,* 123–132. New York, NY: Association of Computing Machinery.

General Data Protection Regulation [GDPR]. 2019. "2018 Reform of EU Data Protection Rules." Accessed March 12, 2019. https://ec.europa.eu/commission /priorities/justice-and-fundamental-rights/data-protection/2018-reform-eu-data -protection-rules_en.

Guarcello, M. A., R. A. Levine, J. Beemer, J. P. Frazee, M. A. Laumakis, and S. A. Schellenberg. 2017. "Balancing Student Success: Assessing Supplemental Instruction through Coarsened Exact Matching." *Technology, Knowledge and Learning* 22, no. 3: 335–352.

Hajian, S., F. Bonchi, and C. Castillo. 2016. "Algorithmic Bias: From Discrimination Discovery to Fairness-Aware Data Mining." In *Proceedings of the 22nd ACM SIGKDD International Conference on Knowledge Discovery and Data Mining,* 2125–2126. New York, NY: Association for Computing Machinery.

Hall, G. E. 1979. "The Concerns-Based Approach to Facilitating Change." *Educational Horizons* 57: 202–208.

Hobsons. 2019. "Intersect by Hobsons." Accessed January 15, 2019. www.hobsons .com/intersect.

Hora, M. T., J. Bouwma-Gearhart, and H. J. Park. 2017. "Data Driven Decision Making in the Era of Accountability: Fostering Faculty Data Cultures for Learning." *Review of Higher Education* 40, no. 3: 391–426.

Hora, M. T., and J. Holden. 2013. "Exploring the Role of Instructional Technology in Course Planning and Classroom Teaching: Implications for Pedagogical Reform." *Journal of Computing in Higher Education* 25: 68–92.

Irvin, M., and J. Longmire. 2016. "Motivating and Supporting Faculty in New Technology-Based Student Success Initiatives: An Exploration of Case Studies on Technology Acceptance." *Journal of Student Success and Retention* 3, no. 1: 1–25.

Jaffee, D. 1998. "Institutionalized Resistance to Asynchronous Learning Networks." *Journal of Asynchronous Learning Networks* 2: 21–32.

Januszewski, A., and M. Molenda. 2008. *Educational Technology: A Definition with Commentary.* New York, NY: Routledge.

Jayaprakash, S. M., E. W. Moody, E. J. Lauría, J. R. Regan, and J. D. Baron. 2014. "Early Alert of Academically At-Risk Students: An Open Source Analytics Initiative." *Journal of Learning Analytics* 1, no. 1: 6–47.

Johnson, J. A. 2014. "From Open Data to Information Justice." *Ethics and Information Technology* 16, no. 4: 263–274.

Johri, A. 2018. "Absorptive Capacity and Routines: Understanding Barriers to Learning Analytics Adoption in Higher Education." In *Learning Analytics in Higher Education,* 140–159, edited by J. Lester, C. Klein, H. Rangwala, and A. Johri. New York, NY: Routledge.

Junco, R., and C. Clem. 2015. "Predicting Course Outcomes with Digital Textbook Usage Data." *The Internet and Higher Education* 27: 54–63.

Kagan, D. M. 1992. "Implication of Research on Teacher Belief." *Educational Psychologist* 27, no. 1: 65–90.

Klein, C., and R. M. Hess. 2018. "Using Learning Analytics to Improve Student Learning Outcomes Assessment: Benefits, Constraints and Possibilities." In *Learning Analytics in Higher Education,* 140–159, edited by J. Lester, C. Klein, H. Rangwala, and A. Johri. New York, NY: Routledge.

Klein, C., J. Lester, H. Rangwala, and A. Johri. 2019a. "Adoption of Learning Analytics in Higher Education at the Intersection of Institutional Commitment and Individual Trust." *Review of Higher Education* (Winter): 565–593.

———. 2019b. "Technological Barriers and Incentives to Learning Analytics Adoption in Higher Education: Insights from Users." *Journal of Computing in Higher Education* (online first): 1–22. https://doi.org/10.1007/s12528-019-09210-5.

Knight, D. B., C. Brozina, T. J. Kinoshita, B. J. Novoselich, G. D. Young, and J. R. Grohs. 2018. "Discipline-Focused Learning Analytics Approaches with Users Instead of for Users." In *Learning Analytics in Higher Education,* 93–117, edited by J. Lester, C. Klein, H. Rangwala, and A. Johri. New York, NY: Routledge.

Knox, D. 2010. "Spies in the House of Learning: A Typology of Surveillance in Online Learning Environments." Paper presented at *Edge2010,* Newfoundland, Canada, October 2010.

Koba, M. 2015. "Educational Technology Soars—But Is It Working in the Classroom?" *Fortune Magazine.* April 28, 2015. http://fortune.com/2015/04/28/education-tech-funding-soars-but-is-it-working-in-the-classroom/.

Kosba, E., V. Dimitrova, and R. Boyle. 2005. "Using Student and Group Models to Support Teachers in Web-Based Distance Education." In *International Conference on User Modeling,* 124–133. Berlin, Germany: Springer.

Kraemer, F., K. Van Overveld, and M. Peterson. 2011. "Is There an Ethics of Algorithms?" *Ethics and Information Technology* 13, no. 3: 251–260.

Kwong, T., E. Wong, and K. Yue. 2017. "Bringing Abstract Academic Integrity and Ethical Concepts into Real-Life Situations." *Technology, Knowledge and Learning* 22, no. 3: 353–368. https://doi.org/10.1007/s10758-017-9315-2.

Lane, P. J., B. R. Koka, and S. Pathak. 2006. "The Reification of Absorptive Capacity: A Critical Review and Rejuvenation of the Construct." *Academy of Management Review* 31, no. 4: 833–863.

Leony, D., A. Pardo, L. de la Fuente Valentín, D. S. de Castro, and C. D. Kloos. 2012. "GLASS: A Learning Analytics Visualization Tool." In *Proceedings of the Second International Conference on Learning Analytics and Knowledge*, 162–163. New York, NY: Association of Computing Machinery.

Lester, J., C. Klein, H. Rangwala, and A. Johri. 2017. "Learning Analytics in Higher Education." *ASHE Higher Education Report* 43, no. 5: 9–135.

Lewin, A. Y., S. Massini, and C. Peeters. 2011. "Microfoundations of Internal and External Absorptive Capacity Routines." *Organization Science* 22, no. 1: 81–98.

Lewis, T., S. Marginson, and I. Snyder. 2005. "The Network University? Technology, Culture and Organisational Complexity in Contemporary Higher Education." *Higher Education Quarterly* 59, no. 1: 56–75.

Liu, S. H. 2011. "Factors Related to Pedagogical Beliefs of Teachers and Technology Integration." *Computers & Education* 56: 1012–1022.

Locke, L. 1995. "An Analysis of Prospects for Changing Faculty Roles and Rewards: Can Scholarship Be Reconsidered?" *Quest* 47: 506–524.

Lockyer, L., E. Heathcote, and S. Dawson. 2013. "Informing Pedagogical Action: Aligning Learning Analytics with Learning Design." *American Behavioral Scientist* 57, no. 10: 1439–1459.

Long, P., and G. Siemens. 2011. "Penetrating the Fog: Analytics in Learning and Education." *EDUCAUSE Review* 46, no. 5: 30.

Lyon, D. 2007. *Surveillance Studies: An Overview*. Cambridge, UK: Polity Press.

Macfadyen, L. P., and S. Dawson. 2012. "Numbers Are Not Enough. Why E-Learning Analytics Failed to Inform an Institutional Strategic Plan." *Journal of Educational Technology & Society* 15, no. 3: 149–163.

Mangaroska, K., K. Sharma, M. Giannakos, H. Trætteberg, and P. Dillenbourg. 2018. "Gaze Insights into Debugging Behavior Using Learner-Centered Analysis." In *Proceedings of the Eighth International Conference on Learning Analytics and Knowledge*, 350–359. New York, NY: Association of Computing Machinery.

Markets and Markets. 2019. "Education and Learning Analytics Market by Application (Performance Management, Curriculum Development and Intervention Management, and People Acquisition and Retention), Component, Analytics Type, Deployment, End User, and Region—Global Forecast to 2024" Markets and Markets. Accessed January 15, 2019. https://www.marketsandmarkets.com/Market-Reports/learning-analytics-market-219923528.html.

Market Research Future. 2019. "Learning Analytics Market Research Report: Forecast to 2023." Market Research Future. Accessed January 15, 2019. https://www.marketresearchfuture.com/reports/learning-analytics-market-5634.

Mazza, R., and V. Dimitrova. 2007. "CourseVis: A Graphical Student Monitoring Tool for Supporting Instructors in Web-Based Distance Courses." *International Journal of Human-Computer Studies* 65: 25–139.

Norris, D. M., and L. L. Baer. 2013. *Building Organizational Capacity for Analytics*. Louisville, CO: EDUCAUSE. http://www.educause.edu/library/resources/building -organizationalcapacity-analytics.

Ochoa, X., F. Domínguez, B. Guamán, R. Maya, G. Falcones, and J. Castells. 2018. "The RAP System: Automatic Feedback of Oral Presentation Skills Using Multimodal Analysis and Low-Cost Sensors." In *Proceedings of the Eighth International Conference on Learning Analytics and Knowledge*, 360–364. New York, NY: Association of Computing Machinery.

Oster, M., S. Lonn, M. D. Pistilli, and M. G. Brown. 2016. "The Learning Analytics Readiness Instrument." In *Proceedings of the Sixth International Conference on Learning Analytics & Knowledge*, 173–182. New York, NY: Association of Computing Machinery.

Ottenbreit-Leftwich, A. T., K. D. Glazewski, T. J. Newby, and P. A. Ertmer. 2010. "Teacher Value Beliefs Associated with Using Technology: Addressing Professional and Student Needs." *Computers & Education* 55: 1321–1335.

Palmer, I. 2018. *Choosing a Predictive Analytics Vendor: A Guide for Colleges*. Washington, DC: New America. https://www.newamerica.org/education-policy /reports/choosing-predictive-analytics-vendor-guide/.

Papamitsiou, Z. K., and A. A. Economides. 2014. "Learning Analytics and Educational Data Mining in Practice: A Systematic Literature Review of Empirical Evidence." *Educational Technology & Society* 14, no. 4: 49–64.

Pardo, A., and G. Siemens. 2014. "Ethical and Privacy Principles for Learning Analytics." *British Journal of Educational Technology* 45, no. 3: 438–450.

Park, Y., and I. H. Jo. 2015. "Development of the Learning Analytics Dashboard to Support Students' Learning Performance." *J. UCS* 21, no.1: 110–133.

Peña-Ayala, A. 2014. "Educational Data Mining: A Survey and a Data Mining–Based Analysis of Recent Works." *Expert Systems with Applications* 41: 1432–1462.

———. 2018. "Learning Analytics: A Glance of Evolution, Status, and Trends According to a Proposed Taxonomy." *Wiley Interdisciplinary Reviews: Data Mining and Knowledge Discovery* 8, no. 3: e1243.

Pentland, B. T., and M. S. Feldman. 2005. "Organizational Routines as a Unit of Analysis." *Industrial and Corporate Change* 14, no. 5: 793–815.

Picciano, A. G. 2012. "The Evolution of Big Data and Learning Analytics in American Higher Education." *Journal of Asynchronous Learning Networks* 16, no. 3: 9–20.

Pistilli, M. D., and K. E. Arnold. 2010. "In Practice: Purdue Signals: Mining Real-Time Academic Data to Enhance Student Success." *About Campus* 15, no. 3: 22–24.

Prinsloo, P., and S. Slade. 2013. "An Evaluation of Policy Frameworks for Addressing Ethical Considerations in Learning Analytics." In *Proceedings of the Third International Conference on Learning Analytics and Knowledge*, 240–244. New York, NY: Association for Computing Machinery.

———. 2015. "Student Privacy Self-Management: Implications for Learning Analytics." In *Proceedings of the Fifth International Conference on Learning*

Analytics and Knowledge, 83–92. New York, NY: Association for Computing Machinery.

Rienties, B., L. Toetenel, and A. Bryan. 2015. "Scaling up Learning Design: Impact of Learning Design Activities on LMS Behavior and Performance." In *Proceedings of the Fifth International Conference on Learning Analytics and Knowledge*, 315–319. New York, NY: Association of Computing Machinery.

Rubel, A., and K. M. Jones. 2016. "Student Privacy in Learning Analytics: An Information Ethics Perspective." *The Information Society* 32, no. 2: 143–159.

Salesforce. 2019. "Recruitment and Admissions." Salesforce. Accessed January 15, 2019. https://www.salesforce.org/highered/recruiting/.

Santos, J. L., K. Verbert, S. Govaerts, and E. Duval. 2013. "Addressing Learner Issues with StepUp!: An Evaluation." In *Proceedings of the Third International Conference on Learning Analytics and Knowledge*, 14–22. New York, NY: Association of Computing Machinery.

Selwyn, N. 2015. "Data Entry: Towards the Critical Study of Digital Data and Education." *Learning, Media and Technology* 40, no. 1: 64–82.

Siemens, G. 2013. "Learning Analytics: The Emergence of a Discipline." *American Behavioral Scientist* 57, no. 10: 1380–1400.

Siemens, G., and R. S. Baker. 2012. "Learning Analytics and Educational Data Mining: Towards Communication and Collaboration." In *Proceedings of the Second International Conference on Learning Analytics and Knowledge*, 252–254. New York, NY: Association of Computing Machinery.

Slade, S., and P. Prinsloo. (in press). "Learning Analytics at the Intersections of Student Trust, Disclosure and Benefits." Paper presented at LAK 2019, Tempe, AZ, 2019.

———. 2013. "Learning Analytics Ethical Issues and Dilemmas." *American Behavioral Scientist* 57, no. 10: 1510–1529.

———. 2015. "Student Perspectives on the Use of Their Data: Between Intrusion, Surveillance and Care." *European Journal of Open, Distance and E-learning* 18, no. 1: 291–300.

Steiner, C. M., M. D. Kickmeier-Rust, and D. Albert. 2016. "LEA in Private: A Privacy and Data Protection Framework for a Learning Analytics Toolbox." *Journal of Learning Analytics* 3, no. 1: 66–90.

Sweeney, M., J. Lester, and H. Rangwala. 2015. "Next-Term Student Grade Prediction." In *Big data (Big Data), 2015 IEEE International Conference on Big Data*, 970–975. IEEE.

Tabuenca, B., M. Kalz, H. Drachsler, and M. Specht. 2015. "Time Will Tell: The Role of Mobile Learning Analytics in Self-Regulated Learning." *Computers & Education* 89: 53–74.

Tagg, J. 2012. "Why Does the Faculty Resist Change?" *Change: The Magazine of Higher Learning* 44, no. 1: 6–15.

Taylor, L. 2017. "What Is Data Justice? The Case for Connecting Digital Rights and Freedoms Globally." *Big Data & Society* 4, no. 2: doi: 2053951717736335.

Tempelaar, D. T., A. Heck, H. Cuypers, H. van der Kooij, and E. van de Vrie. 2013. "Formative Assessment and Learning Analytics." In *Proceedings of the Third International Conference on Learning Analytics and Knowledge*, 205–209. New York, NY: Association of Computing Machinery.

Tempelaar, D., B. Rienties, and Q. Nguyen. 2017. "Adding Dispositions to Create Pedagogy-Based Learning Analytics." *Zeitschrift für Hochschulentwicklung* 12, no. 1: 15–35.

Treaster, J. B. 2017. "Will You Graduate? Ask Big Data." *New York Times.* February 2, 2017. www.nytimes.com/2017/02/02/education/edlife/will-you-graduate -ask-big-data.html.

Tsai, Y. S., and D. Gašević. 2017. "Learning Analytics in Higher Education— Challenges and Policies: A Review of Eight Learning Analytics Policies." In *Proceedings of the Seventh International Learning Analytics & Knowledge Conference,* 233–242. New York, NY: Association of Computer Machinery.

Tsai, Y. S., P. M. Moreno-Marcos, K. Tammets, K. Kollom, and D. Gašević. 2018. "SHEILA Policy Framework: Informing Institutional Strategies and Policy Processes of Learning Analytics." In *Proceedings of the Eighth International Conference on Learning Analytics and Knowledge,* 320–329. New York, NY: Association of Computing Machinery.

Van Barneveld, A., K. E. Arnold, and J. P. Campbell. 2012. "Analytics in Higher Education: Establishing a Common Language." *EDUCAUSE Learning Initiative* 1, no.1: 1–11.

Venkatesh, V., and H. Bala. 2008. "Technology Acceptance Model 3 and a Research Agenda on Interventions." *Decision Sciences* 39: 273–315.

Venkatesh, V., M. G. Morris, G. B. Davis, and F. D. Davis. 2003. "User Acceptance of Information Technology: Toward a Unified View." *MIS Quarterly* 27, no.3: 425–478.

Verbert, K., E. Duval, J. Klerkx, S. Govaerts, and J. L. Santos. 2013. "Learning Analytics Dashboard Applications." *American Behavioral Scientist* 57, no. 10: 1500–1509.

Verbert, K., S. Govaerts, E. Duval, J. L. Santos, F. Assche, G. Parra, and J. Klerkx. 2014. "Learning Dashboards: An Overview and Future Research Opportunities." *Personal and Ubiquitous Computing* 18, no. 6: 1499–1514.

Viberg, O., M. Hatakka, O. Bälter, and A. Mavroudi. 2018. "The Current Landscape of Learning Analytics in Higher Education." *Computers in Human Behavior* 89: 98–110.

Whitelock, D., A. Twiner, J. T. Richardson, D. Field, and S. Pulman. 2015. "OpenEssayist: A Supply and Demand Learning Analytics Tool for Drafting Academic Essays." In *Proceedings of the Fifth International Conference on Learning Analytics and Knowledge,* 208–212. New York, NY: Association of Computer Machinery.

Willis, J. E., S. Slade, and P. Prinsloo. 2016. "Ethical Oversight of Student Data in Learning Analytics: A Typology Derived from a Cross-Continental, Cross-Institutional Perspective." *Educational Technology Research and Development* 64, no. 5: 881–901.

Worsley, M. 2018. "(Dis) Engagement Matters: Identifying Efficacious Learning Practices with Multimodal Learning Analytics." In *Proceedings of the Eighth International Conference on Learning Analytics and Knowledge,* 365–369. New York, NY: Association of Computer Machinery.

Worsley, M., and P. Blikstein. 2015. "Leveraging Multimodal Learning Analytics to Differentiate Student Learning Strategies." In *Proceedings of the Fifth Interna-*

tional Conference on Learning Analytics and Knowledge, 360–367. New York, NY: Association of Computer Machinery.

Zahra, S. A., and G. George. 2002. "Absorptive Capacity: A Review, Reconceptualization, and Extension." *Academy of Management Review* 27, no. 2: 185–203.

Zeide, E. 2017. "The Structural Consequences of Big Data–Driven Education." *Big Data* 5, no. 2: 164–172.

Zellweger, F. 2007. "Faculty Adoption of Educational Technology." *EDUCAUSE Quarterly* 30, no. 1: 66–69.

[11]

Using Data Analytics to Support Institutional Financial and Operational Efficiency

Lindsay K. Wayt, Susan M. Menditto, J. Michael Gower, and Charles Tegen

COLLEGE AND university business officers, like their colleagues in other parts of higher education, seek to maximize the use of analytics to make data-informed decisions for their students, institutions, and the higher education sector broadly. The combination of economic changes from the Great Recession and rapid changes in technology prompted the need for college and university officials to move beyond point-in-time financial analyses and rudimentary decision support techniques to a more robust and disciplined effort that informed institutional objectives. To assist its members, the leading professional association for college business officers, NACUBO, added a priority to its strategic plan in 2012 to identify and disseminate effective analytics to support institutional planning efforts. A revision of its strategic plan in 2017 elevated analytics to one of five organizational priorities, calling for business officers to "lead higher education's integration of analytics to achieve institutional goals" (NACUBO 2019a). In this chapter, we explore how higher education business officers have begun making strides on this priority and provide examples of how colleges and universities have used analytics to effectively manage campus resources in support of institutional missions.

Transition from Traditional Business Analysis to Contemporary Data Analytics

In the early years of cost accounting, analysis, and support for internal finance decisions, higher education continued to lag the corporate sector in the use of modern managerial accounting techniques, even as recently as the later part of the twentieth century. Costing techniques were used from time to time but only became broadly applied when the federal government became involved (Patterson 2004). Typical analytic techniques included ratio analysis of standard financial accounting and reporting outputs to help institutions and their stakeholders (if properly explained) understand sources and uses of resources, the ability to pay debt and debt capacity, gauge financial performance, identify financial anomalies, clarify financial viability, and perhaps illuminate liquidity (Prager et al.1999). While traditional financial accounting assumes the responsibility of conveying financial results to stakeholders, through cost reporting and analysis, decision support managerial accounting and analysis focuses on value creation through good decision making (Patterson 2004).

College and university business officers are keenly aware of the responsibility for communicating financial information and assessment in a manner that makes sense to all stakeholders. With this in mind, some business and facilities analyses increasingly use more sophisticated analytics, including predictive modeling and machine learning techniques, to discern patterns followed by contextual judgment to inform decisions. From the higher education finance perspective, three key uses of data analytics were identified as critical: (1) analytics to support and enhance a mission-driven campus, including a focus on improving student outcomes; (2) analytics to ensure institutional financial viability in an increasingly complex funding environment; and (3) analytics to optimize use of facilities, including a focus on cost savings as well as environmental sustainability (Menditto 2018). Business officers who participated in NACUBO listening tour discussions described these three uses for analytics as "core drivers of what we do in higher education" (Menditto 2018). Examples of *how* the business office contributes to the use of analytics in each of these three core campus areas are explored later in this chapter, but first, it is important to understand *why* it is critical for both business and finance officers to use data analytics and why other campus leaders should collaborate with business and finance officers in conversations facilitated by data.

The Need for Analytics in the Business Office

According to a 2016 national survey of higher education chief business officers (CBOs), nearly a third (31.8%) indicated that the most important aspect of their role besides managing their institution's financial resources was strategic thinking and decision making; another 16.8% indicated that it was leading change and fostering innovation (NACUBO 2016). Similarly, Ayers and Goldstein (2015) reported that CBOs of the future will likely continue to maintain responsibilities for all aspects of finance—and likely human resources, facilities, auxiliary services, information technology, campus police, and risk management—and also will likely have a larger role in guiding institutions' strategic planning.

The expectation that the CBOs of the future will continue to manage resource allocation at their institutions while also being more involved with strategic planning means that data will be critical for them. As other chapters in this volume have noted, higher education as an industry is facing many challenges—challenges that data can help them navigate. As business officers are challenged to maintain financial stability for their institution while also ensuring the campus as a whole can meet its mission and help students be successful, analytics will be one tool they can use to be successful.

The Need for Data Integration

Historically, higher education business officers have relied solely on financial data and anecdotal evidence to make planning and budgeting decisions for academic programs and courses. However, the University of California–Riverside began using a new software platform that allowed it to integrate data from multiple sources. Officials at UC-Riverside found that integrating data produces helpful granular information (Vanover Porter 2017). Having analytics that provide insights into course-level revenues, costs, enrollment patterns, and other key data points can allow campus leaders to better plan for the future, thereby increasing their business intelligence.

As noted by Vanover Porter (2017), a critical skill for business officers on college and university campuses that are using analytics is creating and managing campus partnerships so that the campus can take full advantage of its data. As financial data are integrated with student and administrative data to facilitate enhanced decision making, business officers will have a decisive role in core campus decisions, including resource allocation.

Resource Allocation

UC-Riverside is an exemplar of another key tenet in the business office use of analytics. According to a business leader at the school, resource allocation gives academic department officials enhanced information to allow them to plan better for future growth and help deans think about how they put together their portfolio of courses. In short, the real focus of analytics in the business office is resource allocation and not cost cutting (Vanover Porter 2017).

Indeed, relevant data are critical to good business analyses. For example, business officers know that cutting costs may not always optimize use of facilities, but reallocating resources and generating revenue are keys to organizational and student success. It is not possible that all mission-critical programs will break even—meaning that, as financial stewards of institutions, business officers are challenged to allocate financial, facilities, and human resources in ways that ensure an overall mission-driven, fiscally responsible approach.

Data Literacy and Governance

As has been mentioned in other chapters of this book, and as described by Lancaster, Ledford, and Stephens (2019), collaboration with other officials through a strong data governance plan is critical. A clear data governance structure and investment in staff data literacy skills can help solidify consistent and clear data definitions and single-source repositories for data. Clear and consistent data governance policies and processes that are developed through campus collaboration can enable staff in various units, including the business office, to use data effectively. In addition, collaborative campus efforts around analytics can foster a culture where data literacy is valued and where there is a shared understanding of data definitions and which definition is considered "truth."

Going Forward

Since the 2017 analytics listening tour, NACUBO's Analytics Advisory Group has continued to expand on content to support the use of data analytics in the business office on college and university campuses. In doing so, the top three areas of analytics identified by the listening tour continue to be prioritized. One of the ways the group has continued to focus on these three areas is through sharing model practices that have been successful for their colleagues during national and regional professional development events.

In addition, to help business officers understand their role in promoting and using analytics, NACUBO's Analytics Advisory Group expanded Gartner's Analytic Value Escalator (Gartner Pictures 2012; NACUBO 2018), which shows that as analysis moves from hindsight to foresight the level of analysis increases in difficulty, but so does the value of information garnered. As the Higher Education Data Analytics Framework shows (figure 11.1), staff members and campus processes need to foster a culture that values data-informed decision making and also need to build capacity to make full use of analytics.

Student-Centered Analytics and the Business Office

As the cost of higher education continues to grow, college and university officials face increasing pressure to demonstrate student success and the value of a degree to stakeholders (Creusere and Troutman

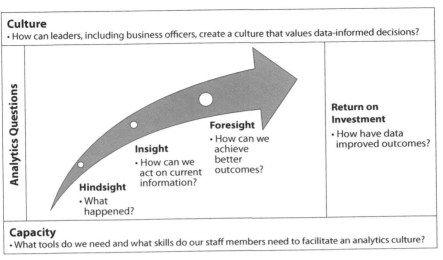

Culture
• How can leaders, including business officers, create a culture that values data-informed decisions?

Analytics Questions

Hindsight
• What happened?

Insight
• How can we act on current information?

Foresight
• How can we achieve better outcomes?

Return on Investment
• How have data improved outcomes?

Capacity
• What tools do we need and what skills do our staff members need to facilitate an analytics culture?

Figure 11.1. Higher Education Data Analytics Framework. NACUBO 2018.

2018). Along with other institutional leaders, this pressure falls on business officers and has guided efforts in ensuring financial sustainability for their institutions.

Optimizing Transportation to Support Student Success at Rutgers University

Recognizing that student success and on-time graduation profoundly influence financial results, business officers at Rutgers University, the State University of New Jersey (hereafter called Rutgers) decided to tackle an issue that was interfering with students' ability to complete required degree coursework (Gower and Hammond 2017). Rutgers is expansive and has the largest college and university bus system in the country. When looking at the institution's master plan, it became obvious that there was room to improve how students were transported across and around campus. Too many students were spending an extraordinary amount of time being shuttled across campus. This became campus lore: You'll spend more time on buses than in the classroom! So, Rutgers leaders decided to improve the student experience and help students succeed—and also had an expectation of a greater return on their mission investment.

Rutgers surrounds the city of New Brunswick, creating a unique problem: One needs to go through the city to get across campus. Given the physical geography of the campus, strategic planners began using data to better inform a new student-centered strategic plan. Initially data were gathered on student movement during an average weekday for course-related student travel in the school of arts and sciences. The data were analyzed by trip origin, based on campus housing as a starting point, and return trips. Subsequently, combinations of trips between classes for all colleges in the system were analyzed. On average, close to 80% of students travel every day. There were over 660,000 records in the final data set used for one week of classes.

Analysis of the data revealed patterns that led to several new institutional objectives:

- Increase the number of students who do not take buses to classes;
- Develop a student communication tool that allows students to make informed decisions about travel and their schedule; and
- Deliver certain large lecture courses in a way that ensures no travel.

In addition to analytics that were used to examine bus schedules, leaders at Rutgers implemented several other strategies that involved data and analytics. A few are described below.

Course Scheduler Planner Project

Leaders at Rutgers sought to reduce student travel. Specifically, to reduce the number of students who regularly traveled at least twice a day and to increase the number of students with zero trips, a new course scheduling platform was developed to work with a web application (app) that optimized class schedules against demand and bus requirements. The app displays "least travel" options for students based on course combinations that students want and/or need. Students can experiment with various combinations of classes and make informed decisions when they choose their schedules and register (Gower and Hammond 2017). After two semesters of using the course optimization software, the campus saw an 8% reduction in course-related travel (Sasaki 2017).

Stagger Time between Course Blocks

Because of the size of the campus and the possibility of fairly wide travel between academic course locations, officials at Rutgers produced a scatter map of the entire campus using student travel and class schedule data, and then they applied additional analytics to assess how more students could reach classes with less travel. Results informed decisions to stagger times between course blocks for certain colleges within Rutgers. Although this decreased student travel, a future student-centered initiative will move classes closer to students but increase faculty movement. Alternate transportation and parking options will be also be examined for faculty.

Understand Student Needs; Change the University Response

After adjusting course times and helping students make informed class selection decisions, Rutgers officials sought to further improve student success. To do this an extensive "student life and academic needs" survey was administered. Results from the data were used to assess differences between four-year graduates and five-year graduates. Responses revealed patterns that helped university officials determine what to change—the availability of required large lecture courses. Analysts discovered that many students motivated to graduate in four years could not because required large lecture courses were not readily available or did not line up with other required courses for a given major. Consequently, Rutgers staff made an informed decision to invest in technology and pilot a program known as immersive synchronous lecture halls (Gower and Hammond 2017).

Lessons Learned from the Use of Data Analytics at Rutgers

The intentional use of data to inform decisions has proven valuable. The number of bus trips (traffic) and number of buses in use is down. There is less campus congestion and wear on the fleet, which reduces overall transportation costs for both individual students and the campus transportation office. In addition, less travel means less wear on students. This, along with staggered course blocks and technology-enabled lecture offerings, increased student success by improving four-year graduation rates (Gower and Hammond 2017). For each initiative, there was a monetary investment, informed by the data, and all indications are that costs will be recovered, thus a return on investment. In addition, more students can be served and will graduate on time or closer to on time, indicating a return on *mission* investment. And, leaders at Rutgers are connecting with other university officials to inform and assist with similar changes.

Innovations at the Minnesota School of Nursing

Ten years ago, the Minnesota School of Nursing's various academic programs were losing money. The school was 58% tuition dependent and running as lean (expenditure-wise) as possible. The school determined that there were minimal costs to cut and instead focused on a strategic approach to increasing capacity and revenue using analytics (Bonneson, Clancy, and White-Delaney 2016). After understanding its cost structures and drivers, the school embarked on an analytics approach to discern patterns in student and course data. A clinical professor and data scientist examined academic programming and faculty effort related to academic programs, courses, course scheduling related to the number of students, distribution of classes by time of day and day of week, workload standards for tenured and clinical faculty, annual faculty contracts, faculty recruitment, and method of instruction.

Modeling software (using histograms and other graphic representations) looked for current trends. For example, slight scenario changes were modified in the model to assess the impact on yield, by examining patterns in the data for many of the variables listed above. Slight changes yielded different results, and each model displayed patterns. Clusters of patterns revealed optimization problems that the school chose to address. In a sense, this was small-scale use of machine learning.

Efficiencies in Classroom Utilization

Minnesota School of Nursing officials were also concerned about the number of classes with a low volume of students and those offered on Mondays and Fridays as well as before 10 am and after 3 pm (Bonneson, Clancy, and White-Delaney 2016). Data analyses revealed that they had many days that did not utilize the classroom space efficiently, so they offered additional classes and scheduled classes more evenly in every time slot throughout each weekday. The increased days and times were given to faculty with capacity. The institution had a simultaneous goal of reducing average faculty effort from 67% to 60% while keeping the distribution equitable among faculty. After multiple scenarios were run, analyses determined that capacity could be improved without adding headcount, with the workload lessened on certain faculty (Bonneson, Clancy, and White-Delaney 2016).

The patterns discerned using data and analytics helped college officials see that it is important to standardize faculty workload, streamline academic programming process, level load course schedules, and gather feedback regularly. Using analytics enabled officials to examine low student volume, to consider if low volume was related to time of day versus curriculum need or student capacity. For the Minnesota School of Nursing, costs remained the same, but the student revenue increased, and the school did not need to augment with adjunct faculty to offer courses during all nonclustered times that students needed or demanded courses. These strategies kept costs stable and increased revenue against the fixed costs as a by-product and consistently increased net revenue by 40% over an eight-year period (Bonneson, Clancy, and White-Delaney 2016).

Leadership and Culture

The dean of the School of Nursing played an important leadership role—and one necessary for a cultural shift in faculty course distribution. According to White-Delaney (the dean), building consensus around faculty workload is an ongoing process, and it must consider class preparation time and clinical obligations (Bonneson, Clancy, and White-Delaney

2016). White-Delaney reinforced the national need for nurses and emphasized to her leadership and faculty that the college could do better if data were used to inform a new way of operating. Although, the absolute essential continuous focus was on mission, faculty were regularly engaged around tweaks to strategies and approach. There was a need to communicate frequently, to be transparent with data, and for everyone to feel part of a close-knit team, to evolve into a culture that is data- rather than opinion-based.

Multi-Pronged Approach Using Data to Improve Student Success at Long Beach City College District

Under the leadership of superintendent-president Reagan Romali, officials at Long Beach City College (LBCC) have recently used multiple sources of data to better understand their student population as well as local workforce needs, have achieved many points of positive success, and have presented some of the results in terms of the financial benefits for students and/or the institution. Not only have they created a culture that seeks student success, leaders have shown how data can inform decisions that result in student success and subsequent contribution to the local economy. In 2018–19, LBCC was noted for having the most improved among all California community college districts in the number of certificates awarded and eighth most improved in the number of degrees awarded (Toda 2020). In addition, it saw a 29% increase in the Associate Degrees for Transfer awarded, particularly high among LBCC students of color. In 2019, LBCC was awarded a $3 million federal Title V grant to improve student success and equitable outcomes for Latinx students in science, technology, engineering, and math (STEM) fields (*Signal Tribune* 2019).

LBCC leaders have developed the culture of data-informed decision making, in part, by analyzing and visualizing data from multiple relevant sources. Analyses used data from student information systems, course registration and enrollment, the early-alert advising system, student financial aid needs, and labor market information. Strategies were identified that matched LBCC institution goals, and success was achieved in multiple areas. For example, data were mined and dashboards were created to better understand current and proposed financial aid awards, and course enrollment patterns were studied to determine when additional course sections needed to be added. In addition, an iterative algorithm that uses student behavior, current schedule, and educational plan was used to recommend course section enrollments. Initial results from LBCC efforts are very positive: more support programs are in place, enrollment and persistence have increased, and more students of color are succeeding. Notably, Romali has pointed to the return on investment (ROI). She suggests that students who are unable to enroll due to seat capacity limits or who fail a course result in lost revenue for the institution. Conversely, students who earn awards will earn on average 8% more in the workplace, and a 6% increase in fall term enrollment would lead to $2.5 million in revenues for the college (Romali 2019).

Cost Management

The primary duty of chief business officers at colleges and universities is to maintain responsibility for their institutions' budgets and financial planning. It should be no surprise then that one primary area of focus for analytics for CBOs is cost management, including activity-based costing. Activity-based costing "looks at how much time is spent on specific predetermined activities and the personnel and nonlabor costs of these activities" (Hurlburt, Kirshstein, and Rossol-Allison 2014, 2) and is a particularly helpful tool that budget and finance leaders use to offer insight into the labor and resources spent on the activities performed by institutions in service of their mission.

Typically, activity-based costing relies on data on labor and nonlabor costs for providing instruction, student service, and academic support activities (Hurlburt et al. 2014). However, as colleges and universities began creating more complex activity-based costing models, some institution officials have begun to analyze expenses at more granular levels to increase the set of activities examined or to more fully measure indirect costs to have a more complete understanding of particular activities. This lends itself well to today's more detailed data analytics.

One institution that uses activity-based costing practices to support resource management decision making is Johnson County Community College (JCCC) in Overland Park, Kansas. Like many colleges, the institution began using this model in order to better understand how resources were being allocated (Gates Foundation 2016). In particular, JCCC was "interested in leveraging new and improved data to inform advanced management analytics and decision making" (Gates Foundation 2016, 3). Thus, over time, the activity-based model used at this institution became more complex in order to better serve the analytical needs of the campus. For example, the model used by JCCC allows for an understanding of program cost margins, analysis of class size and durations, determining capacity utilization of facilities, and normalizing of credit and continuing education courses.

Because of the complex nature of its cost management model, JCCC is equipped to conduct predictive modeling, which allows leadership to plan for the future (Gates Foundation 2016). For example, the institution was able to compare face-to-face and online delivery methods for their courses. Using their Accounting I course as an example, JCCC found that although face-to-face sections for the course had a higher revenue and gross margin (because of larger enrollments in the face-to-face sections), the online sections had a greater percentage margin (due to low expenses).

Officials reported that data and insights gained from cost management data and analytics were being used to help the college make decisions about resource allocation (Dworkis et al. 2019). For example, officials considered whether they should invest more resources into their automotive technology program. Indeed, programs that require investments in technology can be costly to implement or expand. However, analytics that considered costs associated with the program as well as potential enrollment growth provided evidence that this program could grow and support the institution's mission. Ultimately, the institution decided to open a new automotive tech building on the campus.

Campus Facilities: Optimization and Sustainability

As addressed earlier in this chapter (and in other chapters included in this volume), many stakeholders have questioned the rising costs associated with higher education. While business officers are implementing more advanced analytic techniques, so too are leaders of college and university facilities departments. An important core expense for colleges and universities is the operation and maintenance of their physical campus space. As a sector, higher education spends more than $6 billion annually on energy costs, and the industry has an area of about 5 billion square feet of floor space (Better Buildings 2019). This alone may explain the interest of chief business officers in facilities management on their campuses, but there is more cause for interest.

According to the 2018 *State of Facilities in Higher Education* (Sightlines 2018), nearly a quarter (24%) of campus space (by gross square footage) was more than 50 years old in 2017, demonstrating a pressing need for capital investment. In addition, the report noted there had been no growth in facilities' operating budgets for maintaining campus on a daily basis (i.e., for utilities, planned maintenance, and daily service) since 2010.

At the same time that campuses will be called on to address deferred maintenance issues, in an environment where budgets are already tight, there have also been calls from higher education stakeholders for campus officials to be more consumption aware and environmentally conscious. For example, the "Key Facilities Metrics Survey," produced annually by the Association of Physical Plant Administrators (APPA) and NACUBO (NACUBO 2019c), calls on business officers and facilities staff to track the following metrics: energy (BTU), water, waste, electrical, and carbon footprint.

This context—of budget tightening and calls for increased efforts for environmental sustainability—has led many finance and facilities leaders on campuses to use data to guide decisions and ensure efficiency and effectiveness. Although more work has yet to be done, with campuses at varying levels within the higher education data analytics framework, there is evidence that several institutions have employed analytics to gain insight and foresight to maximize the use of their facilities and reduce energy consumption costs, all while making progress toward sustainability goals.

Space Optimization

Several factors have prompted many campus leaders to evaluate how they are using one of higher education's largest resources, its physical space. As budgets tighten, some campus leaders may not be able to consider expansion as an option. In addition, as campuses are increasingly challenged to consider their environmental footprint, the impact of any new construction must be considered carefully. These factors have led some campus leaders to look in rather than out—to critically consider how their space is being used and opting to increase efficiency before considering new construction.

Traditionally, the process for managing classroom space on college and university campuses is decentralized. In this model, departments manage their own course scheduling; although this may give individual departments flexibility with how they use their space, this decentralized process may also mean space use is not being maximized across campus. In addition, since these processes are decentralized, there may also not be a standard approach to collecting and managing data on classroom scheduling, so institutions may not even have access to the information needed to maximize their use of space. Grans Korsh (2013), Hignite (2018), and Motley (2016) highlight case studies of campuses working to address these challenges and lessons learned. For example, centralized scheduling is becoming more common on college and university campuses (Grans Korsh 2013). Analytics play a key role in helping institutions effectively optimize the use of classroom space. Scheduling software can help campuses collect, manage, and use data to track room size and type, seating arrangements and capacity, and daily hours of use. This allows institutions to not only assess what rooms are being used when but also what level of capacity they are being used at for any given course. Patterns revealed through these analytics can facilitate change to optimize the use of space.

Similarly, Queensborough Community College used analytics to establish guidelines for space use and processes for the necessary and difficult decisions of facilities and space assignments (Motley 2016). As with officials at the Minnesota School of Nursing, leaders at Queensbury Community College are using strong analytics to examine classroom space, enabling them to repurpose 35,000 square feet of space and to avoid nearly $14 million in new construction.

Measuring Utility Use and Promoting Sustainability

Some colleges and universities have also begun using analytics to measure energy consumption within spaces. Because the University of Arizona (UA) campus is located in a desert environment, its concerns about water and energy consumption are of particular interest, from both an energy cost perspective and from a sustainability and conservation standpoint. UA's facilities leaders have effectively harnessed key facilities data to meet their goals, including lowered energy costs, reductions in energy consumption, and greenhouse gas emissions, and they have achieved carbon neutrality. In 2011, a metering team was established and energy dashboards were installed. Each of these steps allowed UA to more effectively manage the volume of facilities data generated by a campus of its size and also allowed it to move in the direction of harnessing the power of analytics to meet its goals.

Today, the University of Arizona uses an energy analytics platform to monitor key performance indicators, and facilities staff members, including an energy manager, benchmark energy use in campus buildings and analyze the data for patterns to identify projects for increasing efficiency. In the past, managing energy use was component-based, only allowed for moment-in-time data, and relied on reactive practices to address concerns. With the use of technology and analytics, processes are systems-based, allow for continuous monitoring, and, because of predictive modeling, allow for proactive practices to help the UA campus meet facilities goals (Kopach and Mohammadi 2018). For example, technology allows for real-time monitoring of meter data (captured in 15-minute intervals). These granular data, along with other advanced technologies, allow UA to remotely identify and respond to faults and to continuously optimize energy use. These practices are not only helping the institution to reduce its carbon footprint but also to reduce its utilities costs. For example, in FY10, the utility cost per square foot was $2.68, but because of gained efficiencies, this was reduced to $2.20 by FY16 (Kopach and Mohammadi 2018).

As with the University of Arizona, the University of Nebraska–Lincoln (UNL) is using analytics to identify and address problems with the heating and cooling systems in multiple campus buildings. To ensure that the heating, ventilation, and air conditioning (HVAC) controller dispenses cool air properly, officials are using the Internet of Things, specifically by pairing the use of sensors and analytics software (Joch 2018). UNL installed thousands of digital sensors programmed with an algorithm designed to detect HVAC breakdowns. According to UNL officials, fixing one HVAC default saved the institution $300 per year in excess energy costs, and the total estimate for energy management activities prompted by the use of analytics saved the institution approximately $200,000 in one year.

Along with UA and UNL, smaller, private colleges are also investing in analytics to help reduce energy costs and advance sustainability goals. Macalester College has stated goals to be carbon neutral by 2025 and to have zero waste by 2020 (Macalester 2019a). College officials have indicated that they can achieve their suitability goals, in part, by sharing real-time energy and water consumption data with the students, faculty, staff, and the community (Macalester 2019b). Institution officials have partnered with staff and students from the campus sustainability office to develop an energy reporting dashboard that displays consumption data reported by the electric and condensate submeters installed on campus buildings (Macalester 2018).

With sustainability and student engagement goals identified, staff at Macalester began the dashboard project by considering the cost of implementation. Some of the initial budgetary constraints identified included determining where to start—since the campus has several buildings all with multiple utilities—and considering how to contract the installation of submeters and which software to use for analytics. Ultimately, school officials decided to measure electric and condensate and to begin their efforts with the residence halls.

Two of the early lessons learned from this project were that data, when presented well, can impact behavior and that analytics can support optimization (Miller 2017). The campus installed submeters with the ability to digitally transmit data, which allowed the campus to have access to real-time, granular data on energy consumption. These data were displayed on dashboards that students and other campus community members could access. Because students had access to real-time, granular data, they could immediately see impacts of their actions on energy use at their campus. This encouraged behavior changes among students. In addition, since facilities staff also had real-time access to granular data, they were also able to make changes. For example, Miller (2017) explained that the analytics staff had access to data that allowed them not only to identify an issue with water consumption in a particular building but also to specifically identify which toilet was the root of the issue and to fix the issue to avoid further waste. This ongoing project may continue to help staff and students save their institution energy costs and also promote environmental sustainability.

Conclusion and Implications for the Future

Each of these case studies highlights the growing importance of analytics for business officers in higher education. Although balance sheet and income statement ratio analysis continue to be used in higher education, business officers acknowledge the need to identify and analyze the drivers behind ratios and financial results. It is no longer enough to accept financial information at a point in time and perhaps cut expenses to stabilize the bottom line. Rather, higher education officials must strategically plan, be aware of economic models and constraints, and encourage leadership traits for success (Townsley 2009). Furthermore, with today's sophisticated data analytic strategies, presidents and chief business officers establish objectives, learn from colleagues who have achieved dramatic improvements, and design turnarounds based on data (enrollment and retention statistics, benchmarks, ratios, and management diagnostics).

Decision support in business and facilities management requires the use of available data in support of management decisions. College and university business officers are keenly aware of the responsibility for communicating financial information and assessment in a manner that makes sense to all stakeholders. However, many business officers have noted a widening gap between what the chief business officer reports and what managers, staff, faculty, and deans want and need.

The expanding role of business officers also means an expansion of how they will use data. Earlier in this chapter, we provided a historical view of how data had been used by college and university business officers—from cost analysis to strategic financial analysis and from activity-based costing to managerial accounting and analysis. These uses of data will remain relevant going forward, but the business officer use of data will necessarily expand to analytics as well.

In order for business and finance officers to best support their institutions in meeting their mission (including driving student outcomes), remaining financially viable, and optimizing facilities use, leaders in college and university business and finance officers will need to focus on data integration, approach the use of data from a resource allocation perspective, and hone data literacy and data governance skills and practices.

References

APPA and NACUBO. 2017. "2017 Edition: APPA & NACUBO Key Facilities Metrics Survey." https://www.nacubo.org/Topics/Facilities-and-Environmental-Compliance/Key-Facilities-Metrics-Survey.

Ayers, T., and K. Goldstein. 2015. "Becoming a Renaissance CBO." *Inside Higher Ed.* June 5, 2015. https://www.insidehighered.com/advice/2015/06/05/chief-business-officers-must-broaden-their-skills-and-roles-essay.

Baer, L. L. 2019. "The Rise of Analytics in Higher Education." In *An Analytics Handbook: Moving from Evidence to Impact*, 3–9, edited by L. L. Baer and C. Carmean. Ann Arbor, Michigan: Society for College and University Planning.

Better Buildings. 2019. "Better Buildings Alliance—Higher Education." Accessed April 9, 2019. https://betterbuildingsinitiative.energy.gov/alliance/sector/higher-education.

Bonneson, K., T. Clancy, and C. White-Delany. 2016. "Program Costing: Increasing Net Revenue Through Efficiency," NACUBO Webcast, Washington, DC. https://www.nacubo.org/Events/2016/Program-Costing--Increasing-Net-Revenue-through-Efficiency.

Chester, T. M. 2018. "The IR-IT Nexus: Three Essentials for Driving Institutional Change. through Data and Analytics." In *The Analytics Revolution in Higher Education: Big Data, Organizational Learning, and Student Success,* 55–69, edited by S. Gagliardi, A. Parnell, and J. Carpenter-Hubin. Sterling, VA: Stylus.

Creusere, M. A., and D. R. Troutman. 2018. "What's in Your Data?" *Business Officer Magazine.* October 2018. NACUBO. https://www.businessofficermagazine.org/features/whats-in-your-data/.

DeVries, H. 2019. *The Case for Analytics: Unlocking your Institution's Data to Make Informed Decisions.* Reston, VA: Ellucian, Inc.

Dworkis, P., S. Rider, M. Urmeneta, D. Baker, M. Unterman, and A. Pember. 2019. "Moving from Cost Modeling to Analytics to Achieve Mission and Financial Performance." NACUBO. https://www.nacubo.org/LiveEventsFinal/2019/Moving-from-Cost-Modeling-to-Analytics-to-Achieve-Your-Mission--Financial-Performance.

Gagliardi, J. S. 2018. "The Analytics Revolution in Higher Education." In *The Analytics Revolution in Higher Education: Big Data, Organizational Learning, and Student Success,* 1–14, edited by J. S. Gagliardi, A. Parnell, and J. Carpenter-Hubin. Sterling, VA: Stylus.

Gartner Pictures. 2012. "Analytic Value Escalator." Accessed October 22, 2018. https://www.flickr.com/photos/27772229@N07/8267855748.

Gates Foundation. 2016. "Johnson County Community College: College Cost Management Model." Gates Foundation Grant Whitepaper Addendum. http://www.jccc.edu/about/leadership-governance/administration/files/jccc-abc-whitepaper.pdf.

Gower, M., and L. Hammond. 2017. "Analytics, Immersive Classrooms, and Buses." NACUBO Managerial Analysis and Decision Support Meeting, Philadelphia, PA.

Grans Korsh, S. 2013. "Spatial Concepts." *Business Officer* 47, no. 3: 16–23. Washington, DC: NACUBO.

Hans, J. 1974. *College and University Business Administration.* Washington, DC: National Association of College and University Business Officers.

Hignite, K. 2018. "Reshape Your Space." *Business Officer* 52, no. 5: 18–24. NACUBO. https://www.businessofficermagazine.org/features/reshape-your-space/.

Hurlburt, S., R. Kirshstein, and P. Rossol-Allison. 2014. "The ABCs of Activity-Based Costing in Community Colleges." American Institutes for Research. Accessed April 9, 2019. https://maximizingresources.org/files/The-ABCs-of-Activity-Based-Costing-in-Community-Colleges.pdf.

Joch, A. 2018. "Colleges Use IoT to Save Money on HVAC and Other Facilities." *EdTech Magazine.* February 14, 2018. https://edtechmagazine.com/higher/article/2018/02/colleges-use-iot-save-money-hvac-and-other-facilities.

Kopach, C. M., and A. Mohammadi. 2018. "Analytics, Sustainability, and Cost Savings." Paper presented at 2018 NACUBO Integrating Analytics Forum, Phoenix, AZ, 2018.

Lancaster, J., L. Ledford, and J. Stephens. 2019. "Structure Your Data Governance." *Business Officer* 52, no. 8: 19. https://www.businessofficermagazine.org/features /ethics-at-the-core/.

Lederman, D., and S. Jaschik, 2018. "2018 Survey of College and University Business Officers." *Inside Higher Ed.* Retrieved April 4, 2019. https://www.insidehighered .com/booklet/2018-survey-college-and-university-business-officers.

Macalester College. 2018. "Macalester College 2017–2018 Energy Report." Macalester College. https://www.macalester.edu/facilities/wp-content/uploads /sites/74/2018/08/2017_2018_Campus_Energy_Rpt.pdf

———. 2019a. "About Sustainability." Macalester College. Accessed April 9, 2019. https://www.macalester.edu/sustainability/about/.

———. 2019b. "Reports, Resources, Data." Macalester College. Accessed February 10, 2020. https://www.macalester.edu/sustainability/data-reports/.

Mancini, C. G., and E. R. Goeres. 1995. "Direct Allocation Costing: Informed Management Decisions in a Changing Environment." *Business Officer* 28, no. 10: 40–45.

Menditto, S. 2018. "Final Report for the NACUBO Board of Directors: Ad Hoc Committee on Identifying and Disseminating Effective Analytics." Presented at NACUBO Board Meeting, Long Beach, CA, July 20, 2018.

Miller, K. 2017. "Leverage Sub-Meter Data as Feedback to Engage Community Members and Save Energy on Shoestring Staffing and Funding." Webinar. Association for the Advancement of Sustainability in Higher Education. April 19, 2017. https://www.aashe.org/calendar/leveraging-sub-meter-data/.

Motley, A. 2016. "Keep Pace with Space." *Business Officer* 50, no. 5: 18–24. https://www.nacubo.org/Topics/Facilities-and-Environmental-Compliance /Facilities-Related-Business-Officer-Magazine-Articles.

NACUBO. 2004. *Managerial Analysis and Decision Support.* Washington, DC: National Association of College and University Business Officers.

———. 2016. *2016 National Profile of Higher Education Chief Business Officers.* Washington, DC: National Association for College and University Business Officer.

———. 2018. "Analytics: Information Decisions in Higher Education." https://www .nacubo.org/topics/analytics/analytics-informing-decisions-in-higher-education.

———. 2019a. "Strategic Blueprint." Accessed May 10, 2019. https://www.nacubo .org/who-we-are/strategic-blueprint.

———. 2019b. "2019 Perceptions and Priorities." *Medium.* February 27, 2019. https://medium.com/nacubo/2019-perceptions-and-priorities-6d37a043af26.

———. 2019c. "Key Facilities Metrics Survey." NACUBO. https://www.nacubo.org /Topics/Facilities-and-Environmental-Compliance/Key-Facilities-Metrics-Survey.

Patterson, R. D. 2004. "Managerial Analysis and Decision Support." In *College & University Budgeting: An Introduction for Faculty and Academic Administrators,* 13–26, edited by L. Goldstein and R. Meisinger. Washington, DC: National Association of College and University Business Officers.

Prager, Sealy, & McCarthy, LLC, and KPMG. 1999. *Ratio Analysis in Higher Education.* Washington, DC: National Association of College and University Business Officers. https://www.prager.com/Public/raihe4.pdf.

Romali, R. F. 2019. "Using Data Mining to Drive Student Success, Completion, Transfer, and Revenue Generation." Presentation made at the EDUCAUSE Enterprise Summit, April 17–19, 2019, Long Beach, CA.

Sasaki. 2017. "Implementation Updates on Rutgers' 2030 Plan." Sasaki. Accessed June 5, 2019. http://www.sasaki.com/blog/view/989/.

Signal Tribune. (2019). "Latinx and Low-Income STEM students Just Got a $3 Million Grant to Further Their Education, Long Beach City College Says." Staff reports, *Signal Tribune*, October 24, 2019. Access on February 12, 2020 at: https://signaltribunenewspaper.com/44899/news/latinx-and-low-income-stem -students-just-got-a-huge-3-million-grant-to-further-their-education-long-beach -city-college-says/.

Sightlines. 2019. 2018 *State of Facilities in Higher Education.* Guildford, CT: Sightlines. https://18ux851sis0c8g7t8vm4d0dd-wpengine.netdna-ssl.com/wp -content/uploads/2019/01/2018-State-of-Facilities-in-Higher-Education_updated -1.3.19.pdf.

Toda, S. (2020). "Long Beach City College Makes Phenomenal Progress in Students Earning Degrees and Certificates." Press Release from *Digital Journal*, February 4, 2020. Accessed February 12, 2020. http://www.digitaljournal.com/pr/4578138.

Townsley, M. K. 2009. *Weathering Turbulent Times: A Small College Guide to Financial Health.* Washington, DC: National Association of College and University Business Officers.

Vanover Porter, M. 2017. "Multipurpose Data." *Business Officer* 50, no. 1: 60–66. https://www.businessofficermagazine.org/features/multipurpose-data/.

PART IV. Concluding Comments

Data-Informed Decision Making and the Pursuit of Analytics Maturity in Higher Education

Karen L. Webber and Henry Y. Zheng

THE TRANSFORMATION in the use of data analytics for informed decision making in higher education has begun. Facing growing competition in educational delivery, rising education costs, and shifting demographic trends, the competitive higher education environment today demands a deeper understanding and use of data-informed decision support. Data analytics is beginning to transform the culture, strategy, operations, and outcome assessment of college and university campuses. The use of data, statistical analysis, and explanatory and predictive models to gain insight on complex issues across the business and learning domains of higher education will become pervasive (Bichsel 2012). Supported and informed by position papers from higher education partners such as the American Council on Education (Gagliardi and Turk 2017) and EDUCAUSE (Dahlstrom 2016; EDUCAUSE 2019), institutional leaders have an opportunity to use enterprise-level analytics to drive digital transformation and redefine the student experience and success. To accomplish this, leaders must create and continue to support a data-informed culture that values data and appropriate analytics. While the discussions in this book have focused on data analytics in US higher education, similar trends and activities are happening in higher education around the globe. Although higher education in different parts of the world may face some unique issues, a large number of topics and challenges are similar. Indeed, considerations for the implementation of data analytics, incorporating the use of data amidst growing complexities in higher education organizations, and challenges with data security and privacy resonate comparably with higher education officials in every region of the world.

In the previous chapters of this book, we have seen principles of good practice, examples that have been implemented, and convincing arguments for the use of data analytics to inform admissions and enrollment management decisions, to promote student success via advising and course management systems, to connect and engage stakeholders, to maintain energy-efficient buildings and physical plant practices, and to support the finance and business decisions of colleges and universities. Often, new processes and practices are a bit slower to be implemented in education compared to the business sector. However, data analytics is now moving strongly into many higher education practices and the value received from data analytics is clearer. We agree with Davenport (2006), who believes that organizational leaders who embrace the analytics culture and attempt experimentation are creating competitive advantage.

Data-Informed Decisions Are Better

We framed the discussions in this book around the perspective of *data-informed* decision making (DIDM) rather than the perspective of *data-driven* decision making (DDDM). Where DDDM lets the data "drive" the decision making, removing human consideration of the context, DIDM recognizes that human judgment is a key element in complex, dynamic, and strategic decision making. A number of factors may need to be taken into consideration, thus we define DIDM as the process of organizing data resources, conducting data analysis, and developing data insights to provide the contexts and evidence base for formulating organizational decisions. Even when equipped with sufficient data and excellent analysis, higher education leaders need to draw on their professional experience, political acumen, ethical practice, and strategic considerations in making decisions. Data-informed decisions wisely consider knowledge learned from the data but also factor in unique facets or features that are important in the formulation of a decision. We agree with Lane and Finsel (2014), who purport that data cannot be very useful unless they can be analyzed in a timely way and developed with contextualized meaning.

Technology to assist with data-informed decision making has advanced rapidly in the past half century. While desktop computers became commonplace in the 1970s, computing power to manage higher education institutions advanced significantly in the 1980s and 1990s. Locally developed administrative computing systems were soon replaced with commercial enterprise resource planning (ERP) systems such as Banner and PeopleSoft. These enterprise systems were helpful in linking up some institutional operations such as student records, billing, and budgeting, but they did not capture other important aspects of the institution, including management of learning outcomes, teaching effectiveness, and research outcomes. However, more recent customer relations management (CRM) systems seeking to link multiple systems for areas such as admissions, learning management systems (LMS) for teaching and learning, assessment management systems for educational outcomes, and donor management systems are becoming more prevalent.

Without a doubt, a critical factor in one's success in integrating a strong and successful data analytics program is the use of an actionable and sustainable, but adaptable data governance program. Such a plan includes a system of decision rights and accountabilities for information-related processes, identifies roles and responsibilities for various stewards, promotes high data quality, and emphasizes collaboration and frequent communication to ensure good decision making. Staff members in units such as institutional research are critical for their knowledge of data definitions and nuances of the specific context, and members in IT are valuable contributors for their technical skills in data security, enterprise-level management, and storage.

Institutional leaders who encourage integrated data, stewardship, and collaboration among relevant colleagues for data governance programs are providing leading examples of good practice with data analytics.

Now in 2020, we see an increase in the use of data analytics for informed decision making across campus. Today's advanced educational technologies include learning management systems, early alert or early warning advising systems (EWS), dashboards, and other tools that provide information on student application and enrollment, the management of student performance, course retention, and degree progress. Big Data and other data analytics are also being used to monitor heating and cooling of campus buildings, to examine frequency and length of library and recreation facility use, and to identify the most time-efficient bus routes. Advanced analyses, both traditional inferential analyses based on previous or current data, as well as predictive modeling and machine learning techniques, enable analysts to discern patterns that can be combined with contextual judgment to inform decisions. While the focus of the discussions in this book relate to data analytics that affect student success and institutional administration, we heartily acknowledge that Big Data and techniques such as predictive analyses are being used in faculty member research. Separate volumes are needed to unpack the many ways in which Big Data, AI, and other advanced analytics are contributing to knowledge production across many academic disciplines.

Indeed, the quickened pace of technological developments such as artificial intelligence, machine learning, and blockchain prompt higher education leaders to consider the development and application of data analytics capabilities as an important institutional priority. A survey of papers presented at the 2013–2015 Learning Analytics and Knowledge conferences (Khalil and Ebner, 2016b) found that the largest proportion of papers focused on data mining techniques (N = 31), some papers on visualizations (N = 13) and text mining semantics (N = 13), and the smallest proportion on qualitative analysis (N = 6) and gaming (N = 4). Even since 2015, there has been greater inquiry into all types of analytics and their value in higher education. Further, changes in the higher education marketplace suggest that having strong analytical capabilities and leveraging them to inform decisions will help create more effective strategic and operational capabilities, leading to organizational competitive advantages.

Interesting ideas for data analytics are presented in Kellen (2019). As CIO at the University of California–San Diego, Kellen remarked that old mental models (including data and political silos) hamper efforts to move higher education analytics into the twenty-first century. The model of traditional structured data in a warehouse that requires ETL (extract, transform, load) processes, while familiar and comfortable, hampers improved movement to better ways to think about, organize, and analyze data. Kellen (2019) argues that new technologies enable analysts to capitalize on high-speed, in-memory analytics at lower cost in Big Data environments. New technologies sometimes demand new rules, which Kellen believes serve to turn the old directives on their head, forcing us to consider a new paradigm for how we think about, manage, and use data for decision support. The new analytics environment encourages structures that support maximum flexibility, which will enable very rich analytics environments at a lower price than were available a decade ago. With our emphasis on the need for human interpretation, we are cautiously intrigued by Kellen's (2019) discussion on exploding large data sets (one example given is visualizing an exploded data set to examine classroom room use for each minute of the day, for every day in a year for 20 years). Indeed, such a level of granularity is unprecedented, although we continue to urge caution in collecting data simply because technology allows us to do so at a new low price.

Privacy, Responsible and Proper Use of Data

Along with improved analytics, new techniques and strategies abound for the presentation of data. Visual software packages have improved the ability to present data in colorful charts and graphs, infographics, and dashboards. Interactive visuals can be quite helpful in guiding the reader through the view and can also help ensure clarity through definitions or caveats that appear when the user scrolls over a data point. However, while data visuals can be of great assistance, adherence to principles of good graphic design (e.g., Cairo 2013, Tufte 2001) will lessen the likelihood of misinterpretation. Cognitive psychologists remind us of important principles related to how one "sees" data and how the brain interprets those data into information. Color, spacing, scale, and the calculation of numeric data are important factors to consider when designing graphs and charts. Today's new infographics, while intuitively appealing, may offer challenges to read and understand fully. In designing good graphics, Tufte's (2001) words still ring true: *above all else, show the data.*

As advances in technology allow us to collect more data (both traditional quantitative data but increasingly the qualitative data from social media and other similar sources), senior leaders must be explicitly wary of collecting data for collection's sake. The volume of data currently collected has already shown that many institutions have more data available than are being used for informed decision making. Senior leaders and other lead officials in the institution's data governance program should consider strategies for the addition of data before they are collected. In chapter 2, Hosch wisely suggests that senior leaders keep their focus on strong data governance, not being swayed into thinking that vendor products will solve all data management and analysis concerns. Companies like EAB, Civitas, HelioCampus, and Snowflake can be of assistance in the rapid deployment of technology, but caution is urged when considering the use of numerous vendor products.

Issues of student and staff privacy as well as adherence to data collection and sharing policies (e.g., GDPR, FERPA, HIPAA) must be followed. Transparency and security should be integral aspects of learning analytics technology rather than afterthoughts (Reidenberg and Schaub 2018). It should go without saying that higher education officials and commercial learning vendors should establish appropriate safeguards to govern appropriate access and use of learning analytics data. Khalil and Ebner (2016a) discuss the benefits of de-identification techniques that can help with privacy, and Reidenberg and Schaub (2018) further suggest that legal safeguards for education privacy should reflect the reality of increased use of data in education by expanding privacy protections to clearly cover learning analytics. On a related note, Mathies (2018) urges higher education officials to consider a data sharing mandate that would allow institutional data to be more accessible to campus colleagues but done so within a data governance plan. In such a data bill of rights, institution officials would be required to develop a plan that respects and protects individuals' data, requires programming language that limits coding failures, and includes a data ethics board to review and ensure good data practices. Although Pardo and Siemens believe that "data can be either useful or perfectly anonymous, but never both" (2014, 447), we hold out hope that higher education officials can be thoughtful in developing policies and procedures that enable us to use data to assist in student success yet do so in ways that use data responsibly and ensure privacy.

Across the board, there is an increasing volume in conversations about data analytics in higher education; however, more discussions and actions are needed, particularly in some student support areas—for example, more attention on the use and benefit of data analytics related to career and workforce development. Officials in these areas will likely need to develop standards for the use of state longitudinal data systems and specific data such as unemployment wage records, relationships between educational debt and labor, and other labor-related data sources.

There are a number of critical success factors that have been identified by various chapter authors (consistent with the points made by collaborative conversations and meetings across leaders from AIR, EDUCAUSE, and NACUBO). Many important points have been made and are agreed upon by leaders across the three organizations, including the value and need for a data-informed decision culture. These leaders believe that such a culture requires senior leadership commitments; building a collaborative culture to drive analytics development; securing and sharing data resources that empower the analytics community; building in regular training and professional development for the analytic community; and focusing on key strategic priorities that help determine when best to deploy analytic solutions. It is critical for HEI senior leaders to have a roadmap that will guide their data analytics journey. This roadmap can be effectively supported by a data analytics maturity model and assessed by metrics often designed in a scorecard.

Maturity Models for Data Analytics

Following similar upward growth, expansion, and sophistication in the related processes in the business sector, and despite an overall low level of data analytics (Gartner 2018), leaders in the higher education community are becoming more aware of the need to be focused on the use of data for informed decision making and how that translates into good business practices for the institution. Furthermore, Petty (2019) predicts that by 2022, 90% of corporate strategies will explicitly mention information as a critical asset and analytics as a critical competency.

Senior administrative leaders who are focused on the impact of technology can identify goals to increase the maturity of their institution's analytic structures and capabilities. In general, a *maturity model* is a technique used to explain and project a business process or aspects of an organization, with the goal of moving toward a more organized and systematic way of doing business (Proença and Borbinha 2016). A maturity model typically includes tiered or hierarchical levels that describe how well the behaviors, practices, and processes of an organization reliably and sustainably produce required outcomes related to information technology. It is a tool that is used to develop, assess, and refine one's IT focus, to know where the institution currently sits in relation to the institution's mission and goals, and to help determine where it wants to go in the future. A maturity model can be used as a benchmark for comparison with other institutions and to understand IT practices. Institution leaders can also seek to obtain an IT *maturity assessment* to identify gaps between the current state and future goals. As such, it can include an indication of the institution's strengths, weaknesses, opportunities, and threats. An IT maturity assessment can help establish a path to make improvements over time to create an improved, stronger, and/or more efficient IT landscape.

Maturity models originated in the business sector, but they are relevant and can be used for a variety of practices within higher education. Of interest in this chapter are maturity models that relate to data and analytics in higher education. In addition to the innovations at Northeastern University described by Glasgal and Nestor in chapter 6, a number of maturity models are available for specific aspects such as data governance—for example, the IBM Data Governance Council Maturity Model (Russom 2008; IBM Data Governance Council 2007, in Firican 2018). Further, a number of other leading companies partner with higher education organizations to customize strategies to help the organization improve organizational performance.

In addition to data governance maturity models, several other broader maturity models for the implementation and use of analytics are available. Where data governance maturity examines change in data governance as an enabler of the analytics culture, analytics is the broader use of data within the context of organizational processes used to derive insights for decision making. Both involve technical capabilities, leadership, skills, strategies, and policies, and despite overlap in concepts, we see maturity models for data governance distinctively different from analytics maturity models.

Now refined over a number of years, Davenport's Five Stages of Analytics Maturity (Davenport 2018; Davenport, Harris, and Morison 2010) and the subsequent DELTA model from Davenport, Harris, and Morison (2010) are well known and described here briefly.

Davenport's Five Stages of Analytics Maturity

Most organizations, including higher education institutions, grow in their understanding and complexity of organizational data. According to Davenport (2018), organizations mature their analytic capabilities as they develop their organizational structures and processes related to data. Davenport purports that his Maturity Model (Davenport and Harris 2007), further refined (with Harris and Morison in 2010), helps organizational leaders measure growth in analytic capabilities. The five stages are:

> *Stage 1: Analytically Impaired.* Organization leaders rely primarily on gut feel to make decisions and have no formal plans for becoming more analytical.
> *Stage 2: Localized Analytics.* Analytics or reporting at the institution exists within silos. There is no means or structure for

collaborating across organizational units or functions in the use of analytics. This often leads to "multiple versions of the truth."

Stage 3: Analytical Aspirations. The organization sees the value of analytics, and it intends to improve its capabilities for generating and using it. Thus far, however, it has made little progress in doing so.

Stage 4: Analytical Companies. Companies in this category are good at multiple aspects of analytics. They are highly data-oriented, they have analytical tools, and they make wide use of analytics with some coordination across the organization.

Stage 5: Analytical Competitors. These companies use analytics strategically and pervasively across the entire enterprise. They view their analytical capabilities as a competitive weapon, and they have already seen some competitive advantage result from analytics.

According to Davenport (2018), an institution may have specific analytic strengths or weaknesses that identify them across different levels of the model. For example, an organization may achieve a Stage 4 in analytics leadership maturity but achieve only a Stage 3 in its management and use of data. This assessment enables targeted investment to mature analytics weaknesses based on the DELTA model (Davenport 2018). Furthermore, proceeding through an exercise to gauge the institution's current status of analytics maturity is not a one-time exercise. It should be repeated to measure progress and to ensure that institutional practices and policies related to data and analytics are continuing in the desired direction.

The DELTA Maturity Model

Following earlier versions of an analytics maturity model, including figure 12.1 (Davenport and Harris 2007; Davenport, Harris, and Morison 2010), Davenport developed the DELTA Plus model to enhance the Five Stages of Analytics Maturity (2018). Davenport and colleagues purport that, in order to create meaningful analytics, data must be organized,

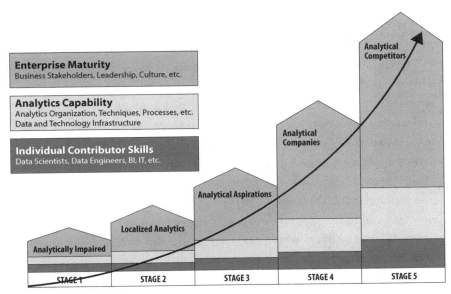

Enterprise Maturity
Business Stakeholders, Leadership, Culture, etc.

Analytics Capability
Analytics Organization, Techniques, Processes, etc.
Data and Technology Infrastructure

Individual Contributor Skills
Data Scientists, Data Engineers, BI, IT, etc.

Analytical Competitors

Analytical Companies

Analytical Aspirations

Localized Analytics

Analytically Impaired

STAGE 1   STAGE 2   STAGE 3   STAGE 4   STAGE 5

Figure 12.1. Five Stages of Analytics Maturity. Davenport and Harris 2007. Used with permission from Davenport 2019.

unique, integrated, accessible, and of high quality (Davenport 2018, 3). Further, Davenport believes that analyses are influenced by the structure, cleanliness, and uniqueness of the data. Unsurprisingly, Davenport believes that organizations need to integrate their data across organizational silos and, where possible, combine and harmonize transactional systems across different business units. The five essential elements are:

D for accessible, high-quality *data*
E for an *enterprise* orientation to managing analytics
L for analytical *leadership*
T for strategic *targets*
A for *analysts*.

Recently, Davenport (2018) added two additional elements to the DELTA model. Spurred by the continued growth of Big Data, and coupled with the introduction of new analytics techniques like machine learning, two additional elements (the Plus factors) that should also be considered are:

T for *technology,* and

A for *analytics techniques.*

Davenport and colleagues clearly advocate for an enterprise approach. This occurs by setting an analytics strategy and building a roadmap for strategy implementation. Integrating data and managing a unified data and analytics platform are essential components of an analytics roadmap, as is promoting a culture of analytics across the organization. Senior leaders must embrace and support this approach, and analytic efforts must be aligned with specific, strategic targets that reach to meet institutional goals. Davenport (2018) also reminds us that while technology was stable for several decades in analytics, it is changing rapidly today. With the advent of Big Data, AI, cloud and open source options, creating an effective technology strategy for analytics is a critical prerequisite for success (Davenport 2018).

Gauging Analytics Maturity

While it is important to begin a campus-wide strategy for data analytics, it is helpful for institutional leaders to understand their progress in analytics implementation. To that end, EDUCAUSE developed maturity and deployment indices to measure and benchmark analytics practices. Gauging the institution's current level of analytics development, identifying areas of strength and challenge, and developing strategies for progress can help officials engage in analytical strategic planning.

Following refinements in the original 2012 version, EDUCAUSE offers (through its Core Data Service, CDS) a current index that measures 32 factors contributing to analytics maturity. The dimensions examine multiple areas of progress such as culture, process, expertise, investment, and governance and are organized into six dimensions:

1. *Decision-making culture,* including senior leadership commitment and the use and cultural acceptance of analytics;
2. *Policies,* including data collection, access, and use policies;

3. *Data efficacy,* relating to quality, standardization, and "right-ness" of data and reports and the availability of tools and software for analytics;
4. *Investment/resources,* consisting of funding, an investment-versus-expense mentality, and the appropriateness of analytics staffing;
5. *Technical infrastructure,* consisting of analytics tools and the capacity to store, manage, and analyze data;
6. *IR involvement,* capturing interaction between the IT and the IR (institutional research or similar analytics functions) organizations.

Each dimension is scored on a scale of 1 (absent/ad hoc) to 5 (opti-mized), and the mean of those scores represents the overall institutional maturity score. The score provides a way for an institution to determine where it is currently and to assess if or to what extent, and in what areas, the institution is moving forward related to analytics. For more informa-tion on EDUCAUSE's maturity index, refer to EDUCAUSE's Benchmark-ing Service at: https://www.educause.edu/about/discover-membership/educause-benchmarking-resources.

Strategies for Success

Managing today's complex higher education institutions requires a thor-ough understanding of issues related to data management and use. It also requires support for campus faculty and staff who are leaders in data analytics, insistence on interpreting data within the institutional context, and regular interactions with external stakeholders to explain the value as well as the limitations of data analytics in higher educa-tion. Strategies must be in place to ensure adequate infrastructure, gov-ernance, security and compliance, process for operations, and ways in which to articulate and promote the value that comes from the analyt-ics. As the role of the chief data officer takes hold, gaining authority and influence on par with other executives, organization leaders will likely move away from merely using data as a resource to analytics as a reporting and decision making support tool. Data and strategic data analytics will likely become the centerpiece of enterprise strategy, focus, and investment (Hippold 2018; Petty 2019).

In many ways, data and analytics have the potential to help higher education students and institutions succeed. Institution leaders who have been on the forefront of these changes have seen benefits, and in some cases strategies that haven't quite hit the mark. In a recent review of over 252 published research and conference papers, Viberg et al. (2018) found high enthusiasm and some evidence that learning analytics improves learning and teaching in higher education. For example, a limited number of studies have examined collaborative problem-solving skills and cognitive gains through self-reflection. In addition, a number of activities have focused on pedagogy and models for implementation of learning analytics to facilitate improved learning. However, Viberg et al. also noted that only 6% of the strategies were used widely and that the vast majority would not "scale to the entire institution or other institutions" (107).

Also mentioned by Klein et al. in chapter 10, more than 1,400 papers were presented at the Learning Analytics and Knowledge conference from 2012 to 2018, and the inertia for research and strategies on learning analytics in higher education is now under way. Along with increased use of course management systems, early warning systems, and other aspects of learning analytics, researchers and senior institution leaders must consider how the tools and techniques are contributing to institutional business practices and student learning. The volumes of data available on students can be used to identify learning environments and student acquisition of skills (Kinnebrew and Biswas 2012). Analysis of learning can occur through traditional human judgment of data results, but newer automated techniques are also being used, including sequence mining (Kinnebrew and Biswas 2012) or classification (Sao Pedro, Gobert, and Baker 2012), collectively called educational data mining (EDM; Baker and Siemens 2014). These forms of assessment can be similar to traditional psychometric approaches or advanced evidence-centered models of complex student skill (Baker and Corbett 2014).

While the advantages of educational data mining can be seen, particularly the possibility of customized analysis of student ability early in a course or academic program, we see value in additional analysis and study of EDM assessment methods and their routine validation of results across multiple populations and for agreement with human judgments.

Institutional Impact

According to Gartner (2018), organizational leaders can follow four steps to move their institution's capabilities to have greater organizational impact:

1. *Develop holistic data and analytics strategies with a clear vision.* Coordination and collaboration among data and analytics, IT, and business leaders can enable continuous and dynamic attention to strategies for data analytics;
2. *Create a flexible organizational structure, exploit analytics resources, and implement ongoing analytics training;*
3. *Implement a data governance program; and*
4. *Create integrated analytics platforms that can support a broad range of uses.*

These steps require a deep and long-term commitment. As the institution moves to a more mature position in data analytics, tasks move from stand-alone disconnected activities to ones that are connected and designed by leaders who are striving for comprehensive solutions and processes.

The Future Forward

The future of Big Data and analytics in higher education has the potential to further benefit student and institutional success. Initial studies, such as those described in this volume offer evidence of benefits to teaching and learning that can come from the use of analytic techniques. The challenges for broader implementation will require student trust and willingness to engage, comprehensive and secure data, and faculty members who see the alignment between the technology and the potential to improve teaching and learning (Leitner, Ebner, and Ebner 2019).

Collaborations among campus personnel as well as collaborations across relevant professional organizations are also important. Similar or joint meetings and published materials can offer a strong and consistent message to members across groups who may have similar interests. The 2019 *AIR/EDUCAUSE/NACUBO Joint Statement on Data Analytics* is an important message that describes the value of data analytics to higher education organizations. The joint statement includes six principles of action to promote the meaningful use of analytics in higher education. The statement and the working committee from these three key associations have taken advantage of their collective knowledge and insights derived from data to suggest an action plan that can help ensure implementation of strong data analytic strategies on campus.

The AIR/EDUCAUSE/NACUBO joint statement reminds us that the use and implementation of data analytics is complex and will require input from many individuals. However, the impact of data analytics across campus will be high, and when accomplished jointly with colleagues across organizations, the outcome can yield even greater benefits that are carried out efficiently. In their suggestions for how to build organizational capacity for analytics, Norris and Baer (2013) offer a framework that considers how to optimize student success through analytics (23). Except for perhaps a too heavy emphasis on data mining, the framework offers relevant suggestions for eliminating impediments for retention and student success, utilizing analyses to respond to at-risk students, and creating personalized learning analytics. In a similar vein, but focused on building capacity in institutional research, Webber (2018) posited four important factors that, collectively, can build capacity in IR. Knowledge of needed skills and analytic techniques is paramount, as is previous research on relevant issues that are related to the analytic task(s) at hand (figure 12.2). As mentioned in several of the previous chapters, clear and accurate communication of the analytics

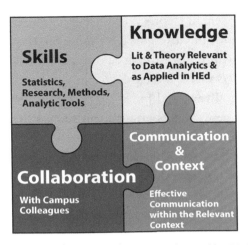

Figure 12.2. Factors in Building Capacity. Adapted from Webber 2018.

results, via printed report, visualization, or face-to-face discussion is critical. Framing results within the context is vital, and working with partners across campus greatly contributes to the success of data analytics tasks. Perhaps the model applies to the ways in which higher education leaders can build and strengthen data analytics in higher education.

This figure is a reminder that data governance and analytics are components of a larger strategic approach. As discussed by Marsh and Thariani in chapter 5, leaders strive for program alignment to ensure student and organizational success. To that end university leaders and trustees seek to leverage data resources and strategic analytics to fully understand the decision contexts and to objectively evaluate the trade-offs, cost-benefits, and long-term impacts of major organizational decisions. These goals require a high-level view.

Many leaders in higher education in the United States and in other countries acknowledge the benefits of building an integrated data environment that empowers informed decision making. For example, MIT's Center for Information Systems Research's advisory board acknowledges that data strategy is a central, integrated concept that works within the larger business strategy (http://cisr.mit.edu/reports/create-a-data-strategy/intro.php). Collaborative efforts between institutions in the University System of Georgia (USG) and data scientists at the UGA Carl Vinson Institute of Governance are using predictive and other data analytics along with innovative visualizations to examine student admissions, pathways through their degree program, and other measures of success (Nolan, Byars, and Jones 2018). Efforts at this USG institution are offering new insights into student success that will likely contribute to institutional success as well.

Describing the framework developed at Stonybrook University, Hosch (forthcoming 2020) purports that a data strategy is an intentional plan to capture, integrate, and use data to advance the institution's mission and goals. While the maturity of each element in the data strategy may vary across institutions, data assets ideally encompass data across an institution and therefore require enterprise-level thinking and planning. In 2012, Picciano surmised that there are not yet enough individuals in higher education trained to use Big Data and analytics appropriately. Along with expertise for database development, Picciano believes more instructional designers who can work with faculty will be needed as well as professionals in institutional research and others who are knowledgeable about statistics, decision trees, and strategy mapping to develop predictive models. While higher education may be making some small advances forward, we believe that the higher education community still needs more carefully considered strategies for training as well as campus policies for governance, data sharing, security, and privacy.

Training for technology, data security, governance, and statistical analysis can be obtained through relevant professional associations, informally from other knowledgeable colleagues, or from intentional formal training that is offered and open to all members of the campus data community. Colleges and universities can no longer put off data governance as an optional function. If data is truly considered a strategic asset, it must be protected, managed, and leveraged just like other valuable assets on campus.

Many industry organizations have created a chief data officer (CDO) or chief analytics officer (CAO) position to lead their data assets management and analytics development efforts. In higher education, CDO or CAO jobs are beginning to emerge, and it is important to recognize that such roles are similar to chief financial officer or chief human resources officer roles, in that they all lead a functional domain, either directly or through a distributive structure. CDOs or CAOs should be entrusted with managing the data assets of an organization, overseeing the translation of data into actionable insights, delivering the data and insights in a timely and effective manner to decision makers, and advocating for the use of such insights to inform strategic and operational decisions. Whether a university chooses to develop a centralized structure with all analytics functions reporting to the CDO/CAO or a coordinated structure with the CDO/CAO serving as the thinker and convener of a distributed analytics network will depend on the university's unique culture, organizational setting, and leadership vision.

Hosch (forthcoming 2020) reminds readers that data strategy should be informed by institutional priorities, goals, and return on investment. All strategies need to be forward-looking, should consider how the institution can accomplish its goals and mission, and must be documented, shared with others, and used to guide practice. We believe that these strategies can be accomplished most effectively when institutional leaders, faculty, and staff have the relevant skills and knowledge needed, ensure that the specific context is considered, communicate effectively, and work collaboratively with relevant colleagues.

Concluding Remarks

As leaders consider options to support or boost their institution's analytic capabilities, the following are some questions to consider. The questions may serve as a useful checklist along four key aspects of technology development: *people, process, technology,* and *culture.*

People

- *Leadership support and commitment:* Do senior leaders have a vision and plan for how data analytics will help transform the campus decision environment? If there is a plan, does it support the incremental progression to a higher level of analytics maturity?

- *Analytics talents development:* Does the institution have a professional development and career progression plan to help move data analytics staff from the more traditional data cleanup and reporting roles to the more skilled data researcher or data scientist roles with the right statistical and analytical knowledge and experience? Is there a formal or informal community or network for like-minded analytics talents to share knowledge and work collaboratively?
- *Acceptance of analytical insights by operational leaders:* Do operational level leaders (directors and managers alike) understand and take advantage of the benefits of analytical insights as they manage their organizations? Even the best research is worthless if the research findings are ignored and not being utilized to effect changes.

Process

- *Breaking down silos:* Do institution leaders make intentional efforts and policies to break down the data silos among different functional areas to improve data transparency and access for integrative analytics development? Analytics is more powerful if data assets are connected to paint a more robust picture of the relationships.
- *Data governance:* Does the institution have a robust enterprise-wide data governance program that effectively addresses the data quality, data curation, data documentation, and data access issues that are key to the enablement of analytics development?

Technology

- *Data quality and integration capabilities:* Does the institution have a cohesive strategy to curate, manage, organize, and transform data as a strategy asset of the organization? A centralized or federated data warehouse or data lake is not the necessary condition for supporting and growing advanced analytics capabilities. However, having a robust data management infrastructure with the right access control will empower and accelerate analytics development.

- *BI platform and visualization tools:* Does the institution invest in business intelligence (BI), data visualization, and reporting tools that empower the analytics community? Analytics development is at its optimal state when BI and reporting tools are not monopolized by a few with access or specialized skills. Wide access to the tools and ease of use will liberate the creative energy among many data professionals as well as business users with an interest in analytics.

- *Ensure data security and ethical use:* Does the institution have a strong data security and data governance program to help ensure compliance with data security, privacy, and ethical use of data assets? Be vigilant that data are well protected so that the information does not get into the hands of those who intend to misuse it. Staff should be trained on implicit bias of model algorithms and the limitations of data. This is especially important for predictive analytics that directly impact the student populations. New America, an advocacy group, has a series of papers on how predictive analytics should be used ethically and its guidelines* are available online.

Analytics Culture

- *Use of data insights for decisions:* Does the institution make intentional efforts to use data to support strategic and operational decision making? This may include the use of performance scorecards for senior leaders' annual reviews, budget allocation decisions, and board conversations.

*New America—Predictive Analytics in Higher Education—"Five Guiding Practices for Ethical Use." Available at https://www.newamerica.org/education-policy/reports /predictive-analytics-in-higher-education/.

- *Achieve value through focus:* Are the institution's predictive analytics efforts oriented toward your strategic and operational priorities? Analytics development efforts need to align with organizational priorities to generate value and support among university stakeholders.
- *Translation of analytical insights:* Do the data analytics professionals know how to translate analytics insights to understandable knowledge? Even the most profound analytics findings must be translated and understood to be actionable and effective. Professional development is needed to help data science professionals to tell stories about data and data discoveries.
- *Communications and acceptance:* Do institution leaders communicate with the campus community about the need and urgency for use of analytics? Higher education is generally more accustomed to incremental changes, and predictive analytics and its findings may point to rapid changes that might conflict with some of the business practices that have been in place for many years. Without clear articulation and communication of how predictive analytics may benefit the campus, even the most brilliant analytic insights may not yield desired outcomes if they are not accepted.

Ideally, the data analytics strategy incorporated in an institution's larger strategy will produce excellent results. However, having the skills, knowledge, people, tools, and processes to develop and implement that strategy requires extensive resources. One great challenge is finding the resources needed, especially for institutions with limited budgets and staffing. No easy answers exist. Perhaps institutional resources can be set aside for this important need; or perhaps local, state, or federal resources can be acquired. Once the large strategy is developed and documented, perhaps small successes can be promoted as a way to build positive community buy-in and work to complete a larger plan over time. The challenge will rest with each institution's leader to chart the best path forward. However that is accomplished, we believe that data analytics in higher education will only grow in importance. We look toward a bright future and believe that the discussions in this book have contributed to the discussion on data analytics in higher education. Due to space limitations, this volume includes case examples that represent only a portion of good programs and practices that exist. We believe that the discussions offered provide insights into a better understanding of data analytics and necessary components of analytics strategies that have been developed and should be considered by those in institutions that may not have reached this step. Indeed, an optimal data analytics plan will require organizational, cultural, and strategic changes, but a beneficial and effective plan is possible, and we hope that this volume leaves the reader with new insights and an excitement for the future of data analytics in higher education.

References

Baker, R., and A. T. Corbett 2014. "Assessment of Robust Learning with Educational Data Mining." *Research & Practice in Assessment* 9, no. 2: 38–50.

Baker, R., and G. Siemens. 2014. "Educational Data Mining and Learning Analytics." In *Cambridge Handbook of Learning Sciences*, 253–274, edited by K. Sawyer. New York: Cambridge University Press.

Bichsel, J. 2012. "The 2012 ECAR Study of Analytics in Higher Education." EDUCAUSE Center for Analysis and Research. Accessed May 10, 2019. https:// library.educause.edu/resources/2012/6/2012-ecar-study-of-analytics-in-higher -education.

Cairo, A. 2013. *The Functional Art: An Introduction to Information Graphics and Visualizations*. Berkeley, CA: New Riders.

Dahlstrom, E. 2016. "Moving the Red Queen Forward: Maturing Data Analytics Capabilities in Higher Education." *EDUCAUSE Review*. August 22, 2016. https://er.educause.edu/articles/2016/8/moving-the-red-queen-forward-maturing -analytics-capabilities-in-higher-education.

Davenport, T. 2006. "Competing on Analytics." *Harvard Business Review* (January): 1–9.

———. 2018. "DELTA Plus Model and Five Stages of Analytics Maturity: A Primer." International Institute for Analytics. Accessed May 25, 2019. https://www .iianalytics.com/delta-plus-primer.

Davenport, T., and J. Harris. 2007. *Competing on Analytics: The New Science of Winning*. Boston, MA: Harvard Business Review Press.

Davenport, T., J. Harris, and B. Morison. 2010. *Analytics at Work: Smarter Decisions, Better Decisions*. Cambridge, MA: Harvard Business School Press.

EDUCAUSE. 2019. "Improving Data Management and Governance in Higher Education." EDUCAUSE. Accessed June 2, 2019. https://www.educause.edu /guides/improving-data-management-and-governance-in-higher-education.

Firican, G. 2018. "Data Governance Maturity Models—IBM." Lights On Data. Accessed on June 6, 2019 at: https://www.lightsondata.com/data-governance -maturity-models-ibm.

Gagliardi, J., and J. Turk. 2017. "The Data-Enabled Executive: Using Analytics for Student Success and Sustainability." American Council on Education. Accessed May 2, 2019. https://www.acenet.edu/news-room/Documents/The-Data-Enabled -Executive.pdf.

Gartner. 2018. "Gartner Data shows 87 Percent of Organizations Have Low BI and Analytics Maturity." Gartner. Accessed May 23, 2019. https://www.gartner.com /en/newsroom/press-releases/2018-12-06-gartner-data-shows-87-percent-of -organizations-have-low-bi-and-analytics-maturity.

Hippold, S. 2018. "Data and Analytics Leaders Must Engage and Train Their Entire Organization to Become Data Literate." Gartner. September 20, 2018. https:// www.gartner.com/smarterwithgartner/build-a-data-driven-organization/.

Hosch, B. (Forthcoming 2020). "Key Elements of a Data Strategy," In *Data Strategy in Colleges and Universities,* edited by K. Powers. New York: Routledge.

IBM Data Governance Council. 2007. "The IBM Data Governance Council Maturity Model: Building a Roadmap for Effective Data Governance." IBM Data Governance Council. Armonk, NY: IBM.

Khalil, M., and M. Ebner. (2016a). De-Identification in Learning Analytics. *Journal of Learning Analytics* 3, no. 1: 129–138. http://dx.doi.org/10.18608/jla.2016.31.8.

———. (2016b). "What Is Learning Analytics All About? A Survey of Different Methods Used in 2013–2015." Conference Proceedings of the 8th e-Learning Excellence Conference, Dubai, UAE.

Kellen, V. 2019. "21st-Century Analytics: New Technologies and New Rules." In *EDUCAUSE Review,* May 20, 2019. https://er.educause.edu/articles/2019/5/21st -century-analytics-new-technologies-and-new-rules.

Kinnebrew, J. S., and G. Biswas. 2012. "Identifying Learning Behaviors by Contextu-alizing Differential Sequence Mining and Action Features and Performance Evaluation." *Proceedings of the Fifth International Conference on Educational Data Mining* (pp. 57–64), Chania, Greece.

Lane, J. E., and B. A. Finsel. 2014. "Fostering Smarter Colleges and Universities: Data, Big Data, and Analytics." In *Building a Smarter University: Big Data, Innovation, and Analytics,* 3–27, edited by J. E. Lane. Albany: State University of New York Press.

Leitner, P., M. Ebner, and M. Ebner. 2019. "Learning Analytics Challenges to Overcome in Higher Education Institutions." In: *Utilizing Learning Analytics to Support Study Success.* Edited by Ifenthaler D., D. K. Mah, and J. K. Yau, 91–104, Chams, Switzerland: Springer.

Mathies, C. 2018. "Ethical Use of Data." In *IR in the Digital Era: New Directions for Institutional Research* 178, 85–97, edited by C. Mathies and C. Ferland. Boston, MA: Wiley.

Nolan, D., J. Byars, and N. Jones. 2018. "'Value-Added' Academic Intelligence." Presentation Made at the NACUBO Integrating Analytics Forum. Phoenix, AZ, November 29–30, 2018.

Norris, D. M., and L. Baer. 2013. *Building Organizational Capacity for Analytics.* EDUCAUSE. Accessed June 1, 2019. https://library.educause.edu/-/media/files /library/2013/2/pub9012-pdf.pdf.

Oklahoma Office of Management and Enterprise Services. n.d. *Data Governance Maturity Model.* Oklahoma Office of Management and Enterprise Services.

Accessed June 2, 2019. https://www.ok.gov/cio/documents/DataGovernance
MaturityModel_IS.pdf.

Pardo, A., and G. Siemens. 2014. "Ethical and Privacy Principles for Learning
Analytics." *British Journal of Educational Technology* 45: 438–450. http://dx.doi
.org/10.1111/bjet.12152.

Petty, C. 2019. "Why Data and Analytics Are Key to Digital Transformation."
Gartner. Accessed June 2, 2019. https://www.gartner.com/smarterwithgartner/why
-data-and-analytics-are-key-to-digital-transformation/.

Picciano, A. G. 2012. "The Evolution of Big Data and Learning Analytics in
American Higher Education." *Journal of Asynchronous Learning Networks* 16,
no. 3: 9–20.

Proença, D., and J. Borbinha. 2016. "Maturity Models for Information Systems—A
State of the Art." *Procedia Computer Science* 100: 1042–1049.

Reidenberg, J. R., and F. Schaub. 2018. "Achieving Big Data Privacy in Education."
Theory and Research in Education 16, no. 3: 1–7. https://doi.org/10.1177%2F
1477878518805308.

Russom, P. 2008. "The Four Imperatives of Data Governance Maturity." TDWI
Monograph Series. Accessed June 2, 2019. http://download.101com.com/pub
/TDWI/Files/TDWI_Monograph_Four_Imperatives_DG_Maturity_July2008.pdf.

Sao Pedro, M. A., J. D. Gobert, and R. Baker 2012. "Assessing the Learning and
Transfer of Data Collection Inquiry Skills Using Educational Data Mining on
Students' Log Files." Paper presented at the American Educational Research
Conference, Vancouver, BC, 2012.

Tufte, E. 2001. *The Visual Display of Quantitative Data*. Cheshire, CT: Graphics
Press.

Viberg, O., M. Hatakka, O. Bälter, and A. Mavroudi. 2018. "The Current Landscape
of Learning Analytics in Higher Education." *Computers in Human Behavior* 89,
98–110. https://doi.org/10.1016/j.chb.2018.07.027.

Webber, K. 2018. "Unpublished Graphic Representation for Factors in Building
Capacity." Based on work developed for *Building Capacity in Institutional
Research and Planning*. K. L. Webber. Dordrecht, Netherlands: Springer Press.

RANA GLASGAL is an associate vice provost at Northeastern University. Her office, University Decision Support, encompasses the disciplines of Survey Research, Analytics, Institutional Research, and Data Governance. Glasgal's work focuses on advancing the quality and ubiquity of evidence-based decision making in higher education through trusted data, analytical efficiency, transparency, collaboration, and communication.

J. MICHAEL GOWER is executive vice president for Finance and Administration at Rutgers University. He is past chair of the board of directors for EACUBO, past chair of NACUBO's Research Universities Council, as well as a member of its board of directors, and he chaired its Committee on the Effective Use of Analytics.

TOM GUTMAN is the associate vice president of Enrollment Analytics at Drexel University. He has a master's degree in economics and has begun his career in institutional research. His work now centers on the use of predictive analytics to facilitate decision making in admissions, financial aid, and budget planning.

BRIAN P. HINOTE serves as professor and associate vice provost for Data Analytics and Student Success at Middle Tennessee State University, where he leads a range of data and technology initiatives. He is a nationally recognized expert in student success, education technology, data analytics, and supplemental instruction methodologies.

BRADEN J. HOSCH is associate vice president for Institutional Research, Planning and Effectiveness at Stony Brook University. In this role, he has led an integration of institutional research with business intelligence operations, transformed student success initiatives with predictive analytics, implemented a data governance system, and developed the university's data strategy.

ADITYA JOHRI is a professor in the Information Sciences and Technology Department at George Mason University. He studies the use of information and communication technologies for learning and knowledge sharing, focusing on cognition in informal environments. Dr. Johri earned his PhD in Learning Sciences and Technology Design at Stanford University.

CARRIE KLEIN is a PhD candidate in the Higher Education Program at George Mason University. Her research agenda is focused on interactions between individuals and the structures, technologies, polices, and practices of higher education organizations, with the goal of creating more equitable outcomes for higher education stakeholders, especially students.

JAIME LESTER is associate dean of Faculty Development and Strategic Initiatives in the College of Humanities and Social Sciences and professor of Higher Education at George Mason University. Her overarching research goal is to examine organizational change and leadership to create and promote data-driven evidence effecting changes in pedagogy, instructional practice, and decision making.

CARRIE HANCOCK MARCINKEVAGE is the CRM Strategy Lead for the Smeal College of Business at Pennsylvania State University. Her role and doctoral research focus on critical success factors for higher education constituent relationship management (CRM) strategy and implementation.

GAIL B. MARSH is the senior vice president and chief strategy officer at the Ohio State University. In this role she formulates and executes key strategic initiatives with the board of trustees, president, and senior leaders, further advancing higher education, health care innovation, and economic impact in the State of Ohio.

SUSAN M. MENDITTO is NACUBO's accounting, financial reporting, and resource allocation expert. She has represented higher education on the Governmental Accounting Standards Advisory Council from 2006 to 2012 and on the AICPA's Revenue Recognition Task

Force from 2016 to 2017, and she is a frequent speaker at higher education professional development conferences.

JILLIAN N. MORN is a Quantitative Research Scientist in the Office of Educational Assessment at the University of Washington. Her research focuses on the intersection of gender, policy, and higher education, with a concentration on the impact of family formation on graduate student persistence in science, technology, engineering, and mathematics fields.

VALENTINA NESTOR is the senior director of Data Administration at Northeastern University. She leads and builds the strategy for the university's data governance program and is a passionate data ambassador with more than 20 years' experience in building partnerships to enable data policies, standards, and processes in driving organizational decisions using trusted information.

CATHY A. O'BRYAN is associate vice president of Client Services and Support (CSS) at Indiana University. She leads the strategic vision for the IU Constituent Relationship Management Initiative as well as enterprise web content, print, and knowledge management systems. CSS provides technical support for IU and Ivy Tech Community Colleges.

HUZEFA RANGWALA is a professor in the Department of Computer Science at George Mason University. His research interests include data mining and applications in learning sciences and biomedical informatics. Dr. Rangwala received a PhD in Computer Science from the University of Minnesota–Twin Cities.

TIMOTHY M. RENICK is senior vice president for Student Success and a professor at Georgia State University. Since 2008, he has directed the student success efforts of the university, overseeing one of the fastest-improving graduation rates in the nation and the elimination of all equity gaps based on students' race, ethnicity, or income level.

CHARLES TEGEN is a lecturer in the School of Accountancy, Clemson University. He has served a distinguished career as associate VP for Enterprise Risk Management and associate VP for Finance and Comptroller. His interests include higher education financial reporting to provide context and meaning to higher education stakeholders.

RACHIT THARIANI is chief population health officer of the Ohio State University Wexner Medical Center and CEO of its Accountable Care Organization. He has held previous leadership roles in strategy, business development, and strategic analytics. He also teaches Healthcare Data and Analytics at Ohio State's College of Public Health.

CHRIS TOMPKINS is the director of the presidential CRM initiative at Indiana University. The enterprise Constituent Relationship Management platform provides a 360-degree view of all constituent populations for each of the nine physical locations of IU across the state. He has led large-scale cross-leveraged IT system implementation and sustainability in higher education for the last 15 years, with a focus on successful development of complex architectures and adoptions.

LINDSAY K. WAYT is director of analytics at the National Association of College and University Business Officers (NACUBO). She helps NACUBO and its members integrate analytics into their organizations by developing and delivering programs, conducting and disseminating research, and working with both NACUBO members and collaborators at other organizations.

KAREN L. WEBBER is a professor of Higher Education, in the Institute of Higher Education at the University of Georgia. Her teaching and research focus on issues related to institutional research and decision support, student success, graduate student educational debt, and faculty workload and satisfaction.

HENRY Y. ZHENG is senior associate vice president for Strategic Analytics at the Ohio State University. He has primary responsibility for working with institutional research, information technology, data analytics, assessment, and organizational effectiveness leaders across the university, the Wexner Medical Center, and affiliated entities to promote a data-informed decision making culture.

YING ZHOU serves as the associate provost for Institutional Planning, Assessment and Research at East Carolina University. With a PhD in higher education, she has over 15 years of experience in higher education as an instructor, researcher, and administrator.

Page numbers in *italics* refer to figures and tables.

Barney, P., 39

Becker, M., 184, 185

behaviors, professional, and adoption of pedagogical innovation, 242–46

beliefs, professional, and adoption of pedagogical innovation, 241–42, 243–46

biases: in algorithms, 10, 95, 146, 305; fear of, in adoption of learning analytics tools, 244; in predictive analytics, 71, 72

Bichsel, J., 18

Big Data, definition of, 31. *See also* data

BI (business intelligence) units, 36, 39, 305

board members and strategic analytics, 109–11, 113–16, 117–19

Boston Consulting Group, 190, 192

branding campaigns, 206–7

Brown, M., 236, 238, 240, 248

budgeting and financial planning, analytics in, 114–15, 117. *See also* financial and operational efficiency

Burdt, C., 206

Burroughs, A., 170–71

business intelligence (BI) units, 36, 39, 305

business offices: cost management and, 271–72; data integration in, 262–63; data literacy, governance, and, 263–64; facilities management and, 273–77; resource allocation and, 263; student-centered analytics and, 264–71; transition to data analytics in, 261–62, 277–78

Cairo, A., 85–86

calculations, misinterpretation based on, 87–88, *88*

Calo, R., 95–96

Campbell, J. P., 231

campus facilities management, 273–77

capabilities and core competencies, assessment of, 110

capacity in IR, building, 300–301, *301*

career services and constituent relationship management, 211

Carlson, S., 155

Carpenter-Hubin, J., 153

Castleman, B. L., 192–93

Central Queensland University, 210

Chai, S., 10

Chamberlain, C., 60

chatbots, 183, 193–94

Chibana, N., 89

chief data officers (CDOs)/chief analytics officers (CAOs), 302–3

Childers, H., 36

Christensen, C., 103, 119, 154

Claremont College, 81

class attendance, tracking, 187–88

classification models, 58

classroom utilization, 269–70, 274–75

Clow, D., 235, 236

clustering models, 58

Codd, E., 33

cognitive science and use of data and visualizations, 81–87, 289–90

Cole, J., 154

collaboration: between analytics and IT communities, 21; importance of, 300–302

collection of data: for constituent relationship management, 217; "opting out" of, 94–95; passive, 37; point of diminishing return in, 91–92; transparency about, 92; use of collected data, 198–99; volume of and purpose for, 291

Columbia University, 213

communication with stakeholders, 111, 206–7

communities: analytics, 13–14, 119; external, interactions with, 22–23, 213–15; interactions between analytics and IT, 21

competitive advantage: identification of sources of, 107; of superior analytics capabilities, 115

competitive forces, evaluation of, 111, 116–17

computing power, evolution of, 31–36

connected campus, concept of, 17–18, 200, 224–25

constituent relationship management (CRM): in admissions and recruiting, 207–9; in alumni and donor engagement, 212–13; in career services and employer relations, 211–12; in communications and marketing, 206–7; complexity of, 203–4, 220; development and uses of, 201–3; in external organization relationships, 213–15; factors in success of, 215–20; at institutions with multiple campuses, 204–5; overview of, 199–201, 224–25; project management approach to, 220–24; in student experience, 209–10

context for learning analytics, 247–48

cost management, 271–72

courses: centralized scheduling and space optimization for, 269–70, 274–75; performance of students in, 233–34, 236, 246; predictive analytics in evaluation and improvement of, 69; prerequisite, tracking grades in, 188

Course Signals (CS), 233

critical data, 129–30

CRM. *See* constituent relationship management

CRM (customer relations management) systems, 18, 35, 166, 199–200

Crow, M., 4–5

culture, institutional: of admitting to failings, 185; in analytics development, 305–6; changing, 195–96; of data, 145–46; of data stewardship, 125, 127; of DIDM, 18–21, 171–73, 291; success of CRM and, 218–19

Cunningham, S., 159–60

curriculum evaluation and improvement, predictive analytics in, 69

customer relations management (CRM) systems, 18, 35, 166, 199–200. *See also* constituent relationship management

DalleMule, L., 21

dashboards: description of, 229; design of, 88, 142

data: categorization of, 129–30, 141; culture of, creating, 145–46; ethical and responsible use of, 71–73, 91–96, 98–99, 289–91, 305; features of, for governance, 130; human interaction, 16–18; misuse or misinterpretation of,

81–83, 86–87, 289–90; privacy and use of, 86–87, 92, 93–95, 167, 289–91; quality of, 125, 128–29, 183–84, 237–38, 304–5; sharing, 36–37, 87, 96, 129, 290–91; storage of, 33–34, 37–38; strategic, 130. *See also* collection of data; data governance; data reports or visualizations; security of data resources

data analytics. *See* learning analytics; predictive analytics/models; strategic analytics

data assets, 126–27

data democratization, 19, 147

data development, key aspects of, 303–6

data-driven decision making (DDDM), 6–11, 286

data governance: business offices and, 263–64; campus-wide involvement in, 134–35; categorization and prioritization of data for, 129–30; characteristics of, 287; creation of programs for, 124; definitions of, 122–23; goals of, 123–26, 143; as helping build trust, 133–34; importance of, 131, 302, 304; maturity models for, 293; need for, 96–98, 132–33; people and people skills in, 139–40, 143–44; principles and pillars of, 126–29; structure for, 15–16, 24–25. *See also* Northeastern University data governance

data-informed decision making (DIDM): DDDM compared to, 8–11; enabling conditions for, 11; expectation imperatives of, 21–25; human judgment in, 7–8, 9, 286–87; institutional culture of, 18–21, 171–73, 291; overview of, 6, 7–8, 286–89; people in, 12–14; as platform and culture, 25–26; process in, 18–21; strategic analytics in, 106–7, 110; in student success and outcomes, 270–71; technology in, 14–18

data lakes, 15, 37–38, 44

data literacy, need for, in personnel, 40, 263–64

data management, 10, 14–18

data mining, educational, 231, 298–99. *See also* learning analytics data models for constituent relationship management, 218

Data Protection Directive (EU), 94

data reports or visualizations: charts or graphics, 87–91, *88, 89, 90*; cognitive science and, 81–87, 289–90; context for, 79–80, 96–97; improving, 97; infographics, 85–86, 88–89, 91, 97; tools for, 16, *17*

data silos, 18–20, 87, 172, 304

data warehouses, 36, 37, 184–85, 289

Davenport, T.: on analytics, 22, 107, 286; analytics maturity models of, 50, 53, *53*; on competition between organizations, 104; on data strategy framework, 21; "Data to Knowledge to Results," 3–4, 5; DELTA Plus maturity model, 294–96; Five Stages of Analytics Maturity, 293–94, *295*; on interpretation of data, vii

DDDM (data-driven decision making), 6–11, 286

decision making: computing power and evolution of, 31–36; data-driven, 6–11, 286; data governance in, 124–25; evidence-based, 81, 96–99. *See also* data-informed decision making

decision tree analysis, 56–57, 62

defensive data strategy, 21

degree audit programs, 7

DELTA Plus maturity model, 294–96

DeMonbrun, R. M., 236

demonstrated interest in admissions, 167

Denley, T., 68, 73

descriptive analytics in enrollment management, 160–61, *161*

descriptive models, 54, 58

de-siloing, 172, 304

Díaz, A., 13

DIDM. *See* data-informed decision making

differentiation and strategic analytics, 107

discount rates on tuition, 152

donors: engagement of, 212–13; identification of, 70

Dourish, P., 93

Drexel University, Enrollment Analytics team, 162–63, 172–73

EAB (Education Advisory Board), 41, 45, 186, 235, 290

early alerts/warnings: for advising systems, 188–90, 228; on student performance, 233–34, 246; on trends and changes in higher education, 110

East Carolina University, Finish-in-Four initiative of, 63–67

Ebner, M., 92, 290

Education Advisory Board (EAB), 41, 45, 186, 235, 290

educational technologies, 228. *See also* learning management systems

EDUCAUSE: analytics definition of, 104; "Analytics in Higher Education" report of, 10–11; information technology issues list of, 4; joint statement of, vii–viii, 300; maturity and deployment indices of, 296–97; predictive analytics and, 51; recommendations of, 25

Eduventures, 52

efficiency and effectiveness, operational, improving, 23, 70. *See also* financial and operational efficiency

Ekowo, M., 71, 74, 93, 96

employer relations, 211–12

energy consumption, 275–78

engagement: alumni and donor, 212–13; predictive analytics in, 63–67, *66*; student engagement lifecycle, 198–99

enrollment management: application of analytics to, 172–73; challenges faced by, 152–53; descriptive analytics in, 160–61, *161*; DIDM in, 153–54; ethical considerations with use of analytics in, 166–71; focus on, 158–59; learning analytics in, 235; overview of, 151; predictive analytics in, 161–63, *162*; prescriptive analytics in, 164–66; strategic decision making in, 159–60

enterprise constituent relationship management (CRM), 202, 203–4

enterprise data warehouses, 15

enterprise resource planning (ERP) systems, 34–36, 45, 203, 287

ethical considerations: biases in algorithms, 10, 95, 146; CRM and, 223–24; for data resources, 24–25; in enrollment management, 166–71; in use of data, 71–73, 91–96, 98–99, 289–91, 305; in use of learning analytics, 239–40; in use of predictive analytics, 71–73, 72. *See also* privacy and data use

European Union, Data Protection Directive, 94. *See also* General Data Protection Regulation

evolution model of cultural change, 219

external organization relations, 22–23, 213–15

Facebook/Cambridge Analytica scandal, 71, 91, 147

faculty: adoption of learning analytics by, 240–46; Big Data in research of, 5; buying in to change, 195–96; standardization of workload of, 269–70

Fairweather, J. S., 242–43, 245

Family Educational Rights and Privacy Act (FERPA), 94, 132–33, 224, 240

fast thinking, 85, 97

Fayerman, M., 202

Ferguson, R., 235, 236

financial aid optimization: predictive analytics in, 67–70, 183; prescriptive analytics in, 165–66

financial and operational efficiency: of campus facilities, 273–77; cost management and, 271–72; data integration and, 262–63; data literacy, governance, and, 263–64; resource allocation and, 263; transition to data analytics in, 261–62, 277–78

financial need of students, 157–58

Finsel, B. A., 287

Five Stages of Analytics Maturity, 293–94, 295

Foer, F., 71, 91

French, K., 89

Frow, P., 199

full-time equivalents (FTEs), calculation of, 10

fundraising, predictive analytics in, 70

Gagliardi, J. S., 19, 153, 155

Gans, J., 31

Gardner, L., 156

Gartner, 199, 264, 299

Gavazzi, S. M., 22

Gee, E. G., 22

Gehlbach, H., 194

General Data Protection Regulation (GDPR, EU), 94, 132, 147, 224, 239–40

Georgia Perimeter College, 181–82

Georgia State University (GSU): graduation rates of, 63, 178; history and students of, 178–80; lessons learned by, 194–96; nursing school predictive model, 234; overview of, 177; as Tier 3 organization, 108; transformation of, 180–85

Georgia Tech, 104

Gilbert, S., 34

Gladwell, M., 32

Goldfarb, A., 31

Goldstein, K., 262

Google, 164–65

governance and ownership of constituent relationship management, 222–23

grades in early major and prerequisite courses, tracking, 188

graduation rates: admissions selectivity and, 180; at GSU, 177–82, 185, 189; at Middle Tennessee State University, 156–57, 157; of Pell-eligible students, 178; at Rutgers University, 267, 268

Grans Korsh, S., 274

grants and microgrants, 191–92

graphical integrity, principles of, 84–85

graphic effectiveness, principles for, 86

graphic excellence, characteristics of, 84

Grawe, N., 152, 153, 155

Great Recession of 2008, 152, 154, 179

Green, K., 34

GSU. *See* Georgia State University

Harel Ben Shahar, T., 95

Harris, J. G., 50, 53

leadership: buy-in to change and, 195, 269–70; CRM success and, 215–16; data governance and, 139, 143; data knowledge gap in, 79–80; role of, in DIDM, 12–14, 287–88; strategic analytics and, 109–11, 113–16, 117–19, 171–72; technology development and, 303–4, 306. *See also* culture, institutional

learning: AI to improve, 42–43; engagement in, and predictive analytics, 63–67, 66; organizational, 8. *See also* machine learning

learning analytics: capabilities of, 230–31; data collection from, 92; evidence of efficacy of, 235–36; factors in success of, 246–49; as field, 5; goals of, 235–36; growth of use of, 232; limitations of, 236; overview of, 228–30, 249–50; predictive analytics in, 68–69; protection of data and, 93–94, 98–99; transparency and security of, 290–91; use and potential of, 232–34. *See also* scalability of learning analytics

Learning Analytics and Knowledge conference, 229, 288, 298

Learning Analytics Readiness Instrument, 248

learning management systems (LMS), 35, 230, 240

Ledford, L., 263–64

Lehigh University, 12–13, 16, 17, 61–63

Levenson, A., 107

Leventhal, B., 54

Lewin, A. Y., 242

Liberman, N., 57

Liu, S. H., 241

LMS (learning management systems), 35, 230, 240

Locke, L., 249

logistic regression, 55–56, 61–62, 65

Long Beach City College District, 12, 270–71

Lonn, S., 238, 248

Lustig, I., 159

Macalester College, 276–77

machine learning, 30, 59–60. *See also* artificial intelligence

Madasamy, M., 59

majors, tracking early grades in, 188

marketing, constituent relationship management in, 206–7

Markov Chain model, 51

Mathies, C., 14, 26, 81, 86, 87, 96, 290–91

maturity models for data analytics, 50, 53, *53*, 292–96, *295*

Maycotte, H. O., 8

Mazzei, C., 117

Mazzei, M. J., 107–8

McCarthy, J., 30

McLaughlin, G., 126

McShea, C., 117

Merz, R., 36

Microsoft Dynamics, 210, 216

Middle Tennessee State University, 156, *157*, 171, 172

Miller, K., 277

Minnesota School of Nursing, 268–70

minority-serving institutions, 179

Minsky, M., 30

Mintz, S., 154

misinterpretation of data, charts, or graphics, 86–91, *88*, *89*, *90*, 289–90

MIT Center for Information Systems Research, 301

Motley, A., 274, 275

multiple linear regression, 55

National Association of College and University Business Officers (NACUBO): Analytics Advisory Group, 264; Discounting Study, 152; Higher Education Data Analytics Framework, 264, *265*; joint statement of, vii–viii, 300; Key Facilities Metrics Survey, 273; listening tour discussion of, 261–62; predictive analytics and, 51; strategic plan of, 260

National Science Foundation, 230

near-peer tutoring, 190

New America, 305

Noble, D., 107–8

nonpayment, dropping students for, 191

Norris, D. M., 238, 248, 300

recruitment: constituent relationship management in, 207–9; predictive analytics in, 9, 60–63. *See also* admissions decisions

registration records, tracking, 187

regression analysis, 54–56, 73

Reidenberg, J. R., 92, 98–99, 290

relevance of learning analytics tools, 246–47

reporting tools, 16

research: data analytics and, 5; statistical software for, 32. *See also* institutional research

resistance to analytics, 117–18, 249

resources: allocation of, 263; for CRM, 216; for technology development, 306

retention and completion rates, 156–57, *157*. *See also* graduation rates

return on education (ROE), 156

return on investment (ROI), 156, 190–91, 196, 268, 271

revenue targets and decline in enrollment, 152

revolution model of cultural change, 219

RioSalado Community College, 248

risk factors for dropping out, 187–88

risk scores of individuals, 40–42

Romali, R., 12, 270, 271

Rowshankish, K., 13

Rutgers University, 265–68

Saleh, T., 13

Salesforce.org platform, 205, 216, 235

Samuel, A., 30

scalability of learning analytics: ethical factors in, 239–40; individual factors in, 240–46; organizational factors in, 238–39; technological factors in, 237–38

Schaub, F., 98–99, 290

scheduling, centralized, 274

security of data resources, 17, 24–25, 98–99, 146–47, 206, 290, 305. *See also* General Data Protection Regulation

Seiner, R., 126

SFFA (Students for Fair Admissions), 169, 170

Shannon, C., 30–31

sharing of data, 36–37, 87, 96, 129, 290–91. *See also* data democratization

Shih, W., 10

Siemens, G., 92, 291

Slade, S., 24, 94–95

smartphones, 37

Smart Sparrow adaptive learning technology, 240

snowflake schema, 37

social media data, 16–18, 91

Solomonoff, R., 30

staffing: for CRM, 216–18; for DIDM, 287

stakeholders, communication with, 111, 206–7

Starfish Early Alert System, 64, 235

star schema, 37

State of Facilities in Higher Education, 273

Stephens, J., 263–64

stewardship of data, culture of, 125, 127

Stonybrook University, 302

storage of data, 33–34, 37–38

strategic agility and differentiation, improving, 24

strategic analytics: data-informed management and, 106–7; as extending capabilities of IR, 105–6; importance of, to leaders and trustees, 109–11; overview of, 104–5; positive feedback loop of, 107–9; in program prioritization, 112–13, *113*, 117; in strategic plan development, 116–17; support as essential to success of, 113–16, 117–19

strategic data, 130

strategic plans, development of, 116–17

Stratford, M., 166

strengths, organizational, identification of, 110, 111

student-centered analytics, 264–71

student engagement lifecycle, 198–99

student experience, 209–10, 234

students: dropping for nonpayment, 191; financial need of, 157–58; Pell-eligible, 168, 178, 179; performance of, in courses, 233–34, 236, 246. *See also* student success and outcomes

Students for Fair Admissions (SFFA), 169, 170
student success and outcomes: academic advising and, 68–69, 182–83, 185–94; CRM in, 210; DIDM in, 270–71; focus on, 158–59; funding models and, 155–56; as mission of higher education institutions, 22; predictions of, 40–42; predictive analytics in, 63–67, 66; transportation optimization to support, 265–68
Student Success Collaborative, 235
success, strategies for: future of, 299–303; institutional impact and, 299; overview of, 297–99. *See also* student success and outcomes
"summer melt," 192–94
Survey of College and University Admissions Directors, 152
sustainability and energy consumption, 275–78
SWOT (strength, weakness, opportunity, threat) analysis, 110

Taei, P., 89
Tagg, J., 249
teaching, improving, 42–43, 244
Teasley, S. D., 236
technology development: analytics culture in, 305–6; people in, 303–4; process in, 304; technology in, 304–5
technology infrastructure: for DIDM, 14–18, 287; for learning analytics, 237–38
Temple University, 81
third-party analytics tools, 82, 96
third-party vendors, 44–45
tiers of organizational value, 108–9
trade-offs and strategic analytics, 107, 111
training and professional development, 20, 320
transformation of decision making and new data ecology, 38–42

transparency: of data collection, 92; of data in performance assessment and institutional planning, 19–20; of learning analytics use, 98–99, 248–49, 290–91
transportation optimization, 265–67
trustees and strategic analytics, 109–11, 113–16, 117–19
Tufte, E., 83–85, 86, 97, 290
Tulane University, 212
Turing, A., 31
Turk, J. M., 19
Tversky, A., 83, 85, 86

University of Arizona, 275–76
University of California-Riverside, 262–63
University of California-San Diego, 210, 289
University of Colorado, 211, 213
University of Michigan, 248
University of Nebraska-Lincoln, 276
University System of Georgia, 301–2
Unizin consortium, 42

Van Barneveld, A., 231
Vanover Porter, M., 263
vendor products, 96, 290
vendors, third-party, 44–45
Venkatesh, V., 245
Viberg, O., 5, 231, 236, 298
Villar, M., 130
visualizations of data. *See* data reports or visualizations

Webber, K. L., 86, 300, *301*
Wells, D., 130
White-Delaney, C., 269–70

Yates, H., 60
Y-axis scales, misinterpretation based on, 88–89, 89, 90, 91